Under the
Pomegranate Tree

Under the Pomegranate Tree

The Best New Latino Erotica

Edited by Ray González

WSP

WASHINGTON SQUARE PRESS
PUBLISHED BY POCKET BOOKS

New York   London   Toronto   Sydney   Tokyo   Singapore

A WASHINGTON SQUARE PRESS *Original* Publication

WSP

A Washington Square Press Publication of
POCKET BOOKS, a division of Simon & Schuster Inc.
1230 Avenue of the Americas, New York, NY 10020

Copyright © 1996 by Ray González

All rights reserved, including the right to reproduce
this book or portions thereof in any form whatsoever.
For information address Washington Square Press,
1230 Avenue of the Americas, New York, NY 10020

Under the pomegranate tree : the best new Latino erotica / edited by
Ray González.
      p.   cm.
   Includes bibliographical references.
   ISBN 0-671-89823-X (pbk.)
   1. Erotic literature, Spanish American—Translations into English.
2. Spanish American literature—20th century—Translations into
English.   3. Erotic literature, Hispanic American (Spanish).
4. Erotic literature, Hispanic American (Spanish)—Translations into
English.   5. Erotic literature, American.   6. American literature—
Hispanic American authors.   7. American literature—20th century.
I. Gonzalez, Ray.
PQ7087.E5U53   1996
860.8'03538—dc20   95-23390
                                                                CIP

First Washington Square Press trade paperback printing September 1996

10 9 8 7 6 5 4 3 2 1

WASHINGTON SQUARE PRESS and colophon are
registered trademarks of Simon & Schuster Inc.

Cover design by Patrice Kaplan
Cover art by John Nickle

Printed in the U.S.A.

Contents

Introduction   xiii

Pat Mora
    Spring Shining   1
    Pétalos Negros   2

Verónica Volkow
    You Are Naked . . .   3
    from *El Inicio*   4

Alma Luz Villanueva
    Free Women   6

Elena Poniatowska
    Happiness   18

Perla Sanchez
    Tongue Cakes   23

Francisco Alarcón
    Love Sequence   26

Tony Guijon
    The Second Time   32
    Cock   33
    Years Ago   34

Xavier Cavazos
    My Dream of Licking   35
    Manteca   35

Maria Madresca
    Face   36
    You   37
    Tool   38

Trinidad Bidar
    A Kiss at Noontime   39
    Hands at Prayer   40

Alejandro Murguia
    Sacred Heart   43

Carlos Fuerza
    Aphorisms   57

María Luisa Mendoza
    Ausencia's Tale   59

Carlos Parian
    Hotel   66

Silvia Curbelo
    *The Blackbirds Take Over
    the Sky*   70
    The Secret History of Water   71

Rosario Castellanos
    On the Edge of Pleasure   72

Coral Bracho
Firefly Under the Tongue   74
Your Borders: Crevices
    That Uncover Me   75
Untitled   77
On the Facets: The Flashing   78

Daniel de Burgos
Collection of Navels   82
Trying Trying   83

Alma Luz Villanueva
The Receiving Blanket   85

Juan Felipe Herrera
Portrait/Nude #30/4×6   91
Portrait/Nude #9/7×11   91
Arc   92
Saguaro   93
The Boy of Seventeen   94

Carlos Parian
Focus   95
Door   96

Kyra Galvan
Bellas Artes   97
My Flaws Among the
    Peach Blossoms   97

Carlotta Sanchez
The Thing in My Mouth   99
Avocado Blues Avocado
    Greens   100

Gilberto Flores
   Resurrection   102

Roberta Medina
   The Brown Woman   105

Wasabi Kanastoga
   Windmills   111

Mara Larrosa
   Ebony Backs   117

Vera Larrosa
   Blue Mouth   119

Antonia Palacios
   A Gentleman on the Train   121

Leroy Quintana
   The Professor   129

Diana Rivera
   The Rose   136
   Death of the Lady Slipper   138

Alberto Alvaro Ríos
   One Woman Turns Her
      Lips Away   140
   The Mouths of Two People   141

Enrique Pardo
   Interminable Rhythm   143
   Untitled   144

Ana Bárbara Renaud Gonzáles
   Conquístador   145

Joe Duran
   Choking the Chicken   146
   Old Man to the Young Man   147

Paul Arturo Cabral Jr.
   Nombre   149

Leo Romero
   from *Crazy in Los Nueces*   157

Enrique Fernandez
   Ms. X   162

Cecilia Rodríguez Milanés
   Haikus for My Honey   167

Rafael Castillo
   Aurora   168

Lorna Dee Cervantes
   Raisins   178
   Le Petit Mal   179
   On the Poet Coming of Age   180
   Isla Mujeres   184

Ricardo Castillo
   Buttocks   185

Hector Manjarrez
   Bogota Transfer   186

Magdalena Gómez
   The Tongue Is Mightier
     Than the Sword   187
   Delirium   189

Francisco Hernandez
   Paura Has No Cunt   190

Jim Cortinas
   from *Sweat Song*   191

Max Martínez
   A Red Bikini Dream   194

Lilia Barbachano
   Aldebarán   226

Marina Fe
   Duel   227

Sabina Berman
   Red   228

Bernardo Galvan
   Journal of a Moving
     Teardrop   229

H. Emilia Paredes
   from *Breath*   239

Virgil Suarez
   Flash Flesh   243

Gina Valdés
　　from *Puentes y Fronteras*　　247
　　Infinite Wheel of Desire　　249

Demetria Martínez
　　Blessed the Hungry　　250

Ricardo Lopez Masarillo
　　Circle of Friends　　255

Juan Felipe Herrera
　　Reversible Lovers　　263

Jose Enrique Pardo
　　Crossfire　　273

Markanthony Alvidrez
　　Researching Frida Kahlo　　294

Rudolfo Anaya
　　The Apple Orchard　　298

Alicia Borinsky
　　*The China Venus Thinks
　　About Making Love*　　310
　　Rumor　　311

Juan Cameron
　　Invocation 13　　312

Ethel Krauze
　　*The Mule Going Round
　　the Well*　　313

Ed Vega
    Home Movies   320

Brenda Cárdenas
    Our Language   328
    A Lover's Resolution on the
    New Year to Thaw Our
    Winter Blood   330

Saúl Yurkievich
    Egyptian Tango   332

John Juan Domingo
    Two Flowers and My
    Tongue   334

Omar Castañeda
    I Tell You This   337

Alma Luz Villanueva
    Sisters   343
    Sassy   345
    Violation   346
    The Lover   347

H. Emilia Paredes
    St. John of the Divine
    Cathedral   350
    Ode to the Firmament Her
    Right Shoulder   351
    Woman in Prayer   352
    Woman in a Velvet Dress   353

Acknowledgments   355

Introduction

Under the Pomegranate Tree is the first major anthology of Latino erotic writings—short shories and poetry by Latin American and U.S. Hispanic writers. The work gathered in this volume is a crucial addition to the study and enjoyment of contemporary Latino literature. It shows how the writing derived from sexual experiences is a key factor in establishing Latin American and U.S. Latino literature as one of the most important and dynamic genres in the world today. Despite the current boom and wide readership of multicultural writing, and the numerous anthologies of Latino literature being published today, Latino erotica has until now, been overlooked.

Under the Pomegranate Tree uncovers the rich and unashamed Latino voices that, by revealing their sexual encounters, fantasies, barriers, and relationships, are redefining the world's notion that Latino culture and art are traditional and conservative. The writing in *Under the Pomegranate Tree* draws attention to itself because the combination of graphic descriptions of sex and highly crafted stories and poems shows how an almost underground genre within Latin American literature has influenced that literature's better-known charactertistics of magic realism in fiction and deep emotion in poetry. The title of this book comes from the metaphor of eating and separating the seeds of the pomegranate fruit as a sexual act. (The pomegranate is found in many countries in Latin America.) Latino writing, which is constantly evolving, must now encompass the erotic to be a complete literature.

Erotica is a vital component of Latino arts and letters. Erotica, within the Latino literary framework, includes fantasies, dreams, heterosexual and homosexual love, graphic encounters, humor, true love, and unusual practices and arts. Though coming from countries and people who have resisted open sexual expression outside the accepted social behaviors of adultery and prostitution, the writers on these pages accept the intellectual and spiritual forces that drive them to create art out of the intense heat of other physical and emotional bodies. Latino erotica takes on, challenges, and attempts to redefine relationships within one of the most conservative and traditional cultures in the world.

Several successful anthologies of erotica in other cultures have appeared in recent years. Ironically, Latino writers, perhaps more than most other groups of contemporary authors, are some of the best creators of this kind of writing, as the passionate Latino character is perfect for erotic expression. But its writers are not just lusting after new territory. They are expanding the traditional boundaries that have restrained many of their predecessors for generations. Despite the evolution and acceptance of Latin American and U.S. multicultural literature, a full collection in this genre has been absent from contemporary literature until *Under the Pomegranate Tree.*

Central, South American, and U.S. Latino cultures are some of the most expressive when it comes to sexual relationships, beliefs, practices, and art. Yet, the fact that Latinos are predominantly Catholic has for generations made eroticism taboo among many writers. When it came to what could and couldn't be said about personal relationships and cultural values, the Catholic Church had a great influence on Latino literature. Their conservative upbringing in patriarchal societies, the suppression of women's art, and the influence of other world literatures kept many modern Latino writers from truly expressing their sexuality. Those who did write about it, like Jorge Luis Borges, Gabriela Mistral, or Julio Cortázar, were branded outcasts or "too experimental" for mainstream publishers and readers. Perhaps the earliest Latin American writer to attempt a free expression of erotica was the seventeenth-century Mexican nun Sor Juana Ines de la Cruz. She created a remarkable sequence of erotic poems amidst the rigid social and religious barriers of colonial Mexico. Yet, she has only recently been acknowledged by critics as a pioneering and influential writer.

In the last twenty years, Latin American literature has grown into one of the most important genres of world literature. While writers such as Pablo Neruda, Gabriel García Márquez, Carlos Fuentes, and Borges were getting the acclaim, a number of Latin American women were affirming the qualities of eroticism in their writing because they saw its possibilities as a force of change and empowerment. In Latin America, writers such as Elena Poniatowska, Isabel Allende, Rosario Castellanos, Mistral, and Luisa Valenzuela broke the religious and male restrictions on eroticism and turned Latin American literature completely around. A number of women writers in this book focus on the new Latina, who makes her own choices when it comes to her sexual identity. By deciding when and how they express their sexuality, and the amount of control and passion they exhibit, these Latina characters define the erotic territory many contemporary Latina women are exploring. Now, as more Latina writers' novels, stories, and poetry appear in international publications, it is clear that their eroticism is a key factor in understanding the many changes Latino literature has undergone. The issues of power and powerlessness and the quest for control over one's self in intimate relationships are concerns that recur in many works by Latina writers. The form their erotica takes is linked to the historical and sociopolitical realities of their countries and societies.

For Latino male writers, the challenge is to create and present erotica that celebrates relationships, whether heterosexual or homosexual, and shows how far Latino men have progressed from the stereotypes of the "macho" rapist, adulterer, and cool "Latino lover." The male authors in this collection present varied points of view when it comes to making love to a woman or a man. Their poems and stories may contain the physical power of males, but they also blend the gentle with the aggressive, the surreal with the realistic. Most important of all, the male writers in this book are not afraid to express themselves within a genre most of them are unused to working in. Almost a quarter of the contributors, men and women, are seeing their first publication of any kind in this book.

The fact that it comes in an anthology of erotica means that readers are not getting the same old thing within these pages. In the U.S., the political struggles of Mexican American, Puerto Rican, and Cuban writers focused on social issues such as racism, poverty, and problems in the cities. Any attempts to write about personal experiences usually involved stories and novels about the preservation of traditional family myths. The folktales of these writers' grandfathers and grandmothers did not contain explicit bedroom encounters. Those experiences were not spoken about. If these U.S. writers were committed to re-creating family myths, their flights of fancy could involve healing customs, superstitions, and beliefs, but sexual fantasies were not a part of this oral tradition.

Mexican Americans were busy writing about revolution in the sixties and trying to establish their place in American literature. If some of them did achieve recognition, their poems and stories were about traditional Mexican family values, their novels about overcoming social injustice. None of these works contained many sexual references. In order to establish a vibrant Chicano literature, the personal had to be given up so that social and political concerns could lead the way. A good example of this is provided by Chicana poet Lorna Dee Cervantes. As one of the leading activists in the sixties, her poetry spoke of racism, oppression, and the realities of growing up in a San Jose, California, barrio. Her first book of poetry, *Emplumada* (University of Pittsburgh Press, 1980), was full of angry political poetry. Poems about her family were mournful ballads about wasted lives in the barrio. Fourteen years later, as Chicano writing has evolved to encompass the personal as well as the political, Lorna Dee Cervantes writes some of the most erotic Chicana poetry to be found in this book. Alma Luz Villanueva and H. Emilia Paredes join Cervantes in turning their poetry in a fresh and bold direction. They have broken the barriers and released their entire poetic selves through erotica. They are just three of the Chicana women represented in *Under the Pomegranate Tree* who show how sexual language is just as powerful and effective as the rhetoric of the sixties.

Puerto Ricans are still highly concerned with the struggle for independent status for their native island. Their literature is filled with the life of New York, but the poverty, drugs, and surviving on the streets has had little to do with sexual privacy and intimacy. With the successful assimiliation of many U.S. Puerto Ricans, and the daily responsibilities that come with it, not much time has been left for such personal needs.

Cuban American writers dream about Cuba and write about their new identities in Florida. Only in recent years has erotica been a way of expressing their freedom in a new country. More of them feel as if they can finally write about every aspect of their lives because they have raised families in the United States and experienced every aspect of the American family and its personal-sexual complexities.

If Latino literature in Latin America and the U.S. has changed and evolved to allow its writers more freedom to write about the personal world, it is because of the recent acceptance and wider audience for multicultural writing. Latinos, African Americans, Asians, and Native American writers have now reached a new plateau in their work. While the political and cultural struggles continue, the fact that more of these writers are being published, studied, and read suggests that erotica is allowing a further expression of the whole character of its creators. It gives the political activist, the street poet, and the feminist writer new life and completes the cycle of their humane quest for identity, both within their own conservative cultures and out in the mainstream world, which has been reading about sex for a very long time.

The search for power and control over one's own sexuality and the freedom to explore erotic fantasies have progressed from the veiled illusions of earlier generations of writers to the frank expression of contemporary authors. Latino writers use a variety of styles and approaches in their erotica. Everything from street "calo" (slang) to bilingual forms and mainstream English are found in Latino erotica. Humor, playfulness, and serious, provocative experimentation give the poems and stories in this book an unpredictable tone, resulting in a collection that adds a new dimension to Latino literature.

Under the Pomegranate Tree combines the work of Latin American and U.S. Latino writers in one volume to show how their writing is rapidly becoming one strong whole. By presenting their erotic writings together, the book traces the influences of these writers on each other, while also showing how the struggle to release sexual art brings this kind of writing together.

Under the Pomegranate Tree will gain further attention by being the first anthology to contain both Latin American and U.S. Latino writers in the same volume. Dozens of previous anthologies of Latin American literature have separated U.S. writers from Central and South Americans to meet geographical, editorial, and marketing needs. The writing in this book shows how the different aspects of sexuality among Latinos is breaking boundaries. The same sexual energies that drive U.S. Latino writers also encourage Central and South American writers to add to the genre, because the religious, familial, and political barriers are common to all Latinos. Their erotica rises out of a response to their shared culture and history.

A variety of Latino erotica has appeared in small-press books and literary journals. It has almost been kept under wraps and has enjoyed only a small audience. *Under the Pomegranate Tree* brings this exciting form to a wide readership at a time when erotic writing from all cultures is being enjoyed by popular and scholarly audiences alike. Their curiosity about this genre tells us that, like the writers in this book, they believe that *every* aspect of Latino arts and culture should be allowed to flourish, in literature as in life.

—RAY GONZÁLEZ

Under the Pomegranate Tree

Spring Shining

Pat Mora

What does he think,
this spring day in the park,
as we watch him
stroke her body,
slim as a stem.

He sees us watching.
What does he think
as he rubs oil, or is it
wax, between his hands,
rubs her shoulders and back,
his strokes slow, circular,
as he moves his hands
over her curves, into her
crevices, down her
legs, rubs oil between
each toe, begins again—
facing her now—massages
her shoulders, arms,
oils her breasts as we
watch, cups them, moves his
hands down her hips, kneels
and strokes calves, thighs,
the folds between her legs,
rises, smooths ointment on her
lips, feels the molding
of her face between his hands,
the nose, downcast eyes,
even her curls now burnished.

She glows like honey
in the setting sun,
silent bronze woman
in the park, lips parted,
speaking always to herself.

Pétalos Negros

Pat Mora

streets dissolve, dusty sighs,
mumbled wishes of women
return to the wrong room

   susurros de lluvia

lips part and green flames
dart, incandescent *quetzales*
into startled trees

   susurros de lluvia

rain's tongue licks windows,
hums in *pétalos negros,* dreams
in the tangle of fragrant hair

   susurros de lluvia

tongue in the fragrant tangle,
skin dissolves, *pétalos negros*
en susurros de lluvia

---

susurros de lluvia: rain's whispers
pétalos negros: black petals

You Are Naked ...

Verónica Volkow

You are naked
           and your softness is immense
you tremble beneath my fingers
your breath flies inside your body

          you are
like a bird in my hands
          vulnerable
as only desire could make you vulnerable
that sweet pain with which we touch each other
that surrender in which we feel
the abandon of victims

pleasure licks us
devours us   like a mouth
and our eyes are extinguished
                are lost

from El Inicio

Verónica Volkow

I.

Hunger is the original eye of the body
primeval eye in the dark of the body
the eye with which flesh first beholds flesh

and a sanguinary darkness draws us inward

                    the eye
with which my feet see you   my teeth
                         my fingers

                    the eye
with which I discover you   centuries long
in one night of touching
                    that night
so like the night of the fish
                    the tiger
                    the snake
so like the first night of life

we close our eyes and are beast again
and our bodies are clamped like throats
                    choking on the shapely flavors

II.

The lovers
have hands solely for loving
            they have only their hands
hands that are feet and wings over their bodies
hands that constantly seek
the breathing animal behind buried eyes
fingers that set their bodies on fire
that are branches on which caresses flower
flowers that are birds that are flames that are hands
hands that are lost in their lightning writing

hands that travel the flesh of bodies
like stars touching at daybreak
like suns rising   like shooting stars
like secret gods who draw the night

X.

Between your body my body
is the print of your body
is the eye   the sound of your body
                    I hear your forearms
                              your teeth
                              your tongue
                              your thighs
I hear the shape of your body with all my skin

between my body your body
is another form of your body
like water turned to incandescent ice
or the open faucet of flames
                    your body
cries out in my body

Free Women

Alma Luz Villanueva

"Aren't you glad you didn't bring your husband? Tell the truth, María. Come on, tell the truth!" Marta teased.

María sipped her piña colada and smiled to herself.

"Well, I'm sure as hell glad I didn't," Yolanda laughed. "Look at those macho hunks over there—not bad, not bad." Then she sighed with self-parodying resignation, "Not that I'd do anything. I'm so chicken."

"You aren't chicken. You're faithful. Wish I had someone to be faithful to. Sort of," Consuelo laughed.

"You've never been married, have you?" Marta's voice was languorous. She was finishing her second piña colada. She was in heaven. She'd made it clear to Luis that this was a convention of analysts, therapists, psychiatrists, nothing exciting. Here, in Mexico, by the ocean? Ha! She laughed out loud and put her hand up to get the boy's attention.

"Decadent bitch!" Yolanda teased, with a slight edge in her voice.

"You bet!" Marta shot back. "Do you mind my asking, Consuelo?"

"Too many macho bastards out there, like those gorgeous macho hunks staring at us. So, I guess, I decided to stay single." Consuelo sipped her margarita. It was exactly as she'd ordered it. After she'd sent it back once, they got it right. Just seeing her, they got it right. Secretly, the bartender called her La Doctora Puta. So when the busboy brought her drink, the bartender would tell him to take it to La Doctora Puta. Consuelo didn't understand the busboy's wide, cheerful smile. She tipped him well for his smile. He was no more than thirteen, but he had the charm of a man.

"I was married in my twenties. But not ever again, I'll tell you." Marta looked over at Consuelo's long, slender, well-shaped legs and felt her usual envy of women with long slender legs stir. Hers were short with saddlebags that refused to go away no matter what she did.

"I know my parents think, deep down, that I'm a little sinvergüenza, but, as they well know, I'm too old now for their harmless criticisms. And, besides, I'm the fuckin' doctor, right?" Marta laughed loudly, keeping her hand up till she caught the bartender's eye.

"Doesn't Luis want to get married?" María asked. She stared at the bright green lime that floated in her benign, listless mineral water. She stared at her stretch marks from her two children. They aren't ugly enough to hide, she thought, but I'm sure not proud of them. And the stomach never got back to flat again. She remembered her son's comment about her "beer belly" as she'd been relaxing in her bikini. She remembered how much she'd wanted to slap him for being ungrateful to her for the imperfection of her body. The sacrifice, she told herself, breathing in the perfect day. There were no symposiums till tomorrow. Just me and my beer belly, my brown beer belly, Maria smiled to herself, letting her breath out softly.

"Oh, he loves me and all that, but I know what lurks beneath that prim Hispanic exterior," Marta laughed sadly. "A Hispanic man who wants to own a woman, a wife, even if you are a doctor and make more than he does. Probably more so because of it, right?" The busboy brought her drink, taking the empty glass. He gave her a small, polite smile as she tipped him. "He's going to be cute when he grows up," Marta said as he retreated to the sound of their appreciative giggles.

"Lecher," Yolanda smiled, imagining his cute brown legs. "Yeah, he'll definitely be hot in a few years, like those guys over there staring at us." She was the only one in the group who wore a one-piece bathing suit. She just couldn't bring herself to wear a bikini. All that proper Chicana upbringing hadn't missed its mark. She was short at five foot three and built nicely. She had no stretch marks or children. She often thought what really stopped her from having children was the image of having to spread her legs in front of a bunch of strangers. Even Alfred had to settle with the lights out—and not that he minded. Yolanda was passionate with the lights out. Then he was anyone she desired.

"I have a question for all of you—colleague to colleague." Marta leaned forward, speaking in a low voice. "And I want an honest answer, no bullshit." She looked at her friends and smiled. "You know, the truth." She paused until the only sound was the gentle waves, the sound of glass clinking in the distance, and a radio playing Mexican songs at the bar.

"What's your fantasy of a perfect orgasm?"

"Oh, come on! That's not fair!" Yolanda laughed. "Do you mean right here, right now? I'm supposed to tell all of you my fantasy of a perfect orgasm?"

"I think it's a great idea! Why not? Don't we pry this sort of thing out of our patients? Why not us for a change?" María laughed excitedly.

"Really, why not?" Consuelo joined in María's laughter, but she felt herself blushing high in her cheekbones.

"Because it's personal, pendeja, I'm not your patient," Yolanda answered, laughing.

"Big deal, who'll know? Just us chickens, Chicanas. What a bunch of prudes!" Marta pretended intense disappointment.

"Will you tell us yours first?" Consuelo smiled teasingly.

"Sure, why not?" Marta took off her sunglasses and laughed. "But first let's jump in the water. I think this is going to be steamy."

"All those guys are staring. I'll just stay here, go ahead," Yolanda whined.

"I bet you've got the hottest fantasy, Yolanda." Consuelo pulled Yolanda to her feet.

"No doubt," María said, wishing her body was as youthful as Yolanda's. No kids, no belly. She sucked her stomach in, angrily.

"Take this to La Doctora Putza. She wants more," the bartender told the boy.

"She always wants more," the boy smiled.

"They don't seem to notice us," one of the men said. "Maybe they like little boys better." All of them laughed as the boy picked up the drink with a shrug of his shoulders. He liked being included in the men's conversation and their secret ridicule of the pochas. His mother had warned him to stay away from the tourist women. "They're all gringas, no matter what color they are. Mujeres sin vergüenza. They pay you for what's between your legs, just like a man pays a woman! ¡Qué putas!"

He watched La Doctora Puta as she lowered herself into the water. Her body was getting a deep brown; only the edges of her ass betrayed her real color. He wondered how much money she'd pay him. He had no real experience, just some kissing and petting that hadn't gone anywhere. Then they'd left in the night to get away from the soldiers that had taken his father and older brother. He'd been at school when they'd come. When he'd come home his mother's eyes spoke eloquently of her terror. Finally, after many months, they'd come to this place. She took in laundry, sewing, catering to the tourists. Between his job and hers they ate well and lived in peace.

Every night she lit two candles for her husband and her first-born, wondering where the soldiers had thrown their bodies. She willed herself not to imagine their torture, their screams, their deaths—but sometimes an image of their mutilated bodies surprised her with a terrible violence, and she'd warn her second son: "Cause no trouble. Draw no attention to yourself, ever, hijo, Madre de Dios. . . ."

The boy set the drink down, picking up the dirty one. He noticed the others were almost empty, so he waited for them to return. La Doctora Puta turned toward him. She adjusted her bikini top unselfconsciously. She has nice ones, he thought. I'd like a motorcycle, a black one. A big black one with silver and a nice motor. He watched her breasts bounce as she approached. My father's dead and I have nothing. He smiled at her and she smiled back at him, but, quickly, she looked away and began to towel herself, aware of his eyes on her.

"I wonder if he's a virgin? No, I shouldn't even think it," Consuelo told herself firmly.

I have nothing, the boy repeated to himself, watching her spread oil to her face, neck, the tops of her breasts. Then the other women came, giving him instructions. He always had to force himself not to laugh at their Spanish. It was forced, self-conscious, too perfect, like from books. Even the one who acted like their women wanted a margarita. Hers was the Spanish that sounded natural, like spoken language. They were laughing as he walked away. "Gringas," he muttered.

The boy returned with their fresh drinks, dropping a napkin in Consuelo's lap. He'd written on it, "I like you, Señora." She read it and looked up at him, completely undone for a moment. He licked his upper lip, staring at her, and then he smiled like a boy seeking approval, with the charm and intent of a confident man. When the boy was gone, Consuelo wiped the sheen of sweat from her face, neck, and breasts with the note—I like you, Señora. She tore the napkin into small shreds and reminded Marta of her promise to be first.

All of them giggled, sounding like teenagers at a pajama party with a joint or two being passed around—the incense lit so the vigilant parents wouldn't know. Their bodies felt young and alive with sexual curiosity, and, miraculously, they felt no guilt—thirteen, fourteen, fifteen. . . .

Marta cleared her throat, laughed nervously, and settling into her reclining chair, she surrendered her body to the hot afternoon sun. Then, with an unusually graceful gesture, she placed a small shell on her dream eye. Marta had suggested they all find one shell to stimulate their dream eye for their perfect fantasy. This could be healing, she thought. She imagined its light, subtle weight made her dream eye quiver, almost itch.

"Girls, if I get too steamy tell me to shut up, okay?" No one answered. They were all oiled, drinks within reach, turning browner by the minute and glad they weren't first in their little game. Marta shut her eyes and her voice became a dreamy monotone.

"I'm in a meadow, it's springtime, warm but not hot, and the meadow's filled with flowers, flowers of every color and the softest green, green grass. I'm wearing a flimsy spring dress with silk panties and bra, a golden silk, which can be seen through the dress, and the wind's blowing through me as though I'm naked." She actually felt the spring wind and opened her eyes for a second to see if the warm sea and hot sand still surrounded her. She felt languid, sensual.

"It's in the mountains, there's a creek close by, and then I hear voices, a woman and a man. They're like twins, only he's blond and she's raven-haired, black, black hair with dark sensual eyes. His eyes are ocean blue, deep blue, powerful. Both of their eyes are extremely powerful, and they're both physically beautiful. Their combined presence is almost overwhelming me." Marta paused, sipping her drink, and lay back down. She rubbed her oily belly once, enjoying her own caress, then she held absolutely still.

"They tell me together, in one voice, 'Take off your dress.' I do. Then he takes off my gold silk bra and his hands are both soft and strong. He takes my breast into his mouth and twirls his tongue around my nipple and he sucks it and licks my entire breast with his tongue and then back to my nipple, teasing it, twirling it with his tongue, and it's like, it's like I'm having an orgasm. He takes the other one in his mouth and I can't stand it. I fall down onto the flowers, and I feel the woman slip my gold silk panties off, licking my belly, pressing her face into my belly, circling my pubis with her wet tongue. He kisses my lips, filling my mouth with his thick tongue, then my breasts again and again. My mouth, eyes, cheeks, eyelids, everything from the breasts up belong to him, and the woman owns the clitoris as she strokes it with her tongue so softly, yet firmly." Marta's breath caught. She raised her leg, squeezing herself, feeling shudders of pleasure run through her body.

"I come and come in swirling colors, flowers, smells, a multitude of sensations and there's no boundary, no place where I can say the orgasm begins here, ends here, it's one continuous, rolling, flowing orgasm . . . like the meadow."

Her friends were silent, each one in her own meadow.

"Then I feel the man penetrate me, and for a moment I want to say no, stop, no, but his possession is complete, his hands clutch me, and his thrusts, deep into my womb, drive the orgasm back into me, back to a kind of frenzied, yet sharper focus. A kind of gathering of my power, yes. Now I want his sperm, all of it. All of it is mine." María couldn't help laughing, softly, with pleasure.

"And the woman?" María asked with admiration. Marta had definitely set the tone and though she felt aroused by the fantasy, she suddenly dreaded she had none of her own.

"The woman's mine too." Marta burst out laughing. "I assume, fellow shrinks, that all of this is highly confidential, right?" She smiled at her friends, wondering how she'd conjured up that meadow, those twins, and missing it at the same time.

"Of course it is. It's absolutely confidential, sister shrink," Yolanda laughed. "What an incredible fantasy."

"Look, we could all analyze that one. It's really healthy, Marta," Consuelo said. "The man *and* the woman. Perfect."

"Plus, it's hot," María giggled.

"Exactly what I was getting to. Let's not analyze our fantasies—that's what we do for a living. Let's just keep it going, okay? You next, María." Consuelo smiled, sipping her drink. "Drink slowly, so you-know-who doesn't sneak up on us."

"We're speaking English, remember?" Yolanda rolled onto her stomach. She glanced at the men at the bar and one of them smiled at her. She smiled back and immediately regretted it. She sipped her drink and laid her head on the soft beach pillow. The sun engulfed her. She imagined taking the bathing suit off and oiling herself, everything. My back, my ass, my legs, my thighs, she thought. Someone else would have to do it. Yolanda smiled as María started to speak.

"I'm in a room of mirrors—walls, ceiling, floor. Well, I'm naked, lying on a giant black futon with colored cushions. There are cushions everywhere—blue, red, purple, yellow, lime, rainbow pillows, name it." María paused, trying to get the image sharper. She saw her belly, slightly rounded, her hips and thighs overweight, yet full and somehow sensual. She smiled at the emptiness of the room—just herself and the mirrors.

"There seems to be a natural light, but I don't see any windows. There's music playing, Brazilian music. I look up at the ceiling and spread my legs and watch myself touch my labia. I spread my labia, placing my fingers inside my wetness. I caress my clitoris, slowly, with my right hand; my left hand squeezes my nipples hard and soft—a door in the mirror to my left opens and a beautiful man walks toward me. He's smiling at me. He asks, 'May I join you?' His voice is so friendly and pitched low, inviting. I nod my head, yes."

María tapped the shell on her forehead. Maybe it really works, she mused, seeing the beautiful man put his tongue in her mouth, in and out, rhythmically, the way she liked it. "Now he's fucking my mouth with his tongue." María became embarrassed and laughed.

"Oh, come, we're all grown women, keep it rolling." Marta complained. "It's just starting to get good, mujer." Marta's shell was still perched on her dream eye, so she imagined she was right there in the room with María.

María took a sip of her drink and continued. "Now a door in the mirror to my right opens and a beautiful blond man walks through. By the way, the first one has black hair."

"I know," Marta murmured.

"The blond man lays to my right, placing his penis on my thigh. It's hard; he wants me. He begins to suck my breasts. One, then the other, moaning. The black-haired man continues to fuck my mouth, and I'm beginning to moan with pleasure like I never have before. I mean, ever—they both want me."

"Holy shit," Yolanda couldn't help saying. "I'm getting hot just hearing about it." The other women giggled; they felt the same.

"A door in the mirror behind me opens and a man with red hair lies to my left and places his penis on my thigh as he begins to stroke my belly, down to my thighs, my knees, my calves, back up, and he finds my clitoris. Now I'm screaming, mutely, in my throat. A beautiful black man comes through a door in the mirror in front of me and falls down, immediately, to eat my pussy. The men begin to moan loudly, in unison, like an ancient chant. The black-haired man puts his penis in my mouth and I want it; I suck it. The men to my side caress me and suck my breasts. The penis in my mouth never goes in too far, doesn't gag me. I'm eating him, the black man is eating me. I come with unbelievable explosions, my body's out of control. I crawl, I writhe, I cry, I laugh. Then each man fucks me, and each one is distinct, different, unique. My vagina continues to convulse, sending messages to my womb straight up to my brain and back to my toenails. I watch each man as we fuck in the mirrors, on top of me, me straddling, on our sides, like dogs, standing, sitting face-to-face. Then they surround me, kneeling; they touch me with their hands, telling me, 'You're beautiful, You're beautiful,' over and over."

"Jesus, these fantasies must be repressed. They're looming up, in full color, right in our faces," Consuelo laughed.

"No analysis, remember?" Yolanda reminded her.

"Yes, please, no analysis. This is wonderful." Marta's voice was soft.

María wept with a strange joy. Each man was so vivid to her, so beautiful, and each one thought she was beautiful. *She was beautiful.* Joy. Strange, strange joy.

"You should see their books, a stack of them. They're supposed to be doctoras, but you'd never know, the way they lay out there in the sun with nothing on," Lupe told the other maid.

"You wonder if they have a man. My husband wouldn't let me go about by myself."

"Only to work, I know." Lupe sighed. "Maybe if we grew up in the North we'd be here with our books."

"And the children?"

"Maybe we'd have no children."

"I'd rather be a mother than a whore."

"They're not whores, they're, as they say, free women." Lupe was startled at the sound of the words: *mujeres libres.* She laughed. "¡Las pochas sin vergüenza!"

"For me, I'll take my husband and my children. We have a good life here, Lupe. The work is plentiful. And, besides, you have a good man, so good-looking too. And your two children are perfect."

"What you say is true." Lupe smiled. "But between you and I, I've always wanted to read books. As a girl I imagined writing them. I used to write poems." Lupe's voice dropped to a whisper. "Of course, I never showed anyone."

"Do you still have them? I'd like to see them. You could read them to me. I'd like that." Her friend's shy longing touched her unexpectedly.

"They're all gone, lost. I wrote them when I was a girl. . . ."

"Write some more. Show them to me. I can't imagine what you'd say, but I'd like to know."

Lupe laughed, putting her hand on her friend's shoulder. "Maybe I will, but it's been so long, and what will I write? After all, I'm a wife and mother now. . . ."

"So? You're not dead!"

They laughed softly, lowering their heads to the afternoon sun, and walked, arm in arm, toward their homes.

"I see you have your bag of shells for the children to paint. Are they selling?" she asked Lupe.

"They are so ethnic, pet shells," Lupe said, imitating the gringa's tone in her accented English.

"Qué ethnic, muchacha. How much do they charge?" she laughed.

"I'm embarrassed to say, it's like stealing. But they do make them cute. They've even begun to glue feathers on them, como los indios."

"Qué chula, save one for me. One never knows about the things children make. They could bring luck. Write a poem about luck, Lupe, for me." She hoped the baby would be clean when she got home and that no accidents had occurred. To hope he'd be home was too much. She knew he was at the cantina.

Lupe squeezed her friend's arm. "I will do it." Her words made her heart race with happiness. She would write a poem for Juanita.

"Did you ever have an orgasm like that?" Yolanda asked. "You don't mind my asking, do you?"

María took the shell off of her forehead and adjusted the lounge to a semi-sitting position. "In the beginning, when I used to have more than one lover at a time, in my early twenties when I was sampling men, I did." María smiled sadly. "And in the first years of my marriage when I thought I was, oh you know, beautiful. Now, I have an orgasm, period. You know."

"I've never had an orgasm like you described." Yolanda lowered her voice. "Not ever."

María laughed softly. "Well, I've never made love to four men at the same time, so why don't you take a shot at it. Don't hold back."

"You give me courage." Yolanda smiled. "Do you all promise not to tell anyone what's heard here today, cross your heart and hope to die, stick a needle in your eye?"

"Stick a needle in my eye."

"Hope to die."

"My lips are sealed."

"Liars!" Yolanda laughed as she lay down on her stomach, pressing the small translucent shell into her forehead so hard it hurt. "Okay, I'm on a stage, kind of dimly lit. I'm laying on an air mattress reading a book." Yolanda paused, trying to see the scene, herself in the scene, as clearly as possible. She laughed with embarrassment, pulling her long, dark hair to one side. The sun felt good on the soft, exposed flesh of her neck.

"Okay, I'm wearing this little girl's dress, full and flouncy, with a white petticoat. I'm wearing white cotton panties and I'm barefoot. I know there're people in the audience. I can almost hear them breathe, but I can't see anyone. An older man, in his fifties, walks toward me from the darkness. He's good-looking, with full, gray hair. He's wearing a suit and a tie and he looks well built. He's handsome but fatherly. 'I've come to make you happy,' he tells me. 'You must do everything I say.' His words scare me, but they also excite me. I just look at him. 'Close the book. If you're very good, I'll give you anything you want, later.' He takes my dress off and carefully folds it, laying it to one side. I'm not wearing a bra and my nipples look pink and girlish, though I look like myself now. He takes my nipples in his mouth, murmuring, 'I bet you like this,' over and over. I'm surprised at the pleasure I feel, but I don't want to let him know. He continues to ask me if I like what he's doing to me—he stays fully dressed. I don't mind that he's fully dressed; I rather prefer it that way, for some reason." Yolanda paused.

"Like I'd rather not see his body, his erection, if he has one. I can't tell. He slips his hand into my panties and begins to stroke me softly, very softly, saying, 'You like this, you like this. . . .' My breath is speeding up and my skin feels like it's starting little fires wherever he strokes me. I want to move, but then he'll know that I like what he's doing, so I lie absolutely still. 'Now I'm going to see what you taste like,' he tells me. He pokes his tongue out at me and smiles, continuing to stroke my neat, folded labia with his smooth, careful fingers. I'm burning up, but I don't move."

Yolanda's breath caught at what she saw next. She felt like masturbating as she spoke, but, of course, that was impossible. She took a deep, full breath. "He lowers my panties to my thighs and slightly parts my legs and he begins to lick my clitoris, making no sound with his mouth. He's so polite, he's exquisite. He's holding my hips between his open palms and he lifts his head. 'I'm not stopping until you come.' His tongue is rhythmic, soft like a puppy's—his hands begin to rotate my hips, making me move. The lights begin to brighten, slightly, but I don't mind. Someone in the audience, a woman, asks, 'Do you think she'll come?' over and over. 'I know you like this,' the man says, and then continues to lick my clitoris. I'm writhing around but I refuse to make any noise. The lights get brighter as I begin to come, feeling his tongue lick my perfect little clitoris. I shut my eyes, just feeling his tongue; the sensation of my orgasm radiates to every part of my body, and the light explodes like the sun as I scream that I love it, I love it better than anything in the world. . . . The man holds me, cradles me. 'I know you do,' he tells me. And it's so fucking wonderful to come this way, just for me. The audience begins to clap, loudly." Yolanda laughed at her own ending.

The women clapped, laughing with her.

"Oh, please don't clap, how embarrassing! What if my husband heard this? He'd croak!" Yolanda laughed louder and her eyes began to tear as she turned onto her back, dropping the shell. It lay on the sand, merging almost perfectly, as though Yolanda had never touched it. "Next fantasy, next fantasy!" And then the word *fantasy* made her sad.

"My turn—last and worst, right?" Consuelo giggled. "Yours were all so great, I'm feeling intimidated, like all the great fantasies are taken."

"Oh, come on, Consuelo, you must have a secret fantasy up your you-know-what," Marta teased.

"You-know-what?" María repeated. "You mean her sleeve?" She kept a straight face, making Consuelo burst into a fit of laughter.

"Okay, okay, I'll tell—"

"Wait, Consuelo, the spy's returning," Marta laughed, indicating the boy walking toward them. They all began to giggle.

As he stood next to Consuelo waiting for them to order, he dropped a note into her lap: "Do you like me?" Consuelo stood up to stretch and adjust her bathing suit. Quickly, she handed him her shell and smiled at him, whispering, "Tonight."

As he walked toward the bar with the word *tonight* ringing in his head, he held the shell tightly in his hand and imagined himself driving the silver motorcycle. He could feel his hands grip the black rubber handlebars that would take him wherever he wanted to go. Wherever he wanted to go. And it would belong to him.

He placed the fresh drinks next to them, carefully. La Doctora Puta was speaking to the other putas in English. Just the sound, the droning, flat sound of the language bored him. It didn't rise or fall like his own language. It has no flesh, he thought. No blood, no heart. He smiled, revealing his white, hungry teeth.

". . . but I have to teach him how to satisfy me, he's still a virgin. So, I tell him to lie next to me. 'Show me your tongue,' I tell him . . ."

"Do you honestly think there's any nineteen-year-old virgins around?" Yolanda interjected.

"It's my fantasy, right?"

"Come on, Yolanda, be quiet," María laughed. "She's right, though. You'd have to snatch a twelve-year-old to get a virgin these days."

"Maybe the busboy's a virgin," Marta couldn't resist adding. She'd noticed the boy staring at Consuelo with interest—and she couldn't help thinking Consuelo noticed the boy as well.

"Never. Do you forget that I'm a child psychiatrist?" Consuelo smiled, spreading her legs to the hot Mexican sun. She wanted her innermost thighs to darken, to burn. She wondered, suddenly, what it felt like to have your heart cut out of your body. Would you be able to see it, for a moment, in the priest's bloody hands? She shivered with fear and excitement and continued to lie to her friends, so leisurely, in English.

Happiness

Elena Poniatowska

Yes, my love, yes I'm next to you, yes, my dear, yes, I love you my love, yes, you plead with me not to tell you so often, I know, I know, these are big words, spoken once and for all life, you never call me love, my paradise, my love, my heaven, you don't believe in paradise love, yes my love, take care of me, I don't ever want to leave these four walls, let me stay in your arms, surround me with your eyes, cover me with your eyes, save me, protect me, love, happiness, don't go away, look there is that word again, I bump into it constantly, give me your hand, later you'll say, but I want to feel it now, say it now, look, the sun, the heat comes in and these tenacious branches from the ivy with their tiny hard leaves that sneak in through the warmth of the window and grow in your room and *interwine* with us, and I need them, I love them, they bind us together, because, love, I need you, you are needed, that's it, you are needed and you know it, my needed man who hardly ever says my name, next to you I don't have a name and when you say this and the other, my name is never present and you reject my words, happiness, love, I love you, because you are wise and you don't like to name things, even though happiness is there, *watching,* with its happy name floating in the air, on top of us, in the twilight of the afternoon, and if I say its name it vanishes, and then shadows come and I say to you, love, give me back the light, then your fingertips travel my body from my forehead to the tip of my toe, along a path selected by you, examining me, and I lay motionless, on my side, with my back toward you and you retrace your fingertips along my sides from the tip of my toe to my forehead, stopping suddenly at my hip and say, you have lost weight and I think of a skinny horse like the one Cantinflas' musketeer used when he hung his feather blanket on its bony rump, because I, my love, I am your old nag, and I can't gallop anymore and I await you watchfully, yes, I watch you, telling you, don't leave me, you have nothing to do but to be with me, with your hand on my hip, no, we won't leave this place, tie me up, put your shirt on me, you laugh because it looks so big on me, don't laugh, go and get lemonade from the kitchen because it's hot and we are thirsty, go on, go, no, wait for me, I'll go, no, I'll go, well you go, wait, don't get up, now it's my turn, I already went running for the lemonade and I'm here again next to you, as you lie on the bed, free and naked like dusk, drink some of it, drink the bright light, don't you realize, I don't want the sun to go away while we drink happiness, I don't want the sun to go away or for you to stop stretching out like that, in the timeless afternoon and evening that come in through the window, our window, look, cover it with your hand, so the night will stay out, a window should be there forever, although you can cover the sun for me with a finger, yes, my love, yes, I'm here, your window to the world, cover me with your hand, dim me like the sun, you can make the night, you breathe and the air ceases to flow through the window, how happy we are, look how warm you are, the window has remained motionless like me, static forever, cover me with your hand, Oh! how I forget it all!, the window protects our only exit, our communication with the stars, I love you, my love, let's go to heaven while the neighbor does the wash in the yard, in her yard, a laundress's yard, while here in your yard no one washes and there is wild ivy in the sink, it's tall and the wind makes it sway because it can't blow clothes on an empty clothesline, you remember, in October a sunflower grew there, small, emaciated, but I felt it swirl over my womb, in my tossed hair, disarranged, sad and yellow like a small abandoned garden, a tiny garden in the outskirts of the city climbing through the thatch and coming here and entering through the window to this house of crumbs, a white bread house, where I am in the heart of tenderness, a golden house, round as hope, ring around the rosie, house of happiness, have pity on us, surround us with your lime walls, don't open your door, don't toss us out in the open, we have filled you with words, look, look, say again: my love, my paradise, my paradise, my love, the heat rises and I don't know what to do anymore to silence my heartbeats and I don't move, you see, don't say I look like a locust, a grasshopper, don't say I look like a dressed flea, I don't move any longer, you see, why do you tell me: be calm, if I'm not doing anything, I only ask you if you want to sleep, and you bring me close to you, I embrace you and I pin myself to your mouth like a medal, and I know you don't want to, you don't want to sleep, you only want us to be still, still and tame while the heat rises from the earth, and grows, throbbing us, I love you, my love, we are the couple, the archetype, I lean against you, I lay my head like a medallion on your chest, I inscribe myself on to you, like a love word coined in your mouth, there are flames on your lips, heat that suddenly melts my being, now on the Pentecost holy day, but we'll never die, right? because no one loves each other as we do, no one loves each other like this because you and I are we and no one is stronger than the two of us, here, locked up in your chest and in mine, let me see you, you are inside of me, look at me with my eyes, don't close them, don't sleep my love, don't go away into sleep, your eyelids are closing, look at me, let me see you, don't leave me, don't let the sun go away, I don't want it to dim, to set, don't yield like the light, the sun, leave everything as it was over my medlar skin, look, you can see me now better than ever because the afternoon is coming to an end, because you are leaving me also, and here I am telling you: don't leave me, be with me forever, strong as the burning sun I stared at as a child with my open eyes, until I saw black, black like the routine ending of fairy tales with the princess living happily ever after with many, many children, don't sleep, don't sleep I'm telling you, anxiously, constantly, with no afterwards, because there is no afterwards anymore for us, even if you leave me, but you'll never leave, you'll have to come to pick me up, to put the pieces back together once again on the bed and here I am in one piece, and you can't leave me because you would have to return and you would miss a part of me forever, like the missing piece from a puzzle that ruins the entire picture, all the life you had given me and you can't take away from me because you would die, you would go blind and you wouldn't be able to find me limping, crippled, maimed by you, without words, mute, with the word final sealing my lips, the final ending of all stories, there is no longer a story, I don't tell you stories, endings, nothing counts anymore, things get transformed, there's no longer an extra hour on earth, look, the window screen has holes, I can see the two butterflies on the wall with their papier-maché wings, yellow, pink, orange, and the cotton candy and that small wooden bird you bought on the street the Friday everything began, the yellow Friday like the tiny bird black and shocking pink that pecks us ever since, a child's toy, like the paper butterflies that fly round the park until the real ones leave their cocoons, like the ones you crucified in the other room, big ones, with their marvelous blue transparent wings, you pierced them with a pin, one on top of the other, with a pin that hurts me and I asked you how you did it, well, doing it, and you strung up happiness, you petrified it there on the wall, happy, again this word, I repeat it, it comes back, it returns and I repeat it, and you get irritated and you tell me, there goes the donkey off again to the wheat field, to the greedy blossom of happiness, don't you understand, no, I don't understand, help me to pull out the weeds, help me to walk through God's wheat fields pinned down with the needle without the other butterfly, you say now we are all alone pinned down with the needle, without the other butterfly, that no one belongs to anyone, that what we share is sufficient, and enough, and is even miraculous, yes, yes, yes, my love, it's miraculous, don't close your eyes, I do understand, don't be silent, don't sleep, open up and look at me, you're tired and in a short while you'll fall asleep, you'll enter the river, and I'll remain on the bank, the bank we walked together, do you remember, under the eucalyptus, walking to the pace of the river, under the leaves, under the swords of light, I'm open to all wounds, here, I brought you my young spreading womb, I give you my teeth big and strong like tools and I don't feel ashamed of myself anymore, I lie, yes, I do feel ashamed, and I tell all the nuns I like roses with thorns and all, under the black skirts, while they play with their rosaries, and the wind and the light can't vibrate between their legs, leave this place birds of ill omen, get out, tiny threads of life, withered corner cobwebs, full of dust, get out, narrow, half-opened doors, go into mourning, spying crevices, get out brooms, let me sweep the world with all of you, you that swept out so many colored papers from my soul, and you love stay, I wish I had met you when I was older, spinning near the hearth my longings for you, even if you had never arrived, and singing to myself the same old song, when I was young he would fall asleep under my window, even if it weren't true, because now you came early, before I had time to get up, and you put your hand on the slit of the door, and you moved the latch, and I liked your pants with their bulging pockets, your pockets that seem to carry inside of them all of life's accidents, and your own thoughts, like little balls of wrapped caramel candy, your thoughts, tell me, what are you thinking my love¿, tell me what are you thinking right now, just right now when you stay like this as if you were with yourself, alone, forgetting that I'm here with you, my love, what are you thinking¿ I always ask the same, do you love me¿, you're falling asleep, I know you'll fall asleep and I'll get dressed without making a sound, and I'll close the door carefully, to leave you there wrapped in the warm red and ocher of the afternoon, because you have fallen asleep and you don't belong to me anymore and you didn't take me with you, you left me behind, today in the afternoon when the

sun and the warm light were pounding through the window, and I am going to walk a lot, a lot, and the neighbor will see me from her door, with her disapproving look because only from time to time do I venture through this path, I'll walk up to the eucalypus trees, until I'm exhausted, until I accept that you are a sleeping body over there, and that I am another one here walking and that together the two of us are
hopelessly,
hopelessly,
madly,
desperately,
alone.

Translated by Carmen C. Esteves

Tongue Cakes

Perla Sanchez

I stuck my tongue in Laura's pussy while she sucked Juan's *chorra.*
She tasted like peppermint and reminded me of what my fingers
tasted like after Tino made me stick them in my pussy, rub them
in there, and lick them with my tongue. That was a few years ago.
I couldn't believe Laura and I were doing this together again. The
first time Laura and I got together, it was with a guy named Hector
who couldn't keep up with us. It was his idea for the three of us
to go for it. I was surprised Laura said yes right away. I was more
hesistant because I thought my best friend and I would be shy about
getting naked together and having some good sex with the same
guy all at once. But, once we got in bed with Hector, I couldn't
believe how exciting it was.

We both tried to suck him at the same time, make a "tongue
cake," as Laura loved to call it. It drove Hector crazy and he squirted
all over our faces. It was great. We were on either side of his big
chorra, running our tongues over it as it beat like a heart. As I pushed
at the tip with my tongue, Laura touched my lips with her tongue
and we wound up kissing each other right over Hector's tip. That
did it. He shot all over us. I had never heard a guy cry out so loud.
But, we also scared him away. He got dressed after that. Laura
asked him if he wanted to watch us lick each other's pussy, but he
said no. That was fine with me because it was our first time and I
think I wanted to enjoy Laura by myself. The thing is, after Hector
left, Laura and I just lay there, thought about what we had done,
and laughed and laughed. It was so funny and there was no way
she and I could get it on with each other. We weren't lesbians.
There had to be a guy there to get us going. So we got dressed and
went home.

We did it the second time with Juan. He was better than Hector
and knew how to fuck and fuck. Here I was kissing Laura's pussy
again while she did a great job on Juan, some guy she worked with
I didn't really like, but she and I had promised each other we would
get another one of these smart-ass guys and show him a thing or
two. I know Pedro and Tino, our two old boyfriends, think all we
know how to do is lie on our backs and let them fuck us. Well, I

got tired of that real fast. I wouldn't let those guys near me any-more. Laura and I are good friends and have always wanted to do something like this together.

I kept thinking about those guys as Laura started moaning. She lifted her right leg higher so I could shift my back onto her other leg and press my face into her pussy. She was really wet. Even though I didn't like Juan, I had to admit he had a better *chorra* than Hector, but the guy wouldn't come. He'd been hard for over an hour and had already fucked Laura once. She was sucking him as he lay back on the bed, her body on his left side with me on my knees leaning over to give her a good licking. Finally, Laura got tired of sucking him, so she climbed on top, and hissed a sigh of pleasure as she slid down on him. She started to move up and down real slow. Juan looked at her, pinched her sharp little tits, and reached for me. I climbed onto the bed, but he motioned to go around to the other side, where he laid his head. I scrambled over the top of the bed and stood over his upturned face. He smiled and pulled me onto his head. I couldn't believe the way his tongue moved inside my pussy. I went wild and started whining! I leaned over and Laura and I kissed and tongued each other. Juan was crazy, but lucky. He was driving me nuts with his tongue and Laura was really fucking him hard. She was jumping up and down so fast, I couldn't keep my tongue in her mouth. I backed off and came and came. Laura reached out and held my shoulders as I gasped. We looked into each other's eyes and shared the pleasure and the pain. Our nipples brushed against each other as we almost suffocated Juan under us. He gave an extra push and Laura started coming. She heaved and moaned and let go of my shoulders as I fell back off Juan's face. Laura spasmed like a string puppet, her long brown hair stuck to her face, the sweat between her breasts glistening in the low lamp-light of the room.

I collapsed next to Juan and watched Laura fall onto him. The two of them panted hard from the fucking, but Juan still wouldn't come. He hugged Laura as she lay on top of him, freshly fucked and tired. He surprised me as the three of us lay naked together in his apartment. I was drifting off to sleep after watching the great fuck when he rolled over her, spread my legs apart with his hands, and slid right into me. I caught a brief look at his swollen red *chorra* as it moved at me. I couldn't believe it and screamed. He was full and hard and smelled great on top of me. Laura was always talking about him. She said the two of them did it in the office bathroom early one morning when they thought they were the only ones there. Arturo, the janitor, walked in on them as Juan was fucking her while she sat on the edge of the sink.

I thought about the two of them in the office bathroom and wrapped my legs tight around his muscular ass. His long black hair spilled down on my face and the whiskers on his chin scratched me. I didn't care because he was really going at it. I had never felt anything so physical stuck inside me. I was crying and tried to look through the long strands of his hair that hung down over my eyes. I felt Laura at my side. I turned to see her face draw near mine. Her eyes were half closed, but she was smiling like she had really liked it. As Juan reached under me and lifted my ass a few inches off the bed, I shifted my legs onto his shoulders. He was really slamming into me and I kept crying out. Laura laughed and tried to stick her tongue in my mouth. Juan started a deep, low grunting sound—the first we had heard him make since we started all this. He kept fucking me faster and the grunts grew louder. Laura and I gasped and laughed and stuck our tongues in each other's throat as Juan came and came and came. He heaved into me and I could feel his *chorra* traveling all the way up. It jumped and shook inside me for several seconds. I don't know how to describe it but I felt like I was flying through the air—my body, Laura's body, and Juan's *chorra* flying through the air as I suddenly came and cried and spit and pushed Laura back so I could breathe, Juan still pointing inside me, the sweat on his chest pouring onto my nipples, Laura's tongue lapping it up like the *gata* that she was.

I don't know how to say it, but Laura and I became closer friends after that. Yet, I have to be honest in saying we have never done a threesome together since that day with Juan. It went on for five hours. He fucked her three times and got me twice. Laura and I were totally fucked every which way you can think of, but we have not done that since. I don't really know why. When I ask her about Juan, she just smiles and says he is fine. Neither one of us has suggested doing such a thing again. I am dating Felipe and she is going out with this new guy named Tony. We don't have to say it, but we know neither one of them would ever do such a thing with the two of us. It's okay. Five hours of tongue cakes with your best friend is enough.

Love Sequence

Francisco Alarcón

Caliente

comienzas
a apuntar
al cielo

Horny

you start
pointing
to the sky

Soother

I tongue bite
your erect
dark nipples

so your heart
won't become
another fist

Puesta de Sol — Sunset

la puesta	with you
de sol	I spent
más larga	the longest
la pasé contigo	sunset
tú	you
juntando	gathering
conchitas	seashells
en el mar	on the beach
yo	I
muy adentro	already
con un árbol	like a tree
de noche	of night
ya en flor	in full bloom

My Bed

it is the raft
on which I navigate
every night
looking to salvage
the remains
of my shipwreck

it is the dock
in my poor
harbor
that with longing
awaits the return
of sailors

it is my lost
island
my cistern
my boxing ring
the trace of Arab
left in me

it is my last
refuge
my nest
my tomb
the only altar
in my home

My Hair

when
you met me
my hair was
black like
the blackest
canvas

with your hair
I'll make the finest
paintbrushes
you would tell me
biting
my ears

and I would run
with my black
hair loose
like a colt
its black mane
shining

with your gray hair
I've made now
a long rope
you tell me
wrapping it
around my neck

Everything Is an Immense Body

everything is
an immense
body

the sierras
extended
thighs

the trees
in the valley
hair on a chest

the bays
mouths
tongue the sea

Bridge

extend
your arms
extend them
until your hands
touch the edge
of my body

I will travel
across your body
like someone
who crosses
a bridge
and saves himself

Un Beso Is Not a Kiss

un beso
es una puerta
que se abre
un secreto
compartido
un misterio
con alas

un beso
no admite
testigos
un beso can't
be captured
traded
nor sated

un beso
is not just
a kiss
un beso is
more dangerous
sometimes
even fatal

Climax Climax

de pronto
en la punta
de la lengua
¡una galaxia!

suddenly
on the tip
of our tongue
a galaxy!

The Second Time

Tony Guijon

I ate her pussy like the swan.
She circled the bed and told me
the red cloud of my tongue
belonged between her legs.

I lay on my back
as she hovered over
the edge of the bed.
"Your tongue! Your tongue!"
she cried.

I stuck my face in her pussy.
The swan became an owl.
The owl became a wrinkled pigeon
from the street near my house,
near the door where
she first kissed me.

The pigeon became a flower
which contained the petal
I moved aside with my finger
as I opened her pussy,

saw myself running toward her,
saw how long it would last
as her weight fell on my
sweating shoulder,
her heavy knee pushing into
my armpit as the room filled
with the panic of sparrows.

Cock

Tony Guijon

My cock looks like an angel.
It falls from heaven without me knowing
who it will protect, which of my prayers it will answer.
When I scratch it, it moves aside
to let me see how men hang themselves
with too much pride.

My cock is not an angel.
It is only my old body growing smaller,
getting older, deciding it will not stick it
to the world as often.

My cock has never spoken
to all the women I have loved.
It only stands when I think
I have something to say
with my mouth, my eyes,
my tongue, my swiveling
sac of balls that trembles
in the air between my spread legs
as I thrust and thrust.

My cock speaks one word.
Its spits it out here and there.
The last woman that shuddered
over my cock closed her eyes
because she couldn't understand
that one word.

My cock looks like an angel.
It will never know hell because
that woman wanted me,
tried to teach my cock
a second word—"love."

Years Ago

Tony Guijon

Thrusting into her from behind,
I see the flame I left burning years ago.
Pushing into her, the shiny marks on her naked back
glisten like the water I spilled years ago.
Having her twist and turn without pulling out,
I know I am not good enough.
Bringing the bowl of blueberries to the bed,
I smell the fruit I hated years ago.
Placing one blueberry at a time in her pussy,
I retrieve it with my tongue.
As she moans and sticks another bead down there, it pops.
I lick the purple juice like the water I drank years ago.
Slurping the entire black opening until it goes back to red,
I become too strong,
know she will push me away,
tell me to go fuck someone else.
Thrusting into her from behind,
I see the smoke that covers my retreat.

My Dream of Licking

Xavier Cavazos

Carmella let me lick your long hair
With my lips   let me braid
Each strand with my red tongue
Weaving & licking & weaving all the same
O mela a   let me lick you wet
O mela   let me lick
O a   let me

Manteca

Xavier Cavazos

Crisco never felt like it felt when
Anna Marie put it on me
The manteca would just melt in
Her hands like summer
I never understood why that never happened
When mom put it on

My hair needed alot &
Anna Marie knew it
Knew how to squeeze the lard just
Right between each hair &
The hair after
Knew how to comb it just right
With her thin fingers

Knew just right
How to make a boy worship a can

Face

Maria Madresca

face of semen
    face of orgasm

it was your turn
    it was your come

when the cry came
    the sky came

the face I saw
    appeared again

face the anus
    face the big toe

when I shove the greased dream
    up your anus

you know me as
    the confessed intruder

when you tickle my stomach
    with your foot

I know you only
    as one man

You

Maria Madresca

I hold you with
      the shattered truce of embrace.
When you weep
      over my nipples,
I cry and don't know you.

Fuck me with a star.
      Force me
to misspell the word "crazy."

I hold you, tell you
      not to talk this way.
When you dance
      far from the bed,
your balls shiver like globes
      of confused light.

I stare at your
      naked body,
hope the hair on your chest
      smells like my smell—

an odor of liking
      and envy—
trail of invisible legs locking
      around your chest
as all your hair falls off,
      makes you stop
dancing so far from me.

I hurt you
      with my thighs.
I squeeze until
      your tears
are the same wetness
      dripping off your balls,
streaming down my bruised ankles.

Tool

Maria Madresca

She saw him fall on the bed and she withdrew the electric thing from the wall. He reached over and plugged it back in, making her recall how the black muscle of his hidden life had hurt her many times. She took the tool with all its colors, but before she could touch him with it, he grabbed it from her. He had done this once before, taken her a long way toward the waterfall she dreamed about as a girl, but that one time several months ago changed the waterfall forever. He had wrapped the tool around her buttocks, shaped it into the mound of flesh that cavorted like the curtain of hungry ice she burned her lips upon. He pulled on the tool and it extended into the sudden strike of her cunt. It hesitated before spilling into her, the growing cascade of her youthful waterfall sending the sharp memory up into her stomach. She knew the tool would be useless to both of them someday, but as she began to reach out toward the falling river, he said something to her she couldn't understand. As she fell, she saw his black muscle come apart in his hands, the cord of his beloved electricity sparking with the mistake he had just made. She hit the water in a perfect dive, the impact drilling her into the green flesh that contained so many fish, eels, and broken electric rocks, that she had no idea how far she descended before his black muscle and his device were completely out of her life.

A Kiss at Noontime

Trinidad Bidar

I visit my baby's house for lunch
the bed sits between cinder blocks and milk crates
we get naked in the afternoon sun
the curtains sunny like lemon pastry

scratchy Al Green record on the box
and her arms spread to hug like a sunflower
she squeezes me tight like a loaf
of sixty-cent wheat bread against the bag

we swim on clean sheets
the soap scent in our eyes
drink some wine from a big cheap jug
it spreads through me like a spill on a blanket

it goes down from neck to shoulders like a cape
I wade through language
and gently cup handfuls upon her wet skin
I make a list of things to kiss

and name the things that meet my lips
her skin is sweet chlorine
her cheeks a spoon of milk
her shoulderblade curve a half-moon

my love feels thick as a river of candle wax
it's sharp as siren lights
it's wet as a child under a fire hydrant
on a summer day

when the chocolate melts
then I kiss down there
a warm marble on my tongue
face dripping like a kid with a melon

her legs rigid, spread like Xmas tree holders
my tongue flaps cheery as the american flag
her eyes crunched up like marijuana leaves
I keep licking peels as she kicks the wall

Hands at Prayer

Trinidad Bidar

" 'How can this be?' said Mary, 'I am still a virgin.' The angel answered,
'The Holy Spirit will come upon you, and the power of the Most High will
overshadow you.'" Luke 1:34–35

"So the Word became flesh; he came to dwell among us." John 1:14

Her bedroom in the attic is children's height,
the ceiling beams of wood folded
like hands at prayer
I can't stand;
only kneel, flatten or sit.

> *That's all I need you for,* she laughs.

We drink gin straight from the bottle,
spilling coins of it on the mattress.
I start kissing chocolate freckles on her skin.

She pushes me away.

> *Why do men talk about sex*
> *all the time*
> *but don't talk*
> *while they're doing it?*

> I say, *I like to hear the bouncy creak*
> *of your boxspring,*
> *the stuttered kick of your breathing,*
> *the heat of your skin,*
> *the rustle of blankets.*

I tickle her milkfat ear lobes,
tongue bundt-cake wax in frowning ear petals,
lick the spicy cointaste of ormulu hoops and rings.

I want you to talk
more.
God whispered to Mary's ear to make Jesus,
the word became flesh,
the word was
pro-creative.

She spends ten minutes lighting candles around the room,
supermarket Virgen de Guadalupes, Josephs and Marys,
their steam rises like snake heat.

Their flames wash a bowl of shadows back and forth
across satchels, rosary beads, pearl necklaces.

Her creamy curtains frayed and moth-eaten
as a thrift store wedding gown
her black clothes droop off wires like nodding monks.

She says, *Women like stories,*
the way men like visions
and porno.

I love the smell of henna powder
and sea plasma on your skin.

That's a start.

We undress each other, slow backward unbuttoning
Under muscled blankets, we exchange favorite kisses:
I mark the small bump of her left shoulder bone,
the chapped whorls of her feet.

Your nipples are like coins on a soft pillow, I say.

Sweat fills the crevices
between the hair on our legs,
my nipples and her back, my penis and her spine.
I make circles with her clitoris.

I feel like I'm touching part of myself.

She turns over to face me
hold her ribs and the small of her back
and I go inside with the first breathless push.

> *I thought of being inside you all week*
> *there's something stupid and primitive*
> *inside of me that wants to be like two*
> *sweaty animals, making babies.*

She says, *Maybe we should try silence again.*

Sacred Heart

Alejandro Murguia

Cristina de la Cruz smoked too much, a mentholated pack a day, sometimes more. She liked smoke-filled bars where brooding men congregated, chasing dreams empty as their pockets. The long mahogany bar at the Kit Kat Klub, for instance. Like tonight—a night of rain, and slick roads, and traffic accidents. The salsa music pounding from the speakers and gyrating couples doing fancy dance steps on the floor and spinning like tops. Cristina de la Cruz sat alone, playing with strands of her hair, checking for split ends; being unloved was worse than being hurt. She crossed her legs. Uncrossed them. She pulled the hem of her dress down but after a while she didn't care how much she showed. She didn't think much of her legs, too short and a little on the heavy side, thought her nose too thin, her face too broad. The rain made her feel unloved, a candle without a fire. She flicked the ashes of her cigarette on the rug, already scarred with a hundred burns. Ashes spilled around her drink and she finished each cigarette with a hard, deliberate crushing in the ashtray. The lyrics of a song kept repeating in her head, but she couldn't remember the name or the artist, only the chorus— *"Cristina . . . Cristina. . . ."* Her red dress dipped low in front and she went without a bra, her dark nipples pressing rings against the silk fabric. She wore red Spanish stilettos, an invitation to a heartache. Sometimes she couldn't stand to be touched. Tonight, though, she wouldn't mind. She could give till her body broke.

Cristina liked men and rum, not always in that order. In her purse she kept imipramine tablets her doctor prescribed, in case the shadows fell on her, in case the light grew cloudy. Her life turned around bars and chance encounters. Depending on her mood she could be a flirt, a bitch, or pin her hair up and play the slut. Often she traded sex with men that left her feeling confused, or cheap and abused, but regardless, the next day when the men woke up in her bed, their strange faces crinkled with sleep, she always felt worse. *Asco.* She ordered them out. Now. Without even asking their names.

Afterwards, paranoia followed her for days; she'd wonder what she might have exposed herself to, vow to change her ways, which never changed. After a few days the repulsion would pass, then anything might make her feel reckless again, and she would go out searching. Return to the Latin Palace, El Rio, Pier 23, the Kit Kat Klub, where all the bartenders knew her. The woman with fire-red lipstick who sat alone. Smoking too much. Enjoying her solitary drinks. And taking home different men. Sometimes a musician. Usually an empty seat besides her, a piña colada in front of her. Like tonight, sitting with her dress hiked up, her legs crossed, her red stilettos swinging back and forth, twirling the straw around in the tumbler and licking the foamy tip.

Pablo had been watching her do the thing with the straw. He wondered about a woman who'd sit alone in a bar. A smoky, blue-lit bar where people stared eye-to-eye and danced belly-to-belly, where faces were shadows, and love a knife to cut the object of one's desire.

Cristina picked him out first, spotted him hiding in that shadowy corner, his back against the wall. He looked hurt by life. They all did; that's what she liked about them. She raised her drink to him, and smiled. So he smiled back. He liked red because it said so much, revealed everything about a woman. A minute later he slipped into the empty seat next to her. They each wanted a close-up of the mistake they were about to make.

"I've been watching you all night," he said.

"Why is that?" She'd known she was being watched. Her voice was low and with an edge, a switchblade to his throat.

"Because red is my favorite color."

She liked that. A man with a sense of color. She liked his face, his sharp profile that extended in a straight line from his forehead to the tip of his nose, his wide nostrils and the eyes like the sharp edge of obsidian. A downturned mustache added a cruel touch. His mouth contained enough anger to load into a gun. She could see him lining up twenty Federales and shooting them, one at a time, before breakfast.

Pablo wasn't sure of the attraction. Her eyebrows had a nice curve, and he liked the wide cheekbones, but her lipstick was smeared in one corner and a rash marred her forehead. He wasn't that anxious; it'd been months since a woman crumpled his bed, and he didn't mind his room neat and tidy.

She packed words together tight as petates, and jumped from idea to idea like a bird pecking at seeds. "Am I talking too much?" she'd say, and keep going, from the latest Almodovar film to the

Chac Mool in Mayan ritual—detouring through the philosophical implications of the sacrificial heart and its journey to the gods. "The heart is our greatest gift and our biggest mystery. How you give it is the thing. It has to be all or nothing at all. The heart is sacred. Do you follow me?" He nodded to the beat of her words. She matched him drink for drink. After several rums, he asked her to dance. Cristina replied, "I don't know how."

"It's nothing, I'll show you," Pablo said, taking her hand. She squeezed back, digging her sharp nails into his palm.

The silk dress rubbed against her nylons, making a rustling sound, and he couldn't help notice how the fabric clung to her hips, revealing the outline of her panties. Her hips were wide under an average waist. On the floor Pablo took her right hand and held it up at her side, face level. He kept the other hand under her ribs, guiding her, leading her around the dance floor, then spinning her to a rapid saxophone merengue until Cristina laughed like a schoolgirl. And she was thinking—I could go for this one, let him do everything. She pressed close to him during the one slow dance near closing time, pressed her wet face to his cheek, and he bent his face to hers and decided to let the current pull him where it would.

Maybe because of the drinks, or because of the conversation, or the red-and-purple strobe lights flashing in her eyes, or because she was feeling good and didn't care what people thought about her (they always thought the worst anyway; maybe she was loose, so what?) or because of the congeros slapping leather, or those crazy saxophones with their *jalao,* or perhaps it was the honey-voiced singer with his weepy boleros that shredded her insides, or maybe in spite of all this, or maybe just because she wanted him to spend the night, wanted him to tell her she was beautiful—her eyes invited him to guide her home.

Cristina'd taken a cab so she wouldn't drive in the rain.

The door panels of his Volvo were rusty and the inside smelled of sweat and paintbrushes. Pablo carried his tools in the trunk. He'd finished a job this afternoon, a two-week gig painting a Victorian in the Haight—a deep crimson color. Oil-based paint that was hard to remove. The red tint stained the creases of his hands, stuck like nail polish to his cuticles, or bled from under his nails. Saturday night and he didn't know when he'd work again or have money, so he turned and kissed her on the mouth, and her wet hair brushed against his face.

Then he touched the delicate line of her jaw and held her face to the yellow streetlight coming through the car window. He stared at her as he would a blank wall to paint, assessing every angle. She closed her eyes and let him. Pablo followed the rise of her cheekbones, the profile of her little turned-up nose, the pout of her lips. Pablo decided she was not beautiful, and that satisfied him. "You're pretty" was all he said. That's all it took. She knew. Whatever he wanted she'd be willing—any way, any time. Cristina opened her eyes to the painful intensity of his gaze, like the rain in Puerto Escondido. A hard, stinging rain that left her drenched for years. A rain she had swallowed as it dripped down the roof tiles. A rain she equated with pain and hunger and powerful forces that left her bleeding. What did it matter she knew only his first name, Pablo, a name like some romantic poet, common as a Mexican town in the middle of nowhere—but his hands, those hands belonged to the Prince of Darkness, hands to be sheathed in leather, blunt instruments, hands she could worship like primitive fetishes. His hands were on the steering wheel and he was gauging her, wondering—a woman lets a total stranger take her home. Cristina tossed her head back, haughty, daring him; she felt brazen, and bad, and didn't want him to see she was just a little bit scared.

Pablo drove the battered car through the rainy San Francisco night, stealing quick glances at her, but he was thinking of someone else. Cristina's mouth reminded Pablo of the woman who'd left him broken in so many pieces they were scattered like bits of glass over every club in La Mission. That's why tonight he'd gone to the Kit Kat Klub, because no memories of Lydia existed there. Lydia Alianza, his part-time lover and his full-time pain. They had fought through the three stages of love: passion, indifference, and hate. Lydia of the hard lean body—the amor of his amores. Lydia who promised never to abandon him as she cradled his head in her arms. Lydia, his last good-bye, who left him for a stand-up Chicano comedian, or was it a politician? He wasn't sure. It didn't make much difference. His heart sealed now like a nuclear tomb, 25,000 years and counting. He needed the right woman to counteract the fallout from Lydia's devastation.

At first Pablo'd been indifferent to her leaving, had even laughed at her bad taste. "Acuestate con todos los payasos en el circo! Que me importa!" he'd yelled at her. Sleep with all the clowns in the circus. See if I care. That's right.

But as Lydia walked out the door, and out of his life, she'd lobbed this at him: "You're just a housepainter, and that's all you'll ever be." And he had loved her more than the moon did the stars, now that he couldn't find her in his sky.

Days later Lydia's words detonated in his brain like a bomb over Hiroshima. He *was* just a housepainter. But he was a good, honest housepainter. And more than that he could not be.

The view from Cristina's second-floor apartment took in the wet palm trees of Dolores Park and the fragmented lights of downtown. The pale halo of a street lamp floated in a black puddle. Soft sheets of rain fell over the rooftops of the city and on the rows of Canary Island palms lining Dolores Street; the rain washed down the buildings and the cars, sloshed into the gutters, and flooded his wretched heart. It was hard to admit he needed someone to love. Just a painter of houses. Just a working man. As if to say he was a grain of sand on a beach, as if to say, *Nada.*

Cristina switched on a small lamp in the kitchen; a yellow hue lit up her face, the red of her dress, his face, his leather jacket, the framed posters of the Mexican painter Frida Kahlo staring down from the burnt-orange colored walls—Frida with a necklace of thorns scratching out drops of blood; Frida as the goddess Tlazoteotl, a bedsheet over her face, her legs spread, a dead baby half out her womb; Frida with nails hammered into her body; Frida's dual portrait, in love with the man who hurts her; Frida as a deer pierced by nine arrows. The kitchen looked like a monument to suffering and blood, an apocalyptic gallery of pain and despair.

Cristina sat at a round table and ran her hands through her wet hair; the sensation made her feel brave, in control. She removed her red-beaded earrings, leaving just the pair of gold studs. She wanted to hold Pablo's beatific face in her hands and kiss his impassive mouth. *Willing* was the word she wanted. She was willing to be crushed by him. Willing because she was stronger and she knew it. Desire like this always frightened her. As she was frightened now by his aloofness, his standing sullenly, hands in pockets, without a word to say. His eyes, sad as a saint's in this yellow light, at this weary hour. Impenetrable as a Mayan fortress. A series of images, jagged as broken glass, stabbed her in the waist, in the ribs, in the heart. She saw herself in Puerto Escondido, breast being fondled, and a hand plunging between her legs and ripping out her womb like some bloody sacrifice. She could see Pablo was capable of cruelty; perhaps as a child he'd nailed a cat to a board or something, and she wanted to be that cat, have him drive nails into her, splinter her body like pine. An altar she wanted to make of herself.

The room in Puerto Escondido held memories that burned her like matches. Sunlight is filtering through the latticed windows, the light is pure and blinding. She is under the cool sheets, the bed is hard, she has almost fallen asleep listening to the transistor radio under her pillow, the Rolling Stones, "Have You Seen Your Mother, Baby, Standing in the Shadows?" Her mother is downstairs in the cantina offering herself to hungry Mexican men. One day she will marry one but that is still years away, after the mescal has drained her beauty, after the scandals, after everything has been lost. Now Cristina is fourteen and her father, an Anglo engineer, has brought them to Puerto Escondido and leaves her mother to dark men with strange tastes while he ferrets out smooth-skinned boys on the deserted playas. Cristina has her mother's eyes and that same vulnerable mouth, but she's her father's girl, a romantic masochist. Her father's sister, Violet, has come with them on this vacation. Violet smokes cigarettes with gold filters and can drink men under the table. It is Violet's hand that covers Cristina's mouth and wakes her. Violet's hands have the licorice taste of her cigarettes. Cristina wonders where is mother? as Violet's mouth tears a kiss from her that tastes of tequila. It is Violet's hand that pinches her nipples, Violet's hand that probes her sex, forces open her legs and rips her insides. It is Violet's fingers that withdraw the first blood. Afterward, Violet sits on the chair, under the slowly spinning fan, her tanned legs crossed, smoking her gold-filter cigarettes and sipping from a bottle of tequila. "Take a drink and don't ever talk about this—or I'll kill you." Violet says it like she means it.

Puerto Escondido will cleave Cristina in two, a dark half and a light half, with constant pressure between them. On the beach the sun hurts her pale skin, but inside herself she feels she's dark, so she must be. That's why she will be pulled to dark men—they are an affirmation of what she lacks. Cristina washes the blood off her thighs with cold water and learns never to leave doors unlocked. At dinner she will ask her mother if she can have rum. Her mother will say, "Go 'head, find your own vices." Cristina gets drunk for the first time, avoiding Violet's piercing eyes. Later when Pacific storms sweep over Puerto Escondido, forcing them inside the hotel for days, there will be occasions when she won't escape so easily from Violet.

"When I was fourteen, I was sexually abused by an aunt. It

did something to me; I can't have a normal relationship. I tense up when I'm touched." Cristina cannot help speaking these words, almost drowned out by the drumming of the rain on the windows and the Latin jazz purling softly from the stereo.

"I wouldn't hurt you," Pablo said, but he wasn't sure since after Lydia, that's all he'd done. Crushed women like flowers. He'd been getting back at Lydia. He knew that. He'd picked through the personal ads, hooking up with women so far gone they didn't care what he did to them, as long as they felt something; he left miles of rope burns, till he'd grown tired and bored of the scene and withdrawn into a kind of sexual monkhood. But Lydia still owned his heart—owned it like the gold heart on the anklet he'd given her.

On the other hand, Cristina was here, available, with her pear-shaped body, the small, girlish breasts. So vulnerable. Pablo considered pushing apart her soft knees, raising her dress above the waist, and slipping his hand under her garments. Then Lydia flashed in his mind—Lydia liked her wrists tied, sometimes to the bedpost. Thinking of this distracted him, made him withdraw from Cristina.

In some ways Cristina'd been expecting him. Like a letter she knew was in the mail and she'd been waiting and waiting for it. This one man. She had everything else, and flaunted it. The white sports car in the driveway, her stylish Dolores Heights apartment, the jet-set job with the travel magazine. She'd been to more places than he had, and had more money, no doubt. But the poverty of loneliness brutalized her every night.

Her one rule was never to ask questions of a man. It showed too much interest. But now she wished to open his heart.

"Tell me about yourself."

"Born and raised in La Mission."

It was plain to see he was from the school of few words, and most likely, badly chosen ones.

"Same here. My family owns La Casa Mexicana on Twenty-fourth Street."

Nothing could have impressed him less—little Mexican-American princess cruising for a bruising.

Cristina went on, "I have no luck with men; they always hurt me. I expect pain as a sign of love. I bet you're like that. Do you like to hurt?" She sparked a lighter and the flame trembled in her hand. Pablo took the lighter and cigarette from her; after he lit the cigarette he placed in in her mouth.

He wanted her to shut up. Either that or he'd walk out. He

couldn't stand women revealing all the sordid details of their life to someone they'd just met. He wasn't sure he wanted to get involved. "I have no idea what I'll do to you." He barely smiled, not sure why he'd said that, but it sounded right.

She dared him to avoid her gaze—"Unless we give ourselves with conviction, we'll never know our true desires."

It was obvious Cristina would offer herself to him, to any man, without discretion. A woman like her, so lonely. So desperate for love. This hurt him—the loneliness of her life hurt him. Pablo wanted to tell her how bored he was. He wanted to say the degradation wasn't worth it. He wanted to tell her she was beautiful, even if it wasn't all that true. What he didn't want was a mimsy fuck—he wanted to rampage and pillage her body against the laws of God and nature. Against her very will. He sought a battle over every inch of her, and wanted to leave her marked forever. He wondered could she be different from the faceless others, and he knew there was only one way to test her.

Cristina was preparing herself for his hands. She wanted to caress them, put her lips to them. Wanted to kiss the web between his fingers, the faded tattooed cross wedged between left thumb and forefinger. Her body, taut as the last white sail on the horizon, strained to reach port before the storm lashed her to rags. Port would always be dark men who hurt her, who trained her to believe that's what love is. Sergio her first lover, fifteen years her senior, did that to her. But now she was thinking how she could be for Pablo—on her knees, her mouth offered like a vase; on her back, spread-eagled and naked. If he'd ask that. Cristina would please him, she told herself. Because she wanted to. Just because. It could have been any man, but the rain had brought her this one. The light in the kitchen seemed like a witness to the crime. "Even if you leave tomorrow, stay and spend the night."

"Sure, why not?" His voice barely a whisper of wind.

A pale blue vein in her throat pulsed out of control when she stood up. She brushed her hair back from her face and he noticed again the pimples on her forehead.

"Please—take me to bed."

How could he refuse when she said please?

Pablo unzipped her, his hand stopping above the curve of her *nalgas,* and she tugged the red silk dress down over her wide hips. She turned and faced him. A string of candlelight twined around the silver rings pierced through her nipples—her breasts, small as pomegranates, would barely fill his hands. "Why'd you do that?" he asked. She shrugged and said, "I wanted to." Cristina kept her stockings on and the sharp heels, and sat before the vanity, a silk robe draped over her shoulders, her hair pinned up with tortoise-shell combs. He recognized some of the colored portraits of saints that decorated her walls—Our Lady of Perpetual Help, and the one of a woman scorched by flames, her wrists chained, the Soul in Purgatory. And Jesus with his hands opened, stigmata bleeding, his heart on fire.

Pablo stood by the window, smoking a hash-laced joint and peering through the rainy night while she redid her makeup, being careful how she outlined her mouth. Pablo watched intently as she layered the makeup on her face so he barely recognized her under the heavily rouged cheeks.

Bundles of dried flowers were spread on the vanity—brittle, without scent, and bleached of color (he remembered women were thorns, not roses); a black silk shawl with knotted fringe was draped over the wrought-iron headboard; in one corner a full-length mirror captured everything in the room. A crucifix was nailed above the bed. A dozen votive candles released the fatal fragrance of gardenias. This bedroom confessed to secrets and sins; redemption here was an angel locked out of the game.

He held her shoulders and placed the unlit end of the joint to her lips and supercharged her, blowing a stream of smoke into her mouth. For a moment Cristina felt dizzy, could not predict what would happen next, could not imagine the scene she wanted played out. Then her body softened, relaxed; she draped an arm around his neck, playing with the hair that fell over his collar, felt his hands circle her waist. More than anything her bedroom reminded him of Juárez, many, many years ago, when he had visited a house where five dollars bought you the pleasure of young girls, and the older ones went for two. A remorse so heavy his bones hurt told him that whatever the hour, it was late, but it was time.

She flopped on the bed, looking up at him. Without malice, he said, "Your bedroom reminds me of a whorehouse."

"It's on purpose," she said, leaning back, unfurling her robe, watching his eyes cover that swatch of skin between her thighs and her belly. Her small breasts looked even smaller; her thighs, big and heavy, were dimpled with fat. He couldn't be serious about her heavily made-up face. He rubbed his hand between her nearly hair-less genitals.

A spark fired her eyes. "Be rough," she said.

He pinched her nipples till she flinched. "Is that rough?"

Pablo couldn't deny the stirrings he felt gripping her by the nape and kissing her hard, cruel, then raking his fingers over her belly. Her chunky, black-stockinged legs and her red stilettos aroused him. How they came to a point like a dagger to be buried in his chest. Her ankles were small and well-turned, and he gripped them fiercely, wondering if she would let him tie them with a rawhide riata.

He stood her before the full-length mirror, his fingers cinching her waist, the smouldering joint in his mouth, forcing her to see their reflection, forcing her to look at his eyes in the mirror. Then he pulled her hair and hissed in her ear, "I want you to be my puta." These words would take centuries to unfold, these words forged like a threat and a promise of deliverance. These words would haunt her months, even years later, every time she thought of him. He bit one of her nipples—feeling the silver ring in his mouth—till she cried, a small, thin cry, like a kitten's.

Cristina was not afraid of him anymore. Sergio had made her do things that besides being painful, had seemed disgusting to her. Sergio who met her on the beach at Puerto Escondido during another summer after her mother had divorced and they returned to Mexico to relive the ruins. Sergio whose manhood looked like a thick knot beneath his skimpy bathing suit. He watched her eyes like a shark. He devoured Cristina while she sat on her beach towel transfixed, hypnotized like a small animal by his eyes. Sergio had a cabana away from town where the tourist didn't go. It was the day after Cristina's nineteeth birthday, her mother had lost herself in another cantina, and Cristina was alone with Sergio. The Mexican girls were so natural and unencumbered in this corner of the port. She thought of them as azaleas, hibiscuses, trumpet vines. She wanted to be loved like that, innocent as an azalea. But Sergio had other plans, other tastes. Serio turned her young-girl passions into an armoire of razors and thorns. While Sergio was digging into her openings as if she were no more than a clay vessel, exploring her like a cave, Cristina's eyes focused on the *abanico* in the ceiling, and she decided—If I cannot be loved like a flower, I will be loved like a thorn.

Now, that was how she wanted Pablo to love her.

"Go ahead, then. Make me do what you want." She said it because those were her exact feelings.

"I want to tattoo you." He was testing her.

"Where?"

He took her wrist, turned her arm up. "Here."

"What?"

"A heart on fire."

"And if I refuse?"

He puffed on the joint and brought the glowing tip a centimeter from her skin. Her pulse was going wild.

"Were you lying?"

"Do it, then."

The hot ember touched her arm a brief second, then he pulled it away. Pablo wished she'd break and get it over with, but love is never that easy. "You're a brave girl."

"Now kiss me," she said.

Pablo leaned over her and she sucked the smoke from his mouth like a fire-eater in a dusty Mexican plaza. He caressed the spot where he'd bruised her nipple. He thrust his knee against her pelvis, and squeezed her mouth open. "Is this what you like? You like pain?" He didn't want to hurt her; he remembered this was not Lydia.

"Don't stop," she demanded. Cristina drew him back fiercely, unbuttoned his shirt, kissed his chest, swirled her tongue over his nipple, sucked the gold cross hanging from his neck.

"I'm going to make you do things you'll regret," he said, trying to sound threatening.

"Fuck me in the mouth if you want."

"I'm going to make you do more than that," he promised.

There could be no winners tonight, only victims—chingas o te chingan. She wanted to control him by giving in to his whims. His puta, he had said; she would be his entire brothel if he wanted, and she pushed him onto the bed, unbuttoning his pants. Cristina noticed that the head of his penis was shaped like a Valentine's chocolate—she noticed this while condoming him. When she finished, he flipped her on her stomach, on all fours, and grabbing her neck tightly so she couldn't get away, he pushed her face into the pillow. Her *nalgas* were puckered with cellulite. He didn't care. Didn't give a damn about any of that anymore. He straddled her ample thighs and slammed into the back of her legs. He reached around her and stuck his thumb in her mouth and ordered, "Suck." Pablo spanked her once, but hard, leaving a red-welt handprint on her big amorphous ass. He spread her dark hindquarters with his palm. With his middle finger he cirlced the tight bloom of her rosebud, probing gently till she relaxed, then he jammed his finger in to his knuckle. She squirmed and moaned, but he wouldn't let go.

"Stop. You're hurting me."

"You wanted an angry man."

He grabbed a chunk of her *nalgas* and slammed against her *con muchas ganas*. Cristina felt the gold chain hitting her back and pictured herself three Os for him to stretch, pictured him a stone plaza she would have to cross on her knees.

He whispered the ways he wanted her: in black garters like a Tijuana whore—masturbating him with her red-tipped fingers—sucking him till he came in her face. Hoping to scare her, Pablo said he'd prostitute her in that whorehouse he knew in Juárez, but Cristina said, "Yes, yes," so readily she came, releasing a guttural scream that shook the bed and left her splayed and spent.

Once finished, she pushed him away, forcing him to withdraw. Cristina didn't love him. Not yet. But she'd opened up so much her body felt like a cross-channel tunnel with a continent of traffic. Pablo rolled off the bed and groped around in his jacket pocket till he found his Delicados, then he pulled his pants on and sat at the edge of the bed with the matches, his back to her.

"I can tell you didn't really enjoy it," she said.

"You're wrong, it was fine."

"You didn't even come."

"Never do the first time."

"Tell me what you like. I'll do it for you."

"Next time I'll make you do things."

He moved to the window, where she could see only his profile. He struck the match and his face was momentarily lit by the tiny flame. She wanted to be that fire cupped in his hands. When Pablo blew out the match it was like he blew out her breath. Cristina huddled under the covers, feeling that he'd carved his name on her body with a razor blade; she closed her legs tight to keep his energy inside. "Eres muy guapo y varonil." She'd never spoken Spanish to a man before, and it sounded as corny as a telenovela.

He wasn't listening. He stood, as weary as this century, his face to the night. Weariness overtook him like a pale horse; the weight of the moon pressed on his shoulders, but there was no moon tonight, only low-lying clouds and rain. Something out there reminded him of his past. Her bedroom looked out onto a garden; the lights of San Francisco twinkled against the glass. Darkness draped a cloth over the entire city—the rooftops, the palm trees; if he'd had a soul it would have draped over that too, as over a crucifix during Lent. The room was so hushed, so still, she could hear two hearts beating.

"I want you to do those things. All those things." Her voice was clear, unwavering; she meant every syllable.

"You shouldn't say that to me."

"Why¿"

"It's dangerous, soy mucho-fucking-malo."

"I'm not afraid."

"I'm the last bad man."

"Then you're the one I want."

Pablo inhaled a stream of gray smoke as if it were his last breath. He remembered that undefinable nothing that haunted him, that unseen something that rustles the leaves, that certain emptiness without a name. As if talking to a ghost in the garden, he said, "I killed a man once." The smoke escaped from his mouth and swirled over his face, hiding his features. "I was seventeen; it was in a gang fight. I hit this *vato* on the head with a pipe and kept hitting him till he was dead. *Muerto. Muertecito.*"

His words ran her through like a hand-forged stiletto. The terror made her close her eyes. He was the Grand Inquisitor and she was the rack. She had to cross all the boundaries of fear and phobias before she opened her eyes, and now was curious and ready to see his face.

"Why do you tell me that¿"

"I don't know, it bothers me sometimes. I never told that to anyone. Ever."

Outside, the rain fell soft against the windowpane, leaving trails of unfulfilled desire; the overburdened leaves dripped onto the patches of grass and stone. The faint slushing rush of tires reached them, the sounds of cars and buses, the first sad birds singing to the sun, the bell of Mission Dolores tolling, calling to the faithful.

Her words leaped the darkness and touched him. "You need my healing, my hurt dulce man. I can make you whole."

"Nobody can heal me. I'm wounded everywhere."

This is not Puerto Escondido, not the same rain, not the same man or woman she'd known there, she is not fourteen, not nineteen—she is Cristina de la Cruz, thirty-four years old, and she knows what she wants. Wrapping herself in the robe, she went to him. She placed her hands on his chest, hard as the flat stones in her garden. With eyes closed, she felt his heart beat through her fingertips. His body, cruel as granite, rattled her like a seed in a maraca. She kissed the hollow of his throat, the crucifix hanging from his chest, ran her tongue over each dip in his ribs. She knelt before him like a supplicant and kissed his hands, drew the latex-covered, Valentine-shaped part of him into her mouth. Then she clawed her nails into his thighs till she left mini-roses of blood pressed into his skin.

Pablo didn't even flinch. His were the eyes of Jesus revealing the stigmata, the wound bleeding under his rib, the heart on fire—he tried to keep the surge from rising in his hips but she drew him out, urging him to hold nothing back.

Cristina felt him tremble in her mouth like lightning before the storm strikes, felt him bend to her touch, to her will, felt his body give as when the earth parts, releasing deformed monsters doomed by morning's first light. Then he lost all hope and gave himself totally, completely. He whispered, "Ay . . . Cristina. . . ." There was so much his words didn't say—he needed her, more than she needed him, more than she would ever dream of needing him. And Cristina de la Cruz knew—he wouldn't leave her, not this one, this one was too broken to fly.

Aphorisms

Carlos Fuerza

* Taste the cunt with the energy it gives you.

* Decide how many times and complete each one as if it were the last.
* Demand sounds from her throat.

* Let her listen to your breathing as if you were another man.

* Surprise her with what you have because it is you.

* When you are in her from behind, standing on the floor as she leans over the edge of the bed, stamp your right foot hard on the floor and the shock will send a vibration up your leg, through your cock, and into her.

* Watch what happens.

* Don't answer her cries with a false sound.

* Be honest, but don't stop fucking.

* Demand a new dimension to the space between her spread buttocks.

* Let her throw you into the shower with the lights off.

* Return to the bed with the wetness of the man who knew where to place his dripping lips.

* Reveal your hardest position, the one where your heart runs out of breath.

* Listen as she tells you how she parted her cunt for the man at the office.

* Listen as she tells you she knows what to do with the weakness of men.

* Listen as you make up the best story about how you, too, entered without guilt.

* Keep a journal of the best cries, liquids, belts, expressions on faces,

expressions on breasts, expressions on the trail of come you left on her leg.

* Be honest, but don't stop flicking your tongue at her clitoris when it frightens you.

* Be dishonest, and pretend you are not afraid.

* Tie the dried flower around her finger and have her scratch your scrotum with it.

* Tell her you saw her place the two marbles inside her cunt.

* Always search for the smooth marbles with your fingers, not your mouth.

* Find a gift set of ben-wa balls and give them to her.

* Only the cunt speaks its own words.

* Every time you wake from the fucking, be sure it is you and not someone else.

* A child shows his toy, a man hides his cock.

* A child loves her parents, a woman decides which position.

* The little hairs are what is eternal, the bare flesh yesterday's terrain.

* A bed opens to you. Go in and face the thousand beds you will never lie on.

* Your suffering tongue is so great inside her cunt, her cries will be the slogans of rebellion.

* Suffering does not come after climax. It always owns the moment before.

* When she swallows your cock, lie back and dream of the river you couldn't cross.

* When she swallows your cock, lie back and dream of the root that spread under the river.

* When she swallows your cock, lie back and dig the root up.

* When you let go in her mouth, you will be the last man to swim across.

Ausencia's Tale

María Luisa Mendoza

Former militia officers with pretensions to dandyism who served in the Dardanelles and the Yser condemn—if not violently at least with firm conviction—the wearing of coattails for formal dinners, theater events, or other ceremonies that without exaggeration can be considered obligatory in daily social life. Coattails are only worn by poor devils with no clue about men's fashions or by newcomers to pseudo-bohemian circles. It's just that the tendency of gentlemen who have held commisions in military campaigns leans towards a relaxed elegance that had formerly been antagonistic to true distinction. But let's not be too inclined to severity in matters of current fashion. We can very well forgive—those of us who understand the vastness of our nation, isolated amidst wheat and corn fields and millions of head of cattle—local ignorance in matters of fashion, though we have noted that smoking jackets are now the trend in London, but worn with matte silk linings, that shiny lapels are unacceptable, not even as a joke—crows' mirrors, my father used to call them—as are felt hats and outrageous spats, that Parisian design has maintained silk-like bindings on the lapels, although cut of the same fabric, that's true. Besides, we all know that only waiters don American-style tuxedos.

The wardrobe situation is in continuous metamorphosis, my dear lady. You can very well understand, given your obvious financial position, that it's been a long time since plush hats were the item of choice to cover the old noggin . . . they're only worn by niggers . . . that a belted overcoat—a coachman's dead giveaway—has been soundly defeated by the perfectly cut evening cape or the greatcoat. And, begging your pardon, boxer shorts that fall below the knee, and shirttails reaching below the hip, have been relegated to what is impossible, unforgivable to wear.

(how long will my skin last without a final go at it. In what coming day, tomorrow, today even when I get to my hotel room, will it show the imprint of so many stories—stories lived, heard, tangled in the dark lines that seem even more pronounced when I speak and remain in the r's or the m's that brush against them, like fishes heaped on a net, quivering, their mouths open, with scales like knives capable of scraping away the softness, leaving behind only dead flesh, fishes of words? Why in heaven's name this downpour of sadness? Ausencia seemed to absent herself from this game of oneupmanship, not giving logical answers, more than normally forgetful about names, titles, synonyms in French, designer labels, breeds, definitions, qualifiers or nouns of real, independent, and individual existence. More past than pluperfect. Then, distracted by the feast of oysters and white wine, of asparagus and "centurion eggs," as she blushingly called the caviar, making an effort to focus her beam of light, which had nearly faded without warning after spending a sleepless night in order to catch the grand zeppelin, the lady understood that she didn't give a hoot about Reinaldo Olavarrieta, this man from Tabasco who inspired in her such grammatical ideas: ferns, lizard-fish, swamp, new corn, gnats, coconut tortillas, sweat, beans and plantains, hammock, green turtle, crocodile, cocoa, laughter, vice, alcohol, chewing gum, heresy, liberalism, terms of endearmeant . . . , and that nothing was more absolute than the subtle beige of the restaurant with its private alcove where they lunched on delicious tidbits, or than her mind's hopeless efforts to conjure more words to identify this man from Tabasco with the sexual impulse that her companion left behind like forgotten cards on a game table in a run-down ship detained in a jungle customs station and seized without further inquiries, the police taking away sequined prostitutes and frock-coated card sharps among gringa heiresses of tobacco plantations, vacationing delegates, uneven pairs of faggots caught in the act, or sweet grandmothers accompanying a grandchild with a penchant for mad escapades but without capital or friends to finance them. Ausencia thus resigned herself to one of those floodings of her lacunae, from exhaustion, "you'll have to forgive me, there are moments in which fatigue makes me seem absentminded," and stopped trying to climb the hill of names. And without further ado she said:)

"I would very much like to eat seafood, Reinaldo, but I very much prefer the catholic diet of green and red, maybe accompanied by a smattering of yellow, a bit of white, absolutely no purple, never any beige, and frankly nothing black; I will take a little something, pink maybe, but I'm only doing it for you who are my compatriot and whose voice, despite what you're telling me, Olavarrieta—a very distinguished and elegant voice, by the way, without any s's—fills me with such an ebb and flowing of nostalgia, familiar airs, revolutionary revolts, profanations of church virgins, and lots of textile-plant money since I assume that's the source of your wealth, or am I mistaken?"

Reinaldo opened his eyes wide, understanding the latter but ignoring, like any intelligent, conceited, and solemn being, the former. He let his rambunctious and lusty tropical laugh loose as he listened to this teaser regaling him with such absurd perspicacities which he supposed, not making an effort despite himself, referred to the food in her diet and which, contrary to what his companion, exhausted from the effort of calling green by its proper name, salad—red was for tomato, yellow for mustard, white for bread, purple for beets, beige for butter, black for caviar, pink for salmon— would have expected, did not disappoint him, nor did they make him pick up his hat and take off running to look for someone who spoke Spanish properly, it didn't even make him lose interest, right now the woman looked even more adorable than in the zeppelin, more than in the car that took them at breakneck speed to the La Cupola Restaurant, specializing in sunfish and not in steak alla fiorentina.

Ausencia was not too keen—between little sips of coffee and cognac—on going to bed at dusk with this compatriot of hers who had plunged headlong into a rigmarole of tailoring and high fashion. Reinaldo was not precisely enthusiastic about the idea of taking his pants off that sunset, and then dressing again. He was just back from that, from the nonchalant squeeze-me-tightly-there, with God's help he was retracing his steps to his homeland, where one made love like drinking a mammee juice, even though that pulpy fruit was short of juices, just like he and Ausencia were short of lusting to trot in bed. But despite this sluggish calm in both their loins, Reinaldo proposed and Ausencia accepted.

(it was the rush, the sleepy Sunday, it was the obstinate stiffness of my legs, the unknown, the rustling of my petticoats, the whiteness of the linen below his navel, it was his youth, it was mine. All that panting, all that pricking, first gently and then hard and then nothing but the comings-in and the goings-out and then the cascade in my squeezing neck from his bulging rod. It was that Virginia didn't know about it and I would have to explain it to her, it was that Enedina wasn't absent, nor was Ausencia—I, Virgin, she—each one of us in a room separated only by blood, Virginia thinking of me, I thinking of her, Enedina thinking of both of us, the three of us with him who came that afternoon for a Scotch; he with me in that my bed which then was made for him, only him.

It was the exhaustion of our flesh and his electricity which led to so many unknown streets, towers of lace, and ships' sirens, sounds never heard by me who only knew of the chants of gold and the sighs of urine ... It was his joy, yes, it was the mad generosity of his dark youth, it was the game of The Pussy in the Well—no sense in covering it up now—it was the delight of all those new Sundays, one on, one off, and his voice like a closed mine, his broad-shouldered back, well-muscled and lean under my breast and the charade of my violation of his delicious behindnesses. It was the ceremony of his dancing in the buff for me, veiling himself with an Arabian cloth, with linen that had belonged to the other, the one that "had been," it was the way he raised the banner to let his sex peek out, up, down, sideways, and ending up bursting out laughing with feminine then masculine grave in a naked boxing match which I watched in a trance seeing the fluttering of the dove between his legs, whirling like a kite wanting to fly away but being held tight by a boy's string, as if that dark-skinned append-age had been expressly made by God to gyrate against the pubis and the pouches of pleasure that could barely keep up with its rhythmic adorability as it spun in the air and then the uppercut, the jab, and the final knockout which released that watered-down paste over me and my bed, his bed now, in order to start again ... it was that.)

"What are you thinking of, queen, sitting there so pierced with silences?" The blue-eyed youth once undressed had given evidence of slightly twisted knees, not quite knock-knees or bow-legs, just somewhat curved legs, as if the well-made patrician trunk, perfect in all its attributes, weighed more than it should have, giving eloquent evidence of sound nourishment, ablutions, brushes against good fabrics with fine labels embroidered in En-glish, French, in Italian, but never in Spanish, good beds, good daybreaks, good evenings, good horsebacks, good berths in luxury liners, good everything, that is.

(when Gerundio died I could have been better, not decent, no, since we cut that word out and made it into paper cones for salted seeds, but better, yes, free. But I didn't want to, I loved my home too much to stray far from it, my ceilings painted with angels and other sillinesses, my former and present properties for me alone ...)

"Sir: my new properties are for me alone. It's like you, Mr. Olavarrieta, you, Reinaldo, for example, sitting here next to me. I don't know you, I don't know much more about you than the language you speak, and you were nonetheless destined for me. You would have to buy a ticket to climb to heaven and let out a scream; your life is a never-ending descending from zeppelins to meet the flashbulbs of the cameras photographing us. And this coming month she'll see our faces, she alone, Enedina, in the Zig-Zags, the monthly magazine she reads looking for me, your photo was in the paper, make believe it's a souvenir . . . Enedina is my maid—if one can call her that. She lives in a very big house of mine, with a door that sometimes—once—resounds like thunder . . . You have no idea. You're the type that springs to life after three o'clock, worried about properties you don't inhabit, like me, and concerned about the statement you make in your elegant clothing, as if the smoking jacket were the answer. I was thinking of my silences, do you understand?"

"No, beauty, I don't understand."

"It's just that going to bed with a man it's not what you'd call something out of this world. We women jump into bed with the ease that men boast of but don't actually feel. We like feeling you down there, ah, how we like it!, but it doesn't go beyond that, a matter of doing what one must once one said one would. The bad part is the memories, the damned piling up of what happened to you before, there, a thousand years ago . . . I don't remember."

"Tell me, Ausencia, speak to me . . ."

"You know? One day we buried my father. His name was Gerundio Batista and he was a miner between the blue of the Spanish sky and the dark night of Sonora. I was still very young in those days, but for five years I'd been threading elusive Sundays: a lover at the plant, no less, and a lover at the mine. I drew lots for them on weekends, without working myself up about it. The truth is that houses of many rooms are very tempting. He 'was' a gringo, but with Arab blood, the other 'had been' Mexican. My 'was' and my 'had been.' Was for him, had been for him."

"Tell me."

"I broke the rules of every day, of every hour. Once my father died I was covered in tinsel and coins. On the desk in his study I learned to sign with the constancy of a millionaire, I collected and bestowed, I acquired and gave away, I took and distributed: the kind of first-class deed that is never forgiven by those who only open their mouths to let out their bile—the damnable habit of damning everyone to hell. If I had not thought of anything beyond the giving and taking, I would not have gotten even with the devil, but would be, on the contrary, in the same boat as all the rich people in the vicinity ... I wore mourning for twenty days, complete mourning, with veil and gloves. I wore half-mourning for twenty days, white collar and cuffs on a black dress, I wore white without fail for twenty days, white from head to toe, including my curls. I covered three years in sixty days. On the sixty-first day I gave a farewell tea party for a mining colleague who was leaving for New York on personal business. On the sixty-second day society sent me the normal invitations to shindigs and whatnots ... His name was D. H. Haller, you know?, and I loved him. My first long awakening into sex. His chest tangled with white hairs, his power ... but I'm getting sidetracked ..."

"Tell me."

"I could go on and on telling you the story of a beautiful life since I've never held back before, but the truth is that women chroniclers of their coituses invent fifty percent of their tales, and the true bed-hoppers are the quiet ones. I only narrate my life story to my lovers, in their own manner and style, tailoring my tale to their image, since in their 'tell me Ausencia,' they know what they want to hear. It's different with women; other women's tales leave them cold, since they have their own: jazzed-up stories if they haven't had much luck and want to boast of their nonexistent whoring; and discreet, cleaned-up tales if on the contrary they have run wild horizontally. In other words, whores act like real ladies in front of their friends, and vice versa. That's the way it works, and it's the same with age. All women take years off their age, and the moment one turns forty a woman finds herself celebrating birthdays in a world of contemporaries who'll be thirty-nine forever. I don't have to tell you my story: you're not my lover, not even my acquaintance, a fleeting fuck doesn't count, it fades away, like the face of the customs officer who reads your vital statistics, stamps your passport, and is forgotten. Besides, cheer up, you would end up boring me, everything has been boring me for centuries. And besides, you're not remotely similar, you're not my type, if only you looked like them ..."

Ausencia began to cover the tip of her foot with the listless parsimony of the idle woman who gets out of bed after reading the theater listings in the paper and choosing the play for the evening. She had just finalized her plans and chosen her adventure. If puddle jumpers could buzz from Paris to Mexico in three hours she would take the eleven o'clock express to Balbuena—now an airport. But she was not in such a rush to move. There was Duvivier awaiting her in downtown Rome, and a whole long week before getting to the port and choosing an ocean liner, and countless sleepless nights, and the memories, and time stretching ahead of her in a wretched row of long and identical days. There was the clockwork care of her eyelids that were beginning to sag under their own weight, and which she pressed half an hour mornings and evenings under compresses of chilled tea, rose water, camomile, salt, and banyan flowers. There was just what no longer appeared to her: life, and no other choice but to await old age.

Translated by Lizabeth Paravisini-Gebert

Hotel

Carlos Parian

He waited in the familiar room until she knocked on the door. He rose from the bed and thought he heard someone breathing in the room. He looked behind him, but of course, the bed was still made, clean and wide. He opened the door and let Carlotta in. She wore a red halter top and Levi's cutoffs. Her black hair was braided into two long tails. He had never seen her wear it that way before. She smiled at him without a word. It didn't surprise him because he never expected them to say much to each other and they usually didn't. This was only their fourth time together. He closed the door behind her and thought he smelled Ivory soap. She kicked off her brown sandals and sat gingerly on the edge of the bed.

"I dreamed about you last night," she told him as she pulled off her top.

He didn't know what to say, but felt a tinge of the old feeling he always had when it came to dreams. He pulled his T-shirt off, but stopped unbuttoning his pants when she pulled the tiny camera from her purse.

"Can I?" Carlotta smiled up at him, her small breasts reminding him of someone else.

He wanted to say no, hesitated, and spoke his first words to her. "What kind of pictures? Who are they for?" He climbed out of his pants.

"Just for me," she whispered.

"Go ahead," he said.

His answer seemed to bring new life into her. She jumped up, shook herself out of her cutoffs. He looked down at the black hair between her legs. She still reminded him of someone else and the thought bothered him as he removed his black bikini briefs. She took the first picture close-up even though there was no way he could get a hard-on for any camera. He blinked in the quick flash. She motioned for him to turn around. He turned and stared at the blank TV screen on the dresser as he heard two more clicks and the room blinked white. He had never done this before and was surprised it neither bothered him nor excited him. He turned to her to find she had fallen back on the bed with her legs spread as far as she could spread them.

"Take one of me," she smiled.

He took the camera from her outstretched hand and looked through the viewfinder as she kicked her legs up in the air and held them high with her arms locked under her knees. She spread her cunt open with two fingers. He clicked the camera twice, the flashes shooting into her opening like searchlights. She quietly eased back on the bed.

"Come here," she said.

He put the camera on the nightstand, moved to her and felt her cold hands stroke his hardening cock. She took him in her mouth. He stood over her and closed his eyes, the memory of other photographs finally coming to him as her tongue worked faster. When he grunted and came in her mouth, he suddenly saw the other photo, recalled how the woman had also wanted to take a picture of him. That time he said no, but weeks later, she showed him a photo of him naked, exactly in the same room where they had done it. He couldn't get her to tell him how she got the picture. It was the last time he slept with her. Her name was Anna. It must have been five or six years before he met Carlotta.

He pulled back as a string of his semen ran down Carlotta's chin. She licked it and wiped it off with her fingers. As he slowly got on top of her, he recalled how Anna had rubbed a strange-smelling green jelly on his cock before sucking on it. He asked her what it was, but she wouldn't say, only smiled as he moaned with pleasure, the jelly creating a smooth burning sensation on his stiff cock. As Anna finished him, the fire spread through his tight balls and flowed up his stomach. He looked down at his green cock as it fell at rest.

Carlotta opened for him and he entered her quickly. It usually wasn't like this. The first three times had been more romantic, more casual. Now, as he fucked Carlotta with long, slow pistons, he kept thinking about the jelly, his green cock and Anna with her secret photo. Carlotta swiveled under him and cried out, pushing against him as if trying to take a broken spear out of herself. She cried again and he grabbed both her legs, placed them on his shoulders. As he slid deeper, she sobbed and came. He punched a few more times and heaved an orgasm over her head, the sweat in her hair brushing his chin as he convulsed inside her. It was over quickly. The two of them lay back, their legs still tangled in each other. They didn't say a word. He looked at her. Carlotta's braids were twisted around her head. She pulled them away from her face and closed her eyes with a smile.

He thought about Anna and the green jelly. He remembered how it wouldn't wash off his cock for several days. He never saw Anna again, but tried calling her several times to find out how she got a photo of him naked. He also wanted to ask her why his green cock kept burning. Suddenly, one week after it happened, he woke early in the morning and found the green flame on his cock was nearly gone. He took a shower and it was completely gone.

Carlotta's eyes were green. He looked at them as he held her.

"Why are you so quiet?" she whispered.

"I don't know," he answered, and looked up at the ceiling.

"Why can't we get together at your place for a change?" she asked. "I don't like this hotel."

He turned to her and placed a finger on the wet hair between her legs. "I told you before it is best to meet here."

"But, why?" Carlotta spread her legs as his finger hooked into her. He pulled it out and rubbed the come across her stomach.

"I told you before: I can't have anybody over there. My room-mate wouldn't understand."

She grimaced as he pushed four fingers of his right hand into her cunt. "Fuck your roommate," Carlotta protested as he grabbed his hardening cock.

"Should I get him over here for a threesome next time?" he whispered in her ear.

"Yeah, right. You just said he wouldn't understand."

"That's right, so let's just have fun here." He thought about Anna and her huge breasts as Carlotta rose over him. Her small nipples were round beads of sweat he took into his mouth. She sat on him.

"Oh, that's in deep," she sighed.

She sprung up and down slowly, her breasts turning green in the dim light from the nightstand lamp. He closed his eyes and thought about his green cock inside Anna. After she had rubbed the jelly on it, she had sucked him off. As his cock trembled in her mouth, he had looked down at her. She pulled back, grabbed her big breasts in each hand and squeezed them around his green thing. She rolled it tighter between the mounds and he squirted all over her face and neck. He thrashed a couple of times on the bed, his taut legs extended, his toes pointing hard in the air as she swallowed him.

Carlotta was going wild, her braids swaying in the air as her pained face twisted with a wide-open mouth, his cries and desperate acts of separation keeping her pinned to him. He pushed up and rolled her over. As he fucked her hard from above, he reached out and slapped the tiny camera off the nightstand. The black box flew across the room and shattered against the wall. Carlotta was too busy coming and coming. As she collapsed, he pulled out, dizzy with sweat. She lay exhausted with her eyes closed and didn't see him stagger, with his dripping stiff cock, to the corner of the room. He finished ripping open the cracked body of the cheap camera. He clutched it close to his stomach as he pulled the roll of film out. He looked down at his cock, red from their sudden fury, and he thought he saw green in the lousy light of the room. He closed the broken camera with a snap that opened Carlotta's eyes. He dropped the roll into the trash can under the nightstand and came back to the bed.

The Blackbirds Take Over the Sky

Silvia Curbelo

Tonight a moment unfolds like a word
no one has spoken in years.

Someone writes someone's name,
not desire but the idea

of desire taking shape in her mind.
When she puts pen to paper

she touches the skin of a new language.
What is left unsaid opens

huge wings and waits. The way
across a crowded room

a stranger might offer a drink
and we remember thirst,

a door, a window opening in a city
we haven't thought about in years

and beyond it, the thin,
bright air of possibility.

Desire is a stone that opens,
the lovesick heart of every story

ever written. Something
in the way his voice flies out

of his chest, the moment
landing on her shoulder

like a bird. And hope,
that long migration.

The Secret History of Water

Silvia Curbelo

The body is a stone house   the body
pins you to the ground
crowded with loss   empty
with longing   the weight
of the world falling through it
the way a body falls
fast asleep then suddenly awake   deliberate
in the way it sees you
ladder   stone boat
sailing   impossible
to hold down
The body anchored in sleep   suddenly
lifted   suddenly unfurled
a crawlspace for wind   for rain
falling on a simple
city street   the clean map
of your childhood with its hundred
roads back to the leaky house   the room
where you first opened
your eyes saying *This is the place*
You are the one   the day I felt
my hands wash over you   and the glass
of my desire break and spill   water
we could sink through

after a photograph by J. Tomás Lopez

On the Edge of Pleasure

Rosario Castellanos

I

Between myself and death I've placed your body:
so that its fatal waves might break against you without touching me
and slide into a wild and humiliated foam.
Body of love, of plenitude, of fiestas,
words the winds disperse like flowers,
bells delirious at dusk.
All that the earth sends flying in the form of birds,
all that lakes store up of sky
along with the forest and the stone and the honeycomb.

(Heady with harvests I dance above the haystacks
while time mourns its cracked scythes.)

City of fortune and high walls,
circled by miracles, I rest in the enclosure
of this body that begins while mine leaves off.

II

Convulsed in your arms like a sea among rocks,
breaking against the edge of pleasure or gently
licking the stunned sands.
(I tremble beneath your touch
like a tensed bow quivering with arrows
and sharp imminent hisses.
My blood burns like the blood of hounds
sniffing their prey and ravage.
But beneath your voice my heart surrenders
in devoted and submissive doves.)

III

I taste you first in the grapes
that slowly yield to my tongue,
conveying their silent, intimate sugars.

Your presence is a jubilation.

When you leave, you trample gardens and turn
the turtledove's sweet drowse
into a fierce expectation of wild dogs.
And love, when you return
my raging spirit senses you draw near
as young deer sense the water's edge.

Translated by Magda Bogin

Firefly Under the Tongue

Coral Bracho

From the restless taste of fermentation I love you:
in the festive pulp. Fresh blue insects.
Glazed and pliant in the newborn juice.
A scream distilled by light:
through fruitful crevices;
under the mossy water that clings to shadows. Papillas,
                                             caverns.
In permeating herbaceous hues. From the startled touch.
Radiance that oozes bittersweet: from the fertile pleasures,
of games severed by palpitation.
                    Hinge
(Wrapped in the evening breeze, the violet sound,
purified, the child, with the velvet base of his probing tongue,
                                             touches,
from that smooth, indefensible lust—sensitive iris that submits
to the rocks
if it foresees the stigma,
the scorching light—the substance, the pure
and vibrant tuft—on its relaxed, absorbed petal—(half-opened
gem that quivers; udders), soothing acidic juice,
the marsh, (ice), the lambent sap (cabala),
(nectar of the firefly).

Your Borders:
Crevices That Uncover Me

Coral Bracho

> *We must have died alone,*
> *a long long time ago.*
> —*D.B.*

You have stroked,
you have softened my flesh
in your transparency, my senses (man of fragile
contours, of soft and limpid eyes);
in the vast nudity that overflows,
that dismembers and submits;

(Like a narrow window toward the sea; like the delicate,
    insistent rubbing of your voice).
The waters: paths that reflect you (a submerged canvas of clouds),
    your abundance, your borders:
crevices that uncover me.

—Because a glaze, a dense word, the living and the dead, a fungal
    sourness, of ropes,
of slime, of fruitful carrion, a milky secretion spreads
    over us, contorts us, someone;
was someone speaking here?

I am reborn, like an albino, to that sun:
painful distance toward the neutral one that observes me, that I observe.

Come, draw near; come and see his hands, recent drippings in
this mire;
    come surround me.
Evening taste, radiance of proud lands, of silken passages,
    like a tree, half-obscured;
the sea:

on this beach, among scattered murmurs of glass). You have
    dazzled,
softened

On whom does this light explode?

—You have forged, delineated my body to your emanations,
to their simple outlines. You have overflowed
with roots, with spaces;
you have deepened, flayed, turned vulnerable (because your
fingertips
    tighten
and release,
because your light extracts—sweetest gouge—with its tongue,
    its rubbing,
my membranes—in your waters; luminous ceiba
    of accessible thickness,
of alternating places, surpassed; in your evening dew)
    my limbs.

Listen; feel in that mournful decision, in that harvested intent,
    dissolved into water.
Who is anointed, who refracted, who is revealed? in its miasma

I stare with colorless eyes at that waxy noise
that is alien to me.

(In my body your skin arouses a compliant jungle
    that enriches its boundaries;
a question, vineyard that penetrates, that embraces
    the traced passages.
—From their plottings, from their heights: the irresistible richness.
A crystal that pierces, resinous, glowing, in the vast
    ocher pupils
of desire, exposes them; a meticulous language.)
You have impregnated me, you have warped my flesh;
and who moves about here?
who slips through their fingers?

Beneath that night: who murmurs among the tombs, the trenches?
Its flame, always multiplied, always swollen and concealed,

    your borders;
you have plunged, you have spilled, you have opened me for
    exhumation;
And who
who enshrouds it here, who tightens it, who kisses it?
Who inhabits it?

Translated by Thomas Hoeksema

Untitled

Coral Bracho

I hear your body with the quenched and calm intensity
of someone impregnated (of one who
emerges,
who reclines saturated, covered
with sperm) in the coded moisture
(soft, dense oracle: temple)
in the slime, warm reservoirs, deltas,
of her origin; I drink (your exposed, permeable roots;
on your wanton shores
—seething mire—moors) the mossy designs, your
thick sap (mound of drunken vines) I smell
in your deep, vigilant borders, embers,
cascades within your oily jungles. I hear
(your tactile semen) the lodes, larvae (fertile apse) I feel
in your living marshes, your mud: trails,
in your enbracing forge: the clues
(I yield
to your anointed thighs, oozing, flowing with light) I hear
within the sour clays, your shores: palpus, omens—signs
submerged—Buds in your atriums:
libations,
fertile clods. Crystalline traces
in the seething springs.

On the Facets: The Flashing*

Coral Bracho

> The rhizome, like a subterranean stalk . . .
> assumes, by itself, very diverse shapes:
> from its superficial extension magnified in
> many ways, to its manifestation in bulbs and
> tubers.
>   Desire is the creator of reality . . . it produces
> and moves forward by means of rhizomes.
>   An intensive feature begins to act by
> itself . . .
>   —Deleuze and Guattari, *Rhizomes*

In the parched word, unformulated, it shrinks
rancid brown membrane ((that is: a delicate drop of oil for the
   morning radiance
of the boundaries, for the tepid
line, well-traveled, that crosses, like a limpid hue, above
the vast sizzling, over the burdened back,
bulb—a drop of animal saliva:
for the inflections, for the fertilized dawn (caress)
which expands to the shore, like foam, a
   relief;
a fruit-bearing fur—an ulcer of light, a basting: for
expressions fragrant to the touch, to the wrinkled shadow,
   coveted;
a voice, a loose fiber—a fleece—at random from the chisels,
   from the strum of the pick)
on the crest, at the flank, of the magnetizations;
Strokings

and the hair language of rubbings in the lobed bowl
of the bodies. Purple
at the root;

---

*A rhimzome section seen by microscope; the partridge is a potato cell.
The rest appears to be or forms part of the landscape: examine it for what
is connected to the libido of horses.

a sponge, a lime, an axillary
mirror: and in the echoes,
stature:
a lark. Rhymes in the lavender;
ice: by the liminal rump, smooth restless animal lips.
Hirsute valve,
alliance, in the overturning; plexus and tendon:
a warmth, a synovial point under the veined delights:
    ducts
to the pale hidden summit;
a splinter, a ribbon (cat),
an embryo for the bronze of rampant thickets,
inimitable;
a boiling, a dishevelled mass, a spore:

Cope-tails ajar at the peak of an inguinal taste.
    Above the manes; kicks:

In the customary moulds, challenged, of existing, in
their smoky, ovulating rears:
    a precise icicle,
    an oil-lamp.

Cliffs.

and in the slimy folds, hints of existing,
and on its pungent banks of sand;
pearly figs; laughter;

a lemon on the excited fringes;
tearing; with inaudible glazed currycombs (wine, prehensile
and shaggy),
with thorns the mood, the hooves;

sparking laughter between the inspected
bulbs, the magpies;
    phosphorus, winks, echoes
    in the claw; the partridge
    leaps.

The partridge: fresh bird, plentiful, with solid thighs;
marked sexual dimorphism. Its red feathers,
   ashen,
conceal. Leaps in ejective parabola above the strawberries;
a fluttering fever. Has gray flanks (Boiling
spongy strawberries, they exhale—from their poppy swamps,
from their verbal mesentery—the delectable lye), slender
   legs,
a short flight; it runs (sumptuous overflowing taste)
rapidly.

   Opens its full clean lips:
the juice moistens and scents its harness; on its skin
of random stings, eagerly encircles the graceful one,
kicking; the slippery simultaneous nectar
sinks; amazement; vast amazement
among the high-pitched buds;
kneeling, on dazzling knee-backs, erect.
On the bicep, the scrotums; Radiant, acrid. Trots.
   Curbed by the illuminated
rumps; cadences; convex rhythm; violet-colored
   paroxysms; face down
among deep resonances. Extendible peduncles
   below the belt:

Sucking from the bubbling shapes; the tongue between
   the linking textures, pristine
vulvas in thermal springs, rain for the splintered
nuclei; turbulent rhizomes between the streams, the
   jubilant, foaming furs of existence;
beneath fermentable reins, the blankets.
   Absorbed
in the beds, expansive. Inundated.
Sensitive forms through the exacerbated straw, sprouting. Vital,
imperishable in their sudden impulses, smooth and tainted
   by their ocher,
their splendor, in their yolks; unique to the rubbing
pupils.
Stampede of flames between the furrow, the peppers, the
   traces; dense
and exaltable on their tips: by smell. Mineral

burst. A line, a caboose, a speck of dust; Gargoyle.
An ant in the joyful tufts, by the thighs,
the belly; in words)) taut, murky,
it shrinks, harsh membrance ((citric. The perpetual
   shrillness on the
edges)) drab; its net dims ((on the lubricated boundaries,
the pistil.

—His voice: savoring, performing, plundering it—Light;
in excitable spaces, the seditious act. Labial,
expandable below the cool forefinger, its smoothness; they
press.

Magnetism aroused to tasty excess,
the grating. The tickling summits.
—Turning sour, squeezing—in wild splittings,
tender. Vortex. Between the irons, the thistle,
instinct. Stubborn rodents
among the threads, the squares, the sieve. A clod,
a lanceolate breath, an itch.
To trail below the jammed, intensive zones.
Papillary knots among the grass. On the facets: the
   flashing.
An awl, an insect in the words)) sluggish,
crammed ((between the cracks the caesuras, on the reins.
Sudden and wanton they focus them—His voice: slitting it,
opening it, choosing it—they encircle and cohabit on reflecting
edges)), hollows; their opaque crust ((among the screams,
the fetlocks, the clefts. To exist:))

Collection of Navels

Daniel de Burgos

colorful and tasty
    beside the eye twitching
inside the fingertip
   glowing with cast desire
as if the tongue
   tastes its own feet
as if the mouth
   closes on its tongue
wetness a hope
   springing inside
the finger holding
   two parted vulvas
destroying the party
   of opinion within
each struggle
   to join a pure
heaving pleasure
   as if the curl of
clitoris is harder
   than the tip
of tongue embedded
   between first shudder
and last whole
   stored wave
last hole
where first clitoris
   was discovered
meant to hold
   two bodies
inside their active
   spines
smear of blood
   look of water
taste of cunt
   crossed

with flavor of cock-tip
    flower
where the stem
        is the stem
lowered into heaven
    with a mask on

Trying Trying

Daniel de Burgos

They didn't touch each other—Man and wife sitting on the carpeted
floor, naked, not touching—each of them having to do something
to themselves so the other can watch and be drawn into the plane
of existence—how simple it must be to see her spreading her cunt
lips with her fingers, reaching for the box of chocolate candies as if
melting one of them will bring him closer to her without allowing
him to have her—his cock standing up when she crushes the
chocolate-covered cherry between her fingers and lets the red syrup
drip onto her belly—rubbing the sprinkle of blood-life into her black
hair, smiling at him when the red sticks her cunt lips together, each
of them popping apart silently as he bends closer to look—not able
to touch her—stroking himself so she can stop turning her flesh
red—she does stop when his grunts are louder, afraid he will cover
her with his syrup—wanting him to beat it in a way she has never
seen him do it, his hanging testicles hiding from her vision, his
brown eyes shutting and opening to match his mouth, the strong
answer to her love quickly jumping from between his legs to splash
on her thighs—husband and wife not touching—coming to be
closer—pulling it off so the chocolate cherry and his come form a
new treasure of insistence—a consumer approach to burying his
face in the strong smell of cherries as she pushes him away—falls
back on the floor—legs spread—his eyes becoming the line of tight-
ness that collects the remains of cherry juice on her opening—
the fresh stars of his semen bristling with what he can't have be-

cause they are falling back and loving each other toward a growling fountain of copulating—infused—lightning—march—flute—melting chocolate—her face hard to the ceiling—not looking at him when she comes and comes—signs of love crisscrossing her tossed legs as she raises her pelvis to him and demands he put his face as close to her cunt as he can without touching her—their fainting commotion bringing the melted patterns of self-congratulations toward a teasing that matters—a love that stretches inside the gift they have shared.

The Receiving Blanket

Alma Luz Villanueva

He didn't do it all the time. But once in a while he did it. Today he would do it. He knew it when he opened his eyes and the dreams still burned on his inner eyelids like a magical, dangerous chemical. In fact, he murmured, "The chemistry of dreams," with a sigh of pleasure as he woke, knowing he would do it.

The pregnant woman again, he thought. Every time she's more beautiful, more pregnant. It's like I want to make love to her *and* I want to be her child. "Cut the crap," he muttered, "I want to *be* her: a beautiful, pregnant woman."

He remembered his mother's pregnancy with his little sister— the game his emotions played with him. Repulsion, attraction, repulsion and finally wonder, sheer unmitigated awe. He rememberd his mother's immense belly and the urge he had controlled. The urge to touch, to cradle, her belly, what lived there so invisible. So alive.

I was never jealous of my little sister; I even felt she was kind of mine. Being I was fourteen years older than her, and since my father died in the crash when she was still in our mother's womb, I suppose I took his place. But I certainly never wanted to make love to my mom or ever wanted to go back into her womb, no, not me . . .

He closed his eyes in order to see his dream more clearly: the way she looked at him, the way she smiled. Usually he'd masturbate now, imagining the fullness of her flesh, her swelling breasts, her aggressively protruding belly, the child within just floating unaware of anything but his small world of bliss. He became penetrator and penetrated. He became the impenetrably pure child as he thrust and thrust through his trembling hand. He trembled into bliss with the child, the woman, himself.

He knew all the homework he had to do, but he reasoned he'd be back by sunset. No longer than sunset. "Cinderella had till midnight; I've got till sunset, then the books or I'm screwed Monday, shit the tests." He spoke out loud to emphasize the importance, to himself, of the deadline.

He was pre-med, and when people asked him what he intended to specialize in, he always said he hadn't decided, but he had. Obstetrics. He knew the usual crude jokes: Can't keep your hands out of the cunt ... Want all that pussy to yourself, huh ... Can't ever get enough of that volume tits and ass, etc. ... So, he shrugged his shoulders and smiled without guile, yet closed the matter firmly by changing the subject.

He knew his mother wanted him to be a surgeon, at the very least a family practitioner. His girlfriend didn't care. She herself was considering surgery. She said she wanted constant drama. The challenge. But he hadn't even told her. It was his own sweet secret and it filled him with sudden joy just to think of it: to have access to all those wonderful, utterly feminine, pregnant bodies. To touch their warmth. To spread their legs. To probe the mysteries to his leisure and, he hoped, satisfaction.

He smelled the coffee brewing. Right on time: 8 A.M.

Morning fog still blocked the sun as he made his way to breakfast. The early-morning people were out getting a jump on the day: shoppers, lovers, tourists, parents with small children. A woman caught his eye and patted her own stomach, smiling at him with sisterly conspiracy. It filled him with absolute bliss as he smiled back at her. Most of the men looked away respectfully, or they simply didn't notice him, showed no interest whatsoever; but he watched every passing stranger, man or woman, for some response. Any response. To him. To her. To him. To her.

One man looked full into his face, scanning his entire body with his eyes, and smiled with masculine approval. Oh, bliss, bliss and more bliss. He floated over the cement like Jesus did over the supposed waters. He understood, truly understood, bliss for once in his life. To float, he thought, opening the door to the cafe, over life because you *create* it, life itself.

He came here from time to time for a quick breakfast. The waitress greeted him, "Hi, hon. Look, if you're more comfortable in a booth, go ahead. I've done that twice myself," she laughed, "and I know how it gets toward the end. Go ahead and stretch yourself out and I'll be right there. Coffee?"

"Decaf, please." He smiled, shielding his ecstasy, the overwhelming waves of bliss that threatened to make him lose consciousness, or so it felt. He closed his eyes, pretending to rest (such work, this making life), and tried to placate the urge to pass out—the unrelenting waves of bliss washing over him—with logical thought—I've dressed as a woman from the time I was thirteen, but I never imagined this—okay, if Juana came in, would she recognize me, I bet she wouldn't, what about my mother . . . His eyes flew open, scanned the room and closed again.

The decaf arrived. "Just you take it easy and I'll be back in a minute, hon."

Bliss, bliss, bliss. He wanted to laugh and laugh and laugh until tears ran from his eyes, but of course he couldn't. He wanted to laugh loudly, in his man's voice, to see what she'd do, but of course he couldn't . . . No, no, get a grip, like the time Mom caught me in her clothes, I was sixteen, and I couldn't stop laughing . . .

I remember the feel of the nylons, for the first time, on my legs. I'd shaved my legs, I was all alone in the house, Mom was out shopping with Evita, Dad was on a business trip, so I took my time bathing and shaving my legs, perfume, the bra, the panties, the red dress, her slinkiest one that dipped low to the breasts, yes, it looked a little silly on me, my skinny ass, body, no breasts except for the stuffed toiled paper, I don't even have man-breasts, so I was imagining my beauty, my curves, my feminine allure, as I slipped my man-foot into the silky woman-foot of the black panty hose, when she walked right in and saw me and screamed. I hadn't even heard the car, I was so engrossed in my feminine self.

"Madre de Dios!" she screamed, her face, my mother's face, contorted with fear and anger; disgust.

And then her words, *Madre de Dios,* Mother of God, The Mother, Head Hancha. I thought, Yeah, that's me, and started to roar with laughter, laughing till I fell on the floor in a heap, my one foot still in its silky panty hose foot. Finally, my laughter subsided to a helpless giggle, and I looked up at her. She was frozen to the spot. Livid.

"Are you gay, Ramon?"

"I don't think so," I gasped. "I like girls, you know that."

"I think you like girls *too much* is what I think!" She looked out the window at the car, where Evita waited. "We had an uncle who did this sort of thing—now a son of mine!" She gave me a killing look. "You promise, right now, to never do this again, Ramon! You promise me right this damned minute! Do you hear me? If your father knew he'd either kill you himself or have you locked away, Jesus Santo!"

"I can't promise you that, Mom, but I do promise that I'll never do it here or wear your clothes again." (I still don't know why I didn't just promise her, just lie, but somehow being caught made me strangely proud, brazen.) And then I wanted to laugh again because her clothes didn't even fit. They were too big and baggy on me, and I knew I had to buy my own. Just the thought, the realization that I'd buy my own girl clothes thrilled me with anticipation, a breathless excitement: my very own girl things . . .

"Okay, have you decided?" the waitress intruded, but I liked her eyes, her smile.

He raised his voice and spoke softly. "I'll take the short shack, one fried egg, over hard, and three sausages. I know I shouldn't eat so much, but I'm so hungry this morning."

"I've got two myself and I was always hungry at the end, so I know about being hungry all the time. Do I! It was the first months that was the bummer—you know, morning sickness."

"Oh, I had it so bad I could hardly lift my head first thing in the morning. I could've just died—well, you know. Now I'm just hungry, but I'm trying not to put on too much weight—I hear it's hard to lose—so my biggest meal is breakfast."

"Yeah, that's good thinking, small dinner before you go to bed and snacks will keep it down and not chase your old man out the door later." She cracked herself up.

"*They* don't have them, that's for sure." He said this with exquisite pleasure, but hid it beneath his conversational tone, while pretending to glance down at his watch. "So it falls to us to be pregnant and look like you've never been pregnant. I'd like to see *them* do it!" He allowed himself a dose of a sweet giggle here.

Bliss, bliss and more bliss. He was experiencing orgasms of bliss as he watched the waitress's ass float away. He closed his eyes and thought about the rest of the day, what he'd do next . . . Baby clothes, that's it. I'll buy baby clothes. Little, tiny shirts, booties, and I'll let the women advise me, being a first-time mom and all . . . He melted with pleasure, but he kept his face composed. He realized too much visible ecstasy would be suspect.

Suddenly he remembered, with sharp clear details, his mother pregnant with Evita, her hand over her enormous belly, exhausted, but with an unguarded smile of ecstasy as Evita moved within her. Her face, usually tense and unhappy, held a visible, joyful light. He'd run over to feel the mysterious life move and struggle beneath his hand, but she'd push him away, shouting, "What are you, crazy?"

That night as he folded the tiny baby clothes (all white and yellow, as the wise saleswomen kept telling him after he told them he was doing it "the old-fashioned way": he didn't want to know the child's sex until she/he revealed her/himself voluntarily), after he'd finished his homework and had a long conversation with Juana (he was wearing men's clothes again and felt like *him*self: functional, ordinary, slightly disappointed), he remembered the older sales-woman at the second baby store he'd wandered into. She'd helped him pick out "receiving blankets," as she'd called them, and a thick, warm quilt. In spite of his better judgment, he'd asked, "Why are they called 'receiving blankets'?"

Her face had jerked upward to attention and her sixtyish eyes, suddenly so soft and young, had met his. "When you have a gift, you have to receive it, right?" He remembered how she'd patted his hand as though he were a slightly retarded child. "I had five and I remember each one. Later on they become a pain in the you-know-what, but that's just growing up, dear, inevitable, you'll see, but you have to receive a gift, pain-in-the-you-know-what and all." She'd smiled and looked away.

Tenderly, he placed each baby-sized item into a large plastic bag, and then put the bag into a box. He stacked the box at the very back of his closet, and he knew he'd go shopping again and again until the box was full.

As he reached up to grab a blanket from the shelf where he kept clean sheets and extra blankets, he murmured, "Receiving blan-ket," and laughed softly. He took it to his bed and spread its thick softness out, end to end. Then he lay down right in the middle, grabbing each end, wrapping it around him, feeling the blanket's satin edge graze his face.

His eyes were closed. He wasn't happy, but he wasn't sad either. He felt the tired innocence of a child who's played his or her hardest at the end of a long, long day. He saw Juana's lovely face float in the darkness of his eyes, and he heard her voice: "I want to live with you, Ramon. We love each other and it'll be cheaper, you know that." He knew she'd move in. He knew that. He loved her.

"But will she understand?" he whispered, and wept without a sound. "Or will she think I'm crazy?"

Then the blanket received him into its warmth, completely.

Juana is so pregnant. I've never seen anyone so pregnant in my life. And she's so beautiful. She glows with it, smiling at me, taking my hand, both of them, and putting my hands on her belly. I feel the child, our child, my child, move like a minor earthquake, yes, very much like a little earth-quake, so unexpected and full of its own will. Life.

We walk into the street. It's absolutely sunny, no fog at all, and the sun feels hot and comforting as it meets my face, Juana's face. I know exactly the way Juana feels, so I laugh as I feel her womb move like a little earthquake inside of me, as the child creates itself, is being created. As the created creates.

Now I'm watching us walk down the street, holding hands, and I see that my belly isn't as immense as hers, but I'm so utterly, utterly happy, like a child, like a woman, like a man.

Portrait/Nude #30 / 4 x 6

Juan Felipe Herrera

Her breasts are delicate eternally alone
her hair falls loose
lightning and liquor
something bitter is between her lips
she smokes and strokes herself

Portrait/Nude #9 / 7 x 11

Juan Felipe Herrera

The unending hip stretches to the sea
her navel
spins ebony
her throat pulses
the moon is buried between her legs and disappears
night

Arc

Juan Felipe Herrera

Lean your dark back lean
draw a silent arc
exhale slowly exhale
erode my body erode
beneath your breasts beneath
up
up
down slowly down
your hair your beauty marks your sweat
lean your dark back lean

Saguaro

Juan Felipe Herrera

Water from your shoulders
sky from your womb.

Everything turns
tonight's blood
time buried beneath your skin.

Nocturnal sigh
ten tears like fingernails
the sea divides;

barren
transparent thorns
liquid eyelashes;

vertical
thick lips piercing
black fruit from a hidden lagoon.

Shine on this cruel moon
lightning
abandoned cross;

scar
horizon
your body like a sword.

Deep naked leaf
cut my heart

water
water
water.

The Boy of Seventeen

Juan Felipe Herrera

The boy of seventeen
twists in the sheets
the pages of sex
    the bolts are crying
    the windows are crying
his legs sweat camphor
and his blue lips
are dissolved into his cheeks
the pillows' hollows
are withering
    the door is crying
    seeing the keys
    the clock cries
    burning the curtains
the boy of seventeen
a paragraph of rain
between silk and marble
he measures the nails
in Christ's arms
he wants an X
on the left side of his dreams

    he's searching for his mother
    naked on the red altar

Focus

Carlos Parian

How could you suck me off
without a word
I swallowed your religion
I believed you
but you took it
without a prayer

How could you kiss me
without a tongue
I basked in your lips
I ate your cunt
but you kissed me
without knowledge

How could you fuck me
without life
I fucked you in the tower
at the bottom of the lake
in front of the sun
I burned my back
the sweat on your palms
was never enough

Door

Carlos Parian

I'll undress you
when the black leather
comes alive
with the sin I created
when I whipped
the first red language
across your breasts

Do not interpret
the red marks
My dick has
a line I never saw before
it points to
the black door
where the black bed
elevates unmade

I'll tie you to it
ask me
write me a song
with the torn leather
we soaked in come
when you finish
my dick will also
be underwater
opening the length
of the whip
the strength of our love
the keyhole in the door
that leads to no door

Bellas Artes

Kyra Galvan

While you slept I heard you breathing,
deep and slow.
One would say it sounded young.
Who could tell
that under your heart weighed
so many years of being the expert
in the art of submission
in the virtue of muteness
in the vice of not touching.

Translated by Zoe Anglesey

My Flaws Among the Peach Blossoms

Kyra Galvan

> *Freedoms are not given,*
> *they are taken*
> —Kropotkin

Suns and tormented archangels have been exploited.
Whites swelling into violets.
Beaches on lakes of extinct fish.
Nights of groins and dormant words.
Unknown adventures on the road.
Tastes of pulque and raw meat.
Unforeseen tremblings and shocks.

Telluric movements in the brains
consumed by surrounding obscurantism.

A deflowering of me toward life.
A crevice toward the Andean sky.
A woman crushed by time.
A viscosity toward salt water.
Living flesh in the presence of death.
    An open mouth in the presence of life.

I will tell you: I am cedar woman agony woman
        woman like a wheatfield like a violet
        like a watermelon and storm.
I seek an island for gestation,
to fashion my liberty and my body and all my
movements.
I seek my face in the crowds, my odor,
in my lover's armpits,
my swallows in the final quarters of the moon.
My flaws, among the peach blossoms.

We have been probing our depths
our darkened rooms, calculating
the radiance of our snail star
and our virtuous toads.
Simply caressing our odors
and our accidental skins.
I still don't know your identity my mystery.
Luminous and intricate animal
that has aroused my hordes:
I have declared war against alienation.
I am at war with that solitude.
    I disrobe
exposing the Great Fear of not seizing
freedom.
And I scream my durable abandonment, my sorrow.
I embrace you to hear your life and mine.
A good beginning.

The Thing in My Mouth

Carlotta Sanchez

The thing in my mouth tastes like the world has been reborn.
It is not a good nor bad taste.
It tastes like he will die if I don't show him what I can do.
I know he is not very smart.
I can do what I want with him.
This thing in my mouth thought it had its own life.
It does not.
It belongs with all the others whose life I have stolen many times.
It wants to jump and sing.
I will tell it when it can speak.
I only keep it in my mouth long enough to show him I know.
He doesn't know.
He can't see.
He is too busy thinking and acting like a macho boy.
When I bite down, he screams.
I don't let go.
This thing in my mouth belongs to him.
I will never claim it for my own.
I don't need to own it, lick it, eat it, have it talk inside my mouth.
I have my own tongue.
I know when to speak.
I told him not to think I will do this for very long.
Suddenly, he decides this is it and comes in my mouth.
It is okay.
I swallow what I want and do what I want with it.
It tastes like the end of the world.
It tastes like it is going to nourish me.
I am already nourishing because I won't let go.
He screams and I laugh inside, swallowing,
dreaming, knowing I can have this and that
and this boy of mine can't do a thing about it.
This thing in my mouth tastes like it may come back from the
dead someday.
I won't be around.

This thing in my mouth belongs to those who can't move
and I've been moving and moving ever since I realized I don't need
this thing in my mouth to live.
I only took it to do him a favor
and now, he belongs to me.

Avocado Blues
Avocado Greens

Carlotta Sanchez

She smeared the avocado all over me and I thought I was a lizard
that could rub its green skin all over her naked ass. I rubbed her
blue and green, until the avocado glistened upon her puzzled
nipples. She smeared the second avocado on her palms, pressed
them together until the meat oozed between her fingers and
dripped between my spread legs. She pushed her open hand into
me, the green ripples of avocado forming a pattern around me,
the cold glaze and cold smell of the avocado reminding me this
was it, this was how I was going to be consumed by her magic
and her silence. She ate the avocado off me and I lifted the last
secret from my mind, drifted and blended tastes of blue and green
with the fresh interior of my meal. She rubbed the green all over
my thighs, her mouth and cheeks smeared in the blue and green
of a silent love that called for the strange request of buying the
avocados at the store, laughing all the way to her house, doing
this so I could see what it was like to go to the other side of my
fear, become what I thought I could only have in a dream, be
eaten as if the strong smell of the avocado in my cunt would
unleash the clouds and patterns of a love I could consume. She
ate the avocado inside me, around me, in me and I licked the
green off her ass until she shuddered like a branch that bore

the avocado, dropped it between our rubbing thighs, planted it in the only place that still remains a secret when I think about that day and how I had to write this to be able to eat, sleep, and dream blue and green, blue and green, the fasting period of my tongue and life lasting until the avocado hardened in my dream and I was able to insert it, uncut, the whole fruit perched in her opening, perplexed, wondering what it was that made this woman, this friend, peel it with her fingernails and drive it in deep.

Resurrection

Gilberto Flores

He wore a black tank top and nothing else. He kneeled over the edge of the cot. As naked men walked by the open doorway, they could peer inside to see if they wanted to fuck his bright, smooth ass. He would kneel with his shining ass in the air and rock himself back and forth, waiting for someone to walk in, close the door, and reach for the Vaseline jar that sat on the tiny wooden box next to the cot.

David Morales leaned against the narrow wall of the corridors that separated the dozens of cubicles in the bathhouse. He'd watched two men go into the guy's room earlier. Neither one of them had taken long. He tightened the towel around his waist, closed his eyes, and listened to the random grunts and moans that rose above the partitions. He had fucked this guy several times in the past, but had never seen him with the black tank top. It excited him and he shifted his legs to hide the erection that tried to bulge through the towel. It didn't matter because the whole place was dark and dimly lit. David always felt self-conscious when the endless stream of men walked by. He felt his own nakedness more when some of them paused to study him.

He decided it was the right time to enter. He looked up and down the corridor, then walked into the guy's room. David didn't know his name. They never spoke to each other, unless it was a sudden command to move a leg. The guy was white with dark brown, short hair. He turned to look at David for an instant, then rocked himself faster, his balls hanging below his open asshole. David closed the door behind him, took his towel off, and dropped it on the floor. He touched the grease in the jar and rubbed it on his stiff cock.

He squeezed the guy's waist and drove his cock all the way in. The guy grunted and heaved and started pumping. David held him back, so he would stop moving. As he knelt still, David screwed himself deeper into the guy's tight hole. He leaned forward, until he stood on his toes. He thrust several times and watched the spine on the guy's back stiffen and rise through his skin. He stuck his hands inside the black tank top until they rested on both shoulders.

David took a deep breath and started fucking the guy wildly. It was an incredible sensation. David never felt so free as when he came to this place to get sucked off and fuck several men in one night. He never let anyone fuck him. It was always the other way around. This guy was here every time David came, but they didn't always get together.

This time, David fucked him with a deep sense of pleasure and violation. The guy would grunt and whisper things to himself, but never speak to David. Suddenly, David slid out, and the guy let out a shout of surprise.

"Turn over," David hissed through his teeth.

The guy flipped over. David looked down at the guy's limp cock. It was small and didn't have any life in it. David parted the guy's greased legs, then rubbed his own cock in the area around his asshole. The guy went wild and started convulsing. Without warning, David entered the guy and lifted himself onto the cot. They bound each other, one on top of the other, both of their slick asses heaving and shaking in the blue light of the room. They fucked and fucked, their isolation, despair, and freedom melting them into one body of sweat, lust, cocks, balls, and male muscle. They fucked and fucked and David thought of the time he was in here with the black guy who traded off with him. The two of them had drilled this guy good, until the three of them lay in a pile of sweaty clouds, musk, and the remains of their spouting power.

David wondered who this guy was and why he had to take so many cocks. David had been coming to this place less than a year, a thirty-two-year-old lonely man who was starting to discover a certain kind of freedom he could never explain to his straight friends. To him, it had to do with the unknown and known state of men fusing together to reside in that place where the male existence of flesh and soul was completely uncovered by mouths on cocks, by shooting come, by fucking beautiful hard asses, by watching others get fucked and sucked, by going down to the level of dark freedom that pulled at David's deepest pain, confusion, and conquering need.

David fucked this guy and was exhilarated by the level he discovered on the other side of such physical freedom and imprisonment. He pulled back and climbed off the cot without coming. He motioned to the guy to turn over again. The guy rose, yanked off his soaked tank top, and was barely back down before David went in again.

This time, David danced like never before. On his toes, on his flat feet, on one foot, kneeling on the edge of the cot, smothering the guy, falling deeper and deeper into the tunnel of a complete black condition where the desire to exist and fly beyond the tip of red, swollen cocks sent him toward the crashing moment of climax.

David came and came, crying and shooting into the guy for a very long time. They both fell on the cot out of breath, the smells and sighs and movements cutting shapes against the walls, the blue light of their deep, dark deaths delayed for years until they could get their breaths back, stare at each other for a few moments, and wonder, in their own exposed memories, what it was that had thrown them against this light. What was it that made David get up, grab the towel, and leave without a word? What was it, after he had given himself to the countless dramas of the corridor, that had made David go take a shower and stand in the hot steam for a very long time, his eyes closed, his mind thinking of a mountain where the signatures on the cross told him the Mexican ghost of sins was coming to get him, save him, relieve him, until the dark corridors could suddenly be lighted blindly by great torches and the guy in the tiny cubicle could grab his black tank top and put it on again, always making sure the door was open.

The Brown Woman

Roberta Medina

He left me alone and I couldn't see how I would miss him. Ruben told me it was going to be difficult to be alone, but he said that because I did what I wanted with him. I even showed him how the fire in that thing he brought me worked. He watched while I did it by myself. One night, in the middle of our second fuck, I bent down to him and whispered in his ear, "Buy me a dildo, a cucumber. Whatever works. It'll try it. I want you to fuck me with it. . . ." At first, he didn't know what I was talking about. He never does when I am on top and can't stop fucking and want to try new things. I can't stop because I can do whatever I want to Ruben. I always win, but lately I've been wanting more than he has to give me.

He showed up with this brown thing—a replica or some kind of sculpture of a naked woman, a foot-long object made of soft, claylike material that doesn't dissolve or fall apart. It doesn't hurt even though it's about ten inches long. It is soft and flexible and smells like clay. The woman is crouched down on her haunches, balancing on her legs with her long arms straight up above her head, her large breasts pressed tightly between her shoulders. It is this soft brown woman that Ruben carefully inserted up my cunt. I moaned and took his hand away. I held the clay up inside me on my own and slid it in and out slowly.

The smell of clay grew stronger as Ruben sat on the edge of the bed and watched the brown woman disappear and appear between my legs. Before I knew it, I was all wet and could feel the object get warmer in my hands. I thought it might be too sharp an object to use, but when I put it in, it seemed to grow softer, the woman's protruding breasts sliding quite easily into me, the stretched arms guiding and opening my cunt so she could get in there. I pushed it until only the bottom part of her legs and feet showed.

Ruben started getting excited at this point and tried to lick around the tiny clay object. I pushed him away and finished alone. I didn't want him to touch me this time. I was tired of his touch and knew the slightest contact with him could change everything.

He stared as I jerked and gripped the thing tighter with my closed legs. I came loudly and lay back while Ruben slowly extracted the clay woman out of me. I did let him do that much, though I warned him not to touch my skin as he gently put his fingertips around the object and withdrew it.

She was wet and shiny. It was a wonderful sensation and my fear of hurting myself with such an object went away. I asked Ruben where he had bought the thing and he said he didn't buy it; it was given to him by a friend. A friend? Ruben didn't have any friends cool enough to play with these things. All his friends were the wham-bam-thank-you-ma'am type. He wasn't the kind of guy who would go into an adult bookstore and buy a dildo, even though I had half-teased him and told him I wanted one.

It's not a dildo, he insisted. I know it's not, I said, and told him to please go. I didn't want him in my bed that night, though I still loved him and he was my lover. He didn't tell me where he got the clay woman, but I suspected it may have had something to do with Cristina, the fifty-five-year-old Puerto Rican poet he met at a reading a few weeks ago. Ruben told me she read a poem about a man who sculpted statues of women after he made love to them. Ruben wants to be a poet, but has never sent any of his work out to get published. He is thirty-eight years old and I am thirty-two.

He talked to this Cristina at the reception after the reading and she told him she owned a craft shop in Manhattan. I have never met her, but he has described her to me in detail. I think he may be interested in this older woman, which would really surprise me. I didn't know Ruben had that much adventure in him. I guess with the appearance of this clay woman, some of our true adventures are being exposed. I don't know if Ruben has ever gone to see Cristina, but when he brought this thing over to my place, what he called a "masturbation toy," he wouldn't tell me where he got it. I asked him if it had anything to do with Cristina's poem. He laughed and said no, but bowed his head as he answered. He showed me her poem in the literary journal where it appeared. There is no sex in the poem, but when we unwrapped the brown woman from the tissue and box it came in, I knew he was lying to me.

I agreed to let him watch me try the brown woman and see what it would do. He started to undress, but I told him that I could only do it by myself. He could watch, but he had to keep his clothes on. In a way, this was a turn-on for me, even letting him slide it up my cunt and letting me take over. But, after that point, as I say,

I made sure he couldn't touch my skin. I just knew it had something to do with the brown clay skin of the woman. Its softness. Its smell. The gentle way she slid in and out of me and gave me a chill. The way I knew where a brown clay woman like this came from, without really having to get a straight answer out of my lover.

It was another change in our six-month-old relationship because a few days ago, Ruben and I took our first shower together. I know that sounds weird, but we are so private that we have always cleaned up after sex one at a time in the bathroom. I know that is strange, but I am very particular about my bathroom and its privacies. Despite that, I love Ruben and he is a good lover. We finally just jumped in the shower together the other night. It was very natural and I had no complaints about him messing with my brushes and towels. It was a turn-on for him, too, because he had a huge hard-on the whole time we were in the shower. I had no choice but to suck him off right there. He did the same for me. I recall clutching wildly at the showerhead as I came and he kept flicking his tongue between my legs. The water ran hot and fast, but we enjoyed it.

This thing with the brown clay woman is the next step in our relationship. It is some kind of pleasant intrusion I have been looking for. I don't know why, but I have needed this kind of object to try and wake Ruben to all our possibilities, even if some of them seem weird at first. I'm not really sure why I agreed to use the brown woman on my body. I just know he got the idea from Cristina's poem. There has to be a connection. I know Ruben is fascinated with this older woman who is a successful poet. I have to meet her and find out if she is the source of the clay woman. I guess I will thank her, because this object works great. It felt so warm and powerful. I was not shy at all as Ruben sat on the bed and watched me. I know he didn't understand why I wouldn't let him join me, but I had to do it on my own.

Now that he has left, I can lie back and think about the brown woman inside me, how I closed my eyes and saw Ruben making love to Cristina. He wants to take me to her next reading, but I don't know if I want to go. It is easier to fantasize about Ruben making love to this older woman while I watch. She is naked and has very short white hair. Cristina is a thin woman with small breasts. She wears a purple scarf around her neck and nothing else. She is on top of Ruben and bends over his chest. I am sitting in a chair by the bed and can see her slide Ruben's cock halfway out of her cunt. She leans forward and I get a good look at her spread ass, the fine red layers of love skin hot and glistening as she suddenly pushes herself back down on his thick thing. Ruben makes noise and Cristina reaches behind her to rub his balls with a sharp red fingernail. This sends Ruben into a frenzy and he grabs Cristina by the scarf, rolls her back and forth on top of himself, and fucks her harder. Cristina does not make a sound, until she leans over him again, exposing her asshole high in the air.

I rise from the chair as she expertly lifts her cunt just enough to allow some of Ruben's cock to stay inside her. Suddenly, I grab the brown woman and push the clay figure into Cristina's asshole. I greased the thing ahead of time because I knew I was going to do this. I have been sitting there watching them fuck, waiting for this moment. I push the clay woman all the way in, until nothing shows but her tiny feet. Cristina cries out in pain and ecstasy. She flings the scarf off her neck and turns to look at me. Her mouth is wide open in fantastic surprise. She sits back on Ruben's cock and, with her right hand, rubs the tiny clay feet that stick a few inches out of her asshole.

I reach over, push gently on the brown feet, and watch in awe as Cristina explodes in an incredible orgasm. She falls off Ruben, who just stares at me with his big green eyes, his cock stiff and trembling in the air. Cristina rolls on the bed, gasping and crying Yes! Yes! As I stand frozen on the edge of the mattress, she slowly pulls the clay woman out of her asshole. She trembles and whimpers as it comes out.

My fantasy stops there. Part of me is rather ashamed because it seems like a violent intrusion on my part, yet I know Cristina loved it just like I loved the brown woman inside me. As for Ruben, I don't know how he fits into all of this. When he comes back, I will force him to tell me where he got the brown woman. I lie here and look at it. It seems like it has soaked up a great deal of desire. The clay has become a darker brown since I pulled it out of me. It is wet and pure and confident about fitting into my cunt again.

The woman's arms point up above her head like she is about to rise and do a nude dance for every man who has dreamed about her. She is about to come to life and be my companion. Perhaps, she has already been Cristina's companion. It may be why I feel she gave Ruben this gift to pass on to me. This brown woman belongs inside every woman that enters the life of a guy like Ruben. He needs this kind of help, this kind of intrusion, because he is not enough for any woman on his own. He is hard to figure out, too quiet and shy. I know he can't be the great poet that he wants to be, but he is trying hard. He may be just another writing student at the university; I have slept with three of them from there. Ruben is the youngest. Pablo was with me the longest—one year and a half. But, Pablo can't make love like Ruben. And, as I say, I now know Ruben is not enough.

I try not to think about men as I take the clay figure in my left hand and rub its hard breasts with my right fingers. I was going to get dressed and go get something to eat, but my fantasy of Cristina and Ruben keeps me here with this brown gift. Ruben told me that he hoped these kinds of gifts will make me dream of him, make me want him more, but as I rub the brown woman and gently press her between my breasts, I want and dream for something else.

It has nothing to do with Cristina or Ruben, but with the darkening brown skin of the clay woman. As I hold her, her skin gets darker and darker, as if a special moisture or rain is seeping into her skin—her long arms and hard breasts are a deep brown, a moving color of the earth I last saw when I first realized and could admit I didn't need Ruben to make me come. I could be happy and pleased on my own, locked in the solitude of my apartment so I could do things to myself that no man would understand. It is why I teased Ruben about bringing me a toy. But, why didn't I get one on my own? Why did I still have to depend on Ruben to get me to the next level of what I want? But, I know if I had gone out and gotten a toy on my own, or just used something here like my hairbrush or an unpeeled banana from the kitchen, it wouldn't have been the same. Ruben was the only one who could have brought me this wonderful clay woman.

There is something to that I don't understand, but it doesn't matter now. As I lie back on my bed, I spread my legs wide and place the brown woman on top of my crotch. My black hairs rise around her legs as I press her against my skin. I close my eyes and slowly move her soft body down into my opening. I stop and think about Cristina's surprise as the clay woman invaded her. It is something I want to do to anyone who might try and take Ruben from me. As I insert her over my clitoris, I see Cristina's head moving up and down between Ruben's legs.

I rise from my seat and go to the side so I can see how much of him she can take into her mouth. She has swallowed his cock deeper than I ever have. I open my eyes as the brown woman weaves and parts my lips with her submerging hips. I look down and the clay is halfway in. Her arms still protrude and so do her breasts, rising just above my swollen skin. I push in and cry out because I know she has been inside Cristina. The difference is that she has allowed Ruben to fuck her with this clay woman. As my hips lift up and down on the bed and I start to forget something I saw between Cristina's parted ass, when she straddled Ruben so easily, I smell the new odor of clay, the first and last love between Ruben, Cristina, and myself. It is why she let him have her brown woman. As a gift for me, Ruben's lover who is now opening and closing herself to the woman of clay, the woman who fucks with the scarf around her neck, the man who thinks he can get away with his lust by digging into the clay and flesh of the women in his life and watching as the soil and dirt of their dripping cunts create this smell that softens the clay as it begins to dissolve, enter, and devour me from the inside.

Windmills

Wasabi Kanastoga

Placing her hand over the stick shift of the old VW convertible, she saw the planes one after the other as they cut across the clear blue, like flickering fireflies cautiously avoiding one another's path. They appeared to glide over a vast ocean using stars as resting points en route to an unknown destination, their red and blue lights intermittently dotting the sky.

Nighttime skies reminded Mariana of immense circus tents tightly stretched and pinned to the soil, suspended in the horizon by the pitch-black darkness of desert nights. Nights which meant hiding as movement ceased and silence reigned. Cacti and seclusive animals slowly disappeared into smearing patches, bleeding into and mixing with each other.

Each summer night was different. The shape of the moon was never the same. Pretentious stars glittered, forming distant patterns inviting the unrestricted imagination of the dreamer, eventual death concealed in their radiance. The wind, with its invisible power, blew warm and strong as the end of the hot day brought forth a sigh of relief from the land.

The drive from L.A. to Palm Springs never took longer than a couple of hours. As Mariana approached the lengthy rows of windmills heading into the desert, she knew it was a matter of minutes. A matter of fragmented events which led to what had to become her latest form of employment. "My days at Weiser Locks are over," she said to herself. The wind tousled her hair, and with a deep breath she absorbed the desert night. "No more gold-plated locks. No more silver-plated dead bolts. No more factory nights of swollen hands. Of acid burns. No more prick foremen pumping my ass for free." She smiled and looked to the side of the road, her slightly callused fingers wrapped around the steering wheel.

Mariana traveled this highway enough to have memorized the various branches which led to valleys and mountain ranges, land which afforded enviable solace and unmolested tranquility. Moments where not a thing could be seen or heard, where masquerades dropped for no one to see.

A mile ahead she exited the main road and drove eastbound

until the highway headlights disappeared. She stepped out of the car, pulled her dress over her head and instantly unclothed, except for the brown suede boots which had been a gift at the onset of her weekly ventures.

Soaking herself with perfumed water, and standing with arms extended and legs apart, she embraced the warm breeze which began to dry her body.

In ritualistic steps she slowly shut her eyes, wet her lips and crouched; her chin nudged between her knees; hair fanned against her shoulders.

She imagined the sky being an upside-down cup granting security. Not a thing flowed in. Not a thing dripped out. Using her nails to caress her thighs, Mariana slid her parted fingers down her legs and over the boots. She ran both hands over pebbles and cracked soil, sensing the warm earth below. She tried to sink her nails into the ground, but was unable to. Mariana moved her hands back up, and noticed the material from the knee-high boots give way to her touch. Small hairs ascending her inner thighs catapulted beneath her hands, similar to rows of upright dominoes slapping one another on the back.

Nearby, Ocotillo silently stared, and she knew that. She also knew that prickly pears and saguaro surrounded her. But it didn't matter to her, and it didn't matter to them. After her departure, as before her arrival, everything was and would remain constant. There was no reason for change.

Ceremonial in her motions, Mariana prepared herself for the final step of the night. With cupped hand she stroked her pubis and worked her way over the lips, over the tender portion of skin between the vagina and buttocks, and between both mounds, where she sunk her middle finger while closing her eyes.

Digging into the upper portion of her boot, she extracted twelve marble-size beads pierced through the center and held together by a nylon string. She ran them over her crotch, and one by one inserted the colorful beads into her anus, leaving but two on the outside.

With rubber-band flexibility she snapped to an upright position and leaned against the car, her thirty-nine-year-old body still youthful. Mariana removed her boots and gingerly freed her feet of cellophane, in which each foot had been wrapped to the ankles for the past three days. Now exposed, her feet felt wet and cold. She held her spaghetti-strap dress above her head and let it go; it easily cascaded over her slim dark body. Boots back on, she climbed into the car and sped toward the highway.

The road which took her into town coiled around mountains, then suddenly straightened in apparent salute to the rows of erect palm trees aligned on both sides.

In the short distance, Mariana spotted her destination as the car glided into a driveway half-lit by a shadowy blue light which when on signaled for her to continue as agreed. She turned off the headlights, and total darkness fell upon her. Nothing but desert encircled the mansion. On her first visit the structure had appeared palatial, and she'd wondered how such an endeavor could take place so far from everything. But as summers had come and gone she'd started to pay more attention to what surrounded the structure. To the beauty of what cannot be seen. After a while the allure dissipated. The mansion became more ridiculous than grandiose. Just a temporary ornament of time. A partitioned box. An eyesore.

The ivory plush carpet sunk below Mariana's boots as she shut the entrance door. A faraway candle on a mantel above the fireplace dimly lit the living room. On the opposite end of the shelf a silver bill-file stabbed legal-tender notes. Shadows seemed to bounce from wall to wall as the candle steadily burned. Everything about was white: the long and winding leather sofa; the centerpiece table; sagging drapes; neatly arranged wall decor—all white.

Mariana imagined she'd entered the padded room of a well-to-do asylum where not a spot of dust could be found. A place of frozen objects. Of crystalized emotions. Beauty unnaturally preserved.

Removing from her forehead strands of hair, she allowed the car keys as well as her dress to drop onto the floor. Her dark skin offered a sharp contrast to her surroundings. Mariana took a deep breath and noticed the air was no longer fresh. The scent of melted wax filled the room. The desert suddenly vanished.

Ahead, a long hallway divided the mansion in half. Although it was dark, she still distinguished the marble busts and statues along each wall. She extended both arms horizontally and gently ran her fingers over their heads, thighs and breasts. Cautiously, she headed toward the half-shut door at the end.

As she neared the entrance to the room, the familiar bubbling sound intensified, reminiscent of when her daughter blew air through a straw into root beer floats. In a strange way, the bubbling sound relaxed her. It reminded her that all this was temporary. That one thing would lead to another, as had been the case in her life.

Mariana opened the room door to a multitude of staring eyes; they floated up, down, side to side, always keeping her in sight. Running her hand over the wall, she felt the light switch, and with a simple click the dome ceiling above, which extended indefinitely, rolled open, exposing the starry night.

The process felt magical. Unreal. Something meant for the Hollywood big screen. The room came to life, round and immense. The entire circumference was a giant aquarium extending from top to bottom. The sudden light frightened some of the fish, which scurried behind rocks and vegetation. Others simply remained as they were, their eyes fixed on Mariana, large bubbles zigzagging to the surface.

The whole room took on a blue hue: the aquarium and fish; the vegetation and light showering from above. In the middle of the room rested a large bed with a wheelchair next to it. Mariana walked toward the bed within the soothing blue ambiance, her naked body elastic and firm.

A middle-aged woman sat on the bed, propped up from behind by several large pillows. She looked to the sky through the rooftop window and slowly lowered her head, fixing her eyes on Mariana. Wrinkle lines ran across her forehead and down the sides of her mouth. Her eyes were lackluster, black as tar, sunk in each socket. She ran her fingers through her hair, down her pale face, and extended her arm toward Mariana. In so doing, the bedsheet covering her body dropped to her midsection, allowing the breasts to show. Resembling a couple of wet socks hanging on a clothesline, they drooped flat against her chest, down to her upper stomach.

Without saying a word, Mariana climbed on the bed, parted her legs over the immobile lower torso, and turned her back to the woman, resting her elbows on the bedsheet.

Her buttocks gripped, Mariana arched her back and stared at the fish. "They seem to recognize me," she said beneath her breath. "Even the timid ones are coming out. They're leaving their hiding places to watch. My audience. My ocean of admirers." She closed her eyes, feeling both mounds stretched like the sudden parting of curtains.

Noticing the beads, the woman threw her head back violently and inserted her nails into Mariana's rear. Her breathing became heavier, rapidly intensifying from one level to the next. Blood crept over the woman's gums as she buried her teeth into the lower lips.

Suddenly, she lunged forward, drowning her face within Mariana, and yanked on both boots until they were off. She ran the palm of her hands over the feet and her fingers through the toes. The feet were moist. As she squeezed, her hands slid toward the edges. She bent Mariana's legs up to her face, heels knocking against Mariana's backside.

The moaning grew increasingly louder. Mariana felt her feet squeezed and her toes parted by fingers which slid in and out with ease.

"I want to hide in you," the woman said, shaking her head within the buttocks. "Hide me from everything. Swallow me." As she spoke Mariana's body tightened.

Withdrawing her face, she held the beads between her teeth, and anxiously pulled back, watching them exit one by one, her nostrils flaring like an out-of-breath racehorse. As the last one emerged, the strand swung against her chest and dropped.

"I have failed you, Jesus," the woman said, clenching her teeth. "I have failed you, but you have failed me. You brought me into this world a half woman. I have carried the cross longer than you ever did. You crucify me daily."

The woman's tongue traveled over Mariana's feet, ferociously rubbing her face against them. Her upper body twisted sideways as she switched from foot to foot. Biting on the heels. Nibbling on the Achilles tendon. Covering each toe with her lips.

As the moist tongue slid over her feet, wild thoughts flashed through Mariana's head: oysters dancing in their shells; egg whites wiggling on still cold frying pans; a cow's ripped tongue, cold and curled, resting on a meat market cooler.

By the wall, the floating eyes stared. Mariana, with hands clasped, rocked back and forth, her nipples rubbing against the bedsheet. "My audience," she said. "My ocean of admirers."

Spastic trembling was followed by an extended deep breath that appeared to extract all air from the room. As if a taut balloon had rapidly deflated, the woman let out a long sigh, and the once tense body dropped on top of pillows as if death had paid her a visit; arms outstretched and inanimate, with palms facing the sky.

A thunderous cracking broke the sky, rain unexpectedly spraying both. Drops slapped Mariana's backside. Her hair, which hung over her face, absorbed the rain. It was time for her to leave as she had entered. In silence, without a hello. In silence, without a goodbye.

Eventually, she would reach the living room, dress and, from the silver bill-file piercing ten one-hundred-dollar bills, collect her earnings; an exchange of passion for the right of survival.

Outside, the rain brought with it a cool breeze; the evening awarding the desert its cooling comfort, bidding forgiveness for the day's heat.

Rows of windmills encrusted in flatland and hills sporadically motioned from afar. Thin giants of the desert waving for no apparent reason. Mad Quijotes of steel extending into the sun; signaling the beginning or the end of the desert, depending on which way you're headed.

Ebony Backs

Mara Larrosa

to Roberto Bolaño

I have seen your body woman, man, in the city
I have only been seeing your human eyes
I have been close to so many women with
   painted lips
We are born on this Earth with immaculate skin and there are
   so many women who have worn their muslin bodice
   since adolescence, the salt escapes from the armpits
   and fingers.
After eating moss from the great
   walls, screaming in the primary school baths,
   kissing the penis of Juan Pablo at ten years of age, I
   am afraid to move my arms and legs. Not my voice
   or my body has disordered the space and thus
   we hope to flourish above the urban winter.
The light must penetrate the darkness, that is why
   trees have grown in my ears, why
   I have opened my feminine essence to you, so
   near your sex, your smooth, appealing stomach. Toward
   you trembling, for you overflowing: I have realized
   we are similar. I love your white
   legs, your white arms.
Through others is through whom I love, *for others.*
I am happy to smell so many people.
Now, in Ecuador, the water is filled with brambles; now,
   while our eyes unfold and F asks to be
   served with a glass cup in the cafes, I have sensed
   EVERYTHING we lack to be distinctly human.
F adolescent leaves for a salt mine: his arms will grow,
   and other boys will grow also tending pharmacies,
manufacturing
   fabrics, shoes, and all are similar to the water that
   is hidden in the Earth, we are all those who
   make noise on the sidewalks, in the beds.

I love F because he is made of water and of men.
Gauguin: where are we going? will we achieve the human
   form? what is this lengthy germination that stirred
   before you knew the ebony backs
   with the straight hair? What stirs is perhaps the lingering love
   so that there may be no more
   Charlots in the cities.

Blue Mouth

Vera Larrosa

The two men I love are vicious
but adorable
I have sent flowers to their cabin
as well as good and bad verses,
it seems that I play the gentleman instead of the lady/
One plays the piano
issuing cotton from his fingers
like a smiling, hairy Frankenstein he sings a
    ballad/
The other has crossed many bridges without
    shaking/
and has offered me his language of a good prince/
My blue mouth screams in the muscles
no better cleansing than this:
the steam,
woman/
I love the young and old men without rolling over to see scarlet
    necklaces,
and I have displayed the adornments at the theater and floating
    between bursts of laughter
where my friends/ they say that by forty they will have
    plastic surgery/
I am powdered by the winds/
    the ledge/
also the tiny shadow figures have been approved by
—oh, these winds/—
powdered I approach the mirror to surprise my cheeks,
more than blush/
more pollen/
When will I be loved in hotels and fields?
When will I comb the long or short hair of my
    men?
Will the small bottle of suicidal tablets
travel in my flesh?

There will be a drama down to my socks if the impact
   and the ether flourish/
I can no longer endure the rejections,
reproach has begun to release a flashing of golds
   and sapphires
The two men I love are vicious
but some enchanting
others elephants
To them I am a tiny grain of pepper/
The small bottle,
the grains begin to stir on the dressing table/
My lovers spread their legs throwing themselves at terror
the terror of a cheap whore in miniskirt/
The small bottle of pills is dancing/
I take one then a second of these blue grains
farewell forever flabby ass
you knew nothing about docile clothes/
farewell forever horizon of males/

A Gentleman on the Train

Antonia Palacios

Delia is looking out the train window. She watches the land going by, so different, so much the same. The passing landscape, flat although slightly tilted, upturned in the inclines, in the unavoidable curves, bunched up high in gigantic promontories. She watches the green and distant prairies go by, and the windows of a house already passed. She is sitting very still in the train as the countryside parades by her. Opposite her, a gentleman is reading his paper. Maybe he doesn't know a thing about the landscape, the landscape on parade. He is reading the newspaper which is raised above his knees, level with his hands.

"Are you comfortable, Miss?"

"Yes, thank you. And you?"

Delia continues to watch animals passing by, a fat white cow lying by the rails which the train almost carries off. Delia would like to be a cow, as white as the one left behind, a cow comfortably settled into a fertile field with all sorts of aromas, chewing the green grass, and, chewing them over time and again, with large, unworried melancholy eyes and soft pink udders, just like the cow. A harmless cow, lying on the ground, indifferent to it, the ground passing by with men, women and children. Passing by without them.

"Do you smoke, Miss?"

"No, thank you. Do you?"

There is an enormous silence, then the train strains forward. the countryside in review makes a show of its luxuriant hair and its spotted pelt. The train rolls along and Delia watches with her hands folded over the pleated skirt. Her beautiful hands, so smooth and golden. The train rolls along and Delia watches.

"Are you gong to Quietzco?" the gentleman asks.

"To Quietzco?" she echoes.

And she thinks of a faraway Quietzco, a Quietzco . . . she does not know, whose name she has never heard . . . and wonders where it is. Maybe it is just a dot by the sea in some old atlas or a brown stain on the calcined earth.

"I know a street in Quietzco where there is a small bar. You're welcome to have a few drinks with me by the sea."

Delia imagines the streets of Quietzco to be different, twisted, where one gets lost easily. And she imagines that its people are also different, easy to talk to, and easy to be quiet with just looking at the sea. The sea of Quietzco—if there is one—will be peaceful, with never-ending shores, a smooth sketch on very fine sand. A sea with seagulls flying to almost touch the sea spray and then shooting away and disappearing over the water. Delia imagines Joaquín waiting for her in Quietzco . . . —"You are welcome to have a few drinks with me by the sea"—he will hold her very close while they cross the streets, those streets that Joaquín knows so well. Is Quietzco small? Is Quietzco big? Quietzco is endless . . .

"Please don't worry, this is a brief stop. Would you like something to drink? Coke, Pepsi, something cold?"

"No, thank you."

"Have a soda, or a Seven-Up?"

"No, thank you. How about you?"

"I think I'll have a soda. It'll have to be quick, the stop is very short."

Delia watches the gentleman drinking from the bottle. The train has stopped. The child selling the drinks has also stopped, as have the fields and the big wire fences from which green and yellow branches hang. Delia, also at rest, observes the gentleman as he stands up and stretches his long, long arm covered by the brown sleeve. The bottle tumbles; the train has started. Everything returns to its appointed place and the countryside resumes its procession. Now the people and the animals go by very fast, the ground with its varied planes pulled by strange, different speeds, the fastest and the slowest. Delia closes her eyes and watches her own internal parade, that of the people who live with her on earth. Soldiers, captains, colonels, high-ranking officers, prostitutes and nannies, priests, beggars, presidents and vice-presidents, men in bare feet and men in shining boots, the hungry and the sated, men with gorged stomachs and high-society women with long, undulating dresses, ladies and gentlemen with calling cards, their names, degrees, titles and ancient lineage delineated in a line of the white card. The parade continues with deposed queens and kings, their crowns fallen to the ground where a child snatches them up and waves them above his head. Delia opens her eyes and looks at the dawn.

Summer is warm when the day is being born, the first light peeping out from a hidden place as if still walled in by night. The summer is warm with an inner warmth and light not yet full new, not yet through, before following its course which is also the flow of time. The summer is warm in that decisive instant when the night goes out and the beams of light float in the air, torn from nothingness at that instant that seems to be prolonged forever, forever, forever . . .

"This world has gotten so horrible, so ugly!"

"Which world?" Delia asks.

"This very world," the gentleman answers, "in which we both live."

"Which world?" she repeats.

Delia doesn't know the world. Maybe there are several worlds or just one . . . maybe . . . She thinks of a hidden, very wide world where many people live happily. Delia doesn't know the world. She probably knows her world: walls that rise up, a middle-sized wall, a small wall and a wall grown taller than the others. One wall behind another. They are closing in, forming circles, squares, long angular corridors. Some have roofs; others without them reveal up high a clear summer's sky. Delia knows her world, oh, so small and narrow! Where the walls touch each other. She knows her world: a wardrobe, sofa-bed, two tables, some chairs and a wide couch where Joaquín sits. A large crystal vase with a red flower, a sweet flower Delia watched grow. There are books everywhere: on the chairs, against the walls, in heaps on the floor. There are creased papers, ballpoint pens of several colors and a dry inkwell that belonged to her grandmother. Delia imagines her grandmother writing long letters to her beloved, dipping the fine nib attached to the penholder in the black ink and filling the white pages in her tiny longhand, telling her lover perhaps the same things Delia says to Joaquín. She thinks back in that time of infinite distance—everything so far away, the seas were lost and the skies untouched!—in that time of infinite distance, where lovers were united in spite of the separation.

"This world is in a bad way. Have you seen the horrors in today's paper? A mother strangled her son, a boy of twelve jumped off a tall building, a child molester raped two girls . . . What do you think of this awful world?"

"Which world?" Delia whispers.

"What disgusting times we live in! No more peace, or love, or anything . . ."

Is this man very old? Delia wonders. Maybe not so old . . . He just dressed old. Delia dresses him up differently: tight blue jeans, a wine-colored polo shirt. That's a lot better! As if he were somebody else . . .

ANTONIA PALACIOS • 123

Delia dresses him as a hippie with long hair and a thick beard, faded pants with frayed cuffs and a lot of medallions dangling on long chains around his neck. Oh no! He's not a hippie. Such an outfit! She dressed him in white. Oh yes, white does suit him! Anyone would think him young, as young as Joaquín. With an open-neck shirt showing his chest. The gentleman's hairs . . . and suddenly she thinks of Joaquín's hairs, so stiff and curly. She rests her cheek on Joaquín's chest and his smell envelops her. His own, particular smell! Of cut wood, of recently sawn trees, wafted by the breeze and imbibed by Delia, an aroma that wraps itself around her like a sweet somnolence. The summer is burning in the brilliance of the day, in the exploding exuberant light. The summer is white, with a colorless luminosity, and the earth does not remember that almost invisible shadow folded within itself. The summer is vibrant halfway through the day, as if everything were in a vibrant suspense, as if the sun, in the midst of that incredible brilliance, were stopped in the middle of the day, stopped forever, forever, forever . . .

"Are you comfortable, Miss?"

"Very."

"Why don't you come and sit over here?"

"Thank you, I'm fine here."

"I'm fine here too, but it would be better with you next to me."

"Thanks, I'm all right here."

"I'm sure you'd feel better here. We'd be closer and could talk more comfortably."

"What's being comfortable?" Delia asks as she looks at the gentleman. He looks so serious!

"One doesn't argue about it, one gets comfortable, that's all."

Yes, the gentleman is very serious, but his eyes dwell on Delia's beautiful legs, so fine and nicely turned. Her legs are crossed under the pleated skirt while Delia looks at the countryside parade through the window. But is not the earth passing in front of Delia's eyes? It is the sky and clusters of clouds and birds in it, flying up to almost touch the clouds. Delia would like to be a bird, with feathered skin, smooth and shiny feathers that would shed the rain. She would like to be a lark, or a woodpecker, always probing the hidden heart of the trees with its beak. She would like to be a hummingbird, an iridescent hummingbird turning round in mid-air, held up in space by a mysterious force, turning around a flower, drinking drop by drop love's essence from the calyx. Delia would like to be as free as the birds. Are they really free? She thinks of migrant birds in their long journeys along the same route, she thinks of the exhaustion of crossing the enormous distances in the obligatory flight from frost, hail and wind in a winged search for shelter, warmth and a feeling of protection and welcome ... No, birds are not free. They are prisoners dragging invisible chains through the skies. Delia feels free, tied to Joaquín. Free in his high, high flights, free possessing the earth sky, seas and stream. Delia feels free in Joaquín's arms that surround her tenderly, that hold her strongly, and Delia would love to be held, embraced, sustained forever in his arms.

"I tell you, Miss, we live in an awful world!"

Delia looks at her world—such a small world!—which fills with light when Joaquín is in it. Lying on the sofa-bed, Delia very close to him while Joaquín sits up, and his hands ... his own extra-special hands ... strong and tender, subtle and wise ... those hands caressing her body, lingering on her round breasts and sweetly pressing her nipples. Those hands that travel along her body, now on her belly, now between her legs. And Joaquín's lips right next to hers and his teeth touching hers, mouths together, and within her mouth that thing alive and trembling, a naked fish caressing the innermost corners of her mouth, so deeply ... and Joaquín's weightless weight on her body ... and Joaquín penetrating her and reaching her most hidden being, that most distant being ... and Delia feels fulfilled, frightened with a fulfillment and abandon that leaves her she knows not where ... Delia forgets her name, her birthdate, her fingerprints, those shallow curving designs on her fingertips ... And Delia is moving, moving with the earth alongside Joaquín with an inebriating and all-enveloping sensation and feels lifted and detached from this earth, projected to those infinite heights she may not reach; or maybe descending, slowly, to those depths beyond the subsoil, beyond the seas, beyond the bottoms of the seas ... Delia loses her memory and all notion of time, hours or minutes, seconds or centuries. Delia forgets yesterday's memories and tomorrow's ... Delia loses herself to find herself panting and wet with different dampnesses, of sweat and of her innermost being. And through half-open lids her eyes perceive a semidarkness where the same old things, though apparently different, are waking up ... and Delia sees Joaquín, asleep with his head on her bare breast.

"Relax, young lady, we'll see what happens. Take it easy. What's the matter with this train?"

The train seems to be stunned, dragging its own weariness. Things go by frighteningly slowly and inadvertently Delia thinks

ANTONIA PALACIOS • 125

about death, not knowing why. Maybe because, unknowingly, she is looking backward in time, into her world in shadows, no longer illuminated by Joaquín. His books are closed, the sofa-bed is empty, the pens dusty and untouched, and grandmother's inkwell reveals a dark hollow ... Delia thinks that when somebody leaves you it is like a death and if nobody looks at things, they die ... and ... Joaquín left her. Delia saw him in the streets, his arms around Valentina, so close together their figures became one, Valentina cheek-to-cheek with him, his arm tight around her waist—no, not Delia's, but Valentina's—that night when Delia saw her ... that afternoon? morning? dark night? ... walking slowly, pressed close to Joaquín. And Delia didn't know what to do. She wanted to scream, loudly, and could not, to call for help, shout out loud through the immense, bottomless void. She tried to scream, shout, make somebody hear her, hold her up—was Delia falling?—to hear anybody's voice or feel their shadow. And Delia kept on looking without realizing what she was seeing, watching Joaquín going away, close to Valentina, along a little street which Delia sees as long, infinitely long, dark and empty ... only Joaquín getting further away, smaller ... until there is nothing left, not even his shadow.

"This is a very strange train and there is nobody we can call. I wonder what's the matter?"

Delia watches the gentleman who is very close to her, already on his feet, his head out looking at the tilted train. Is the train tired out? Delia understands if the train feels like that. What an enormous effort to perform hour after hour, each minute of each day and night! How exhausted it must be! The same old red flags waved by the same hands, the same green lamps piercing the darkness to illuminte the rails. The same route, back and forth, back and forth, the same people harvesting the same wheat, plowing the fields, making scratches in the earth. But maybe the train discovers the small and large differences that distinguish one thing from another. It is true that nothing is the same ... people or things, streets or mountains. People are all different ... and most of all ... Joaquín. He doesn't resemble anyone. He is above everybody. Nobody is comparable to him. His laughter is different, his voice is different. Joaquín says "Good evening!" and he makes the day begin.

"Okay, it's beginning to move. Look here, lean forward and you'll see the wheels starting to roll. You see, everything is okay. The train has started again."

The gentleman returns to his seat. He is already opening the newspaper he himself folded up a few seconds before. The paper is raised above his knees, level with his hands, and Delia continues to look at the earth's procession. The earth is not naked anymore, it is covered with layers of different substances: cement, granite, waxed floors. Covered by bricks, mats and large stone blocks. One can no longer see the sky, the roofs reach up to the clouds. Many people crowd the streets without even turning their heads to watch the passing train.

Summer is sweet at sunset before the impenetrable night. Summer offers a dying sweetness with long, oblique rays, a golden, ethereal light. Summer is sweet when late afternoon traces a curved line and suddenly becomes still, as if the dusk, the dying day, could last forever, forever, forever . . .

"Are you going to Quietzco?"

"Quietzco?" Delia asks.

"You don't know what it is to be in Quietzco. It's a magic place. The people are different there. They only think of love. Quietzco's streets love, squares love, the towers love . . . Did you know that Quietzco has seven towers? They are not very tall, but they shine as if they were near the stars. And what a sea Quietzco has! . . . difficult to describe how its waves climb high and then calmly recede to sleep on the shore. Quietzco has a rainbow every afternoon, joining all the towers from end to end. You'll see . . . We're near Quietzco now."

How nicely the gentleman speaks! Nobody would have imagined it. Will Quietzco be as pretty as he describes it?

"How long to Quietzco?" Delia asks in a small voice.

"Not long now; you can feel Quietzco in the air. Can't you smell the fragrance of roses, of honeysuckle in bloom? Can't you feel the air getting lighter, the sun getting drowsy, everything getting smooth and restful? . . . Can't you feel that peace is certain and that love is sweetness, impossible sweetness? . . ."

How beautifully he says what she feels and cannot express herself! How he has changed! He has dropped the newspaper on the floor and with it the world, the awful world he mentioned before. Delia is already forgetting the newspaper world: the mother who strangled her son, the youthful suicide, the sadistic rapist of the two girls . . . Now she wants to sit very near the gentleman to hear what he has to say about Quietzco. To hear him without straining, restfully. Delia doesn't look anymore at the countryside going by and thinks of a distant Quietzco, the gentleman's Quietzco . . . Delia imagines that Joaquín will be there in Quietzco waiting for her to hold her tight, and both will wander through the flower-covered labyrinths with balconies that Joaquín knows so well. Both will walk and walk toward the sea. The train is almost silent, dragged by a growing silence that carries Delia with it, and she is dreaming . . .

The train has left behind all living things, cities, fields, people, animals. It has also left time in its wake and now is slowly progressing into the shadows. Delia opens her eyes and sees nothing; only dark shadows, one after the other . . . one after another as if they were endless. Delia searched for the gentleman in the shadows. The train doesn't move anymore, as if dead. Have we arrived at Quietzco? Delia shouts, "Sir, Sir!" but gets no answer. Where is the gentleman? And in the darkness she stumbles. "Are we already in Quietzco?" Delia asks, out of breath.

"Where? What place? I don't know what you're talking about. Besides," a very different voice says, "I've never seen you before and I don't understand what you're talking about."

"Don't you know me? We've traveled together all the way. I'm asking about Quietzco. Surely you haven't forgotten the things you told me? I'm asking you if the train has reached Quietzco!"

"What's this nonsense about a train? There is no train here. Please, one side, let me go! I'm in a hurry. This woman must be crazy . . ." mumbles the man as he walks away.

Delia doesn't know what to do. She is lost in the night, lost in the darkness. She does not know what to do, she feels alone . . . with a huge, endless loneliness. She can see nothing in the dark. Large, motionless, silent, shapeless shadows.

Delia screams, "Sir! Sir!" and no one answers. She keeps on searching everywhere, further on, all around. She wanders from one place to another in the shadows. She looks for the gentleman from the train, searching high and low. She looks for her own things, but she has nothing. She carries nothing. Her hands are empty, those hands she is waving in the dark.

The night is heavy with summer. Immense, forsaken, endless night. A night that has forgotten what light is like. And the light is lost, buried on the other side of night. A deathly still night, without wind or noise, as if it were inside her, an inner darkness that has found a home in her and is remaining there forever, forever, forever . . .

Translated by Delia Hufton

The Professor

Leroy Quintana

Crystal

He wanted her in nothing but her gray cap with the likeness of Mickey, her ears sticking out a little like Mickey's, rosy nipples large and fervid as Mickey's eyes.

Danielle

He wanted to kiss her nipples, purple and simple under her transparent strawberry blouse, run his lips in dizzying circles sleekly over the silk.

Kim

It was a glimpse of her aquamarine bra that stopped his breathing, his heart, as if she had folded it the way he imagined at the Laundromat: first, the backstraps, the shoulder straps next, and then, somewhat softly, the way she would stuff it into his mouth, one cup thrust into the other.

Maya

She bends down low over his desk to ask a question about the homework assignment, and he remembers he imagined, oh, long ago, that the nipples of the young girls looked like Hershey's Kisses, and how he would pull the strip to open the aluminum foil wrapper and how the candies melted in his mouth, and how the taste lingered, gritty and so overlysweet, and how he wanted now to pull the strap, and swallow first the left, and then the right.

Alliteration

(Susanna slips her slip off slowly slithers towards him, says something sweetly sordid, and they seesaw, Susanna with her sophistry and solecisms, her fallaciousness, from Friday and throughout the Sabbath into Sunday.)

Assonance

Ashley's ass, ah!, abundance, accommodate, accelerate, accomplished, ache, adept, adolescence, adultery, advantage, adventure, affair, afflict, agile, aging, agony, allure, amour, angel, angularity, animal, anonymous, ardor, (arrest), assent, atonement, avoidance, awkward.

Amy

Oh, how her hair springs up in ringlets as large as the hoops of her earrings.

He wanted to see if he could fit the large silver hoop earring into his mouth and still close both lips around her lobe.

Could his lips circle her entire nipple if she had it pierced, the silver hoop dangling like a shameless manacle?

Monique

She takes off her beret.
He presses against her.
Then her coat.
She is facing away from him, hands gripping
the counter.
Her sweater, then
her skirt, slip.
She reaches behind, undoes
her bra with one hand,
nimble fingers,
unhooks his belt,
unzips him.
She whirls.
Her green eyes.
His hands,
cupped as if pleading
for alms or mercy,
sliding under her panties,
follow the sweetcurve
of her ass
down.
She grabs
the countertop again.

He sits,
and she hooks
her heels
on the stool
Up. Down. updown
updownup
Down.

Tania

She is older, those wrinkles at the edges of her gracious green eyes, obvious only when she smiles, sure of herself yet somehow so vulnerable, as when she looked up at him as he sat straining on his cluttered desk, his pants stubborn as shackles around his ankles.

Gabriela

Those long, oh so long legs, so long she's perfect, oh beyond perfect, page 101 of *The New Joy of Sex,* where she kneels facing away from him on the verge of an ordinary chair.

Ursula

Oh, sullen Ursula; unsnapping her burgundy garter belt slowly, so slowly that the scorching lump large as a fifth of Seagram's in his throat suddenly shatters, Oh, the splinters as he shouts her name. Oh sullen Ursula, her dark lashes fluttering almost as fast as his heart.

Paula

Oh, when she wears that white silk blouse that she leaves unbuttoned; that wide V allowing her breasts to spill (at least) halfway out

     or

In those faded jeans with a plain T-shirt, that luminescent black bra

     as

She stands at the blackboard, chalk in hand, knowing full well he is scrutinizing the small curve of her breasts and not her sentence structure.

Jolie

She's ice.
Oh, those black net stockings.
Begin perhaps with both hands cupped
around her heels,
or circling each ankle.
Or grabbing each calf,
knuckles facing each other;
Up to her knees,
and beyond; kissing
perhaps first the right,
then the left:
As he opened her
to the possibilities
of fire.

Katie

Suddenly
he notices
the stubble.
Identical scalene
triangles.
The secret
of her inner
thighs.

When she wears a bikini
there is a faint isosceles of fuzz that,
that runs darker then colorless
from the top of her bottom piece
all the way to her deep belly button.

When she wears her one piece
solid-black bathing suit,
golden curls sprout
along both sides
of her inner thighs,
glisten in the sunlight,
so close to the prized apex.

To be so furtive as
to caress nothing else

with his lips:
the stray hairs between
her pallid thighs and
lampblack satin panties.

Celina

where
her calf muscle begins to bulge:
where
he would begin to memorize
the entirety of her body
with his mouth.

Cristina

He notices the thick blue-green vein
on the back of her hand, that
forks and then drifts into her knuckles,
and he is certain that if he opened
her blouse, there, coursing into
the randiest part of her nipple ...

She's been in jeans all semester; suddenly
on Monday he takes notice of her,
and on Wednesday she is wearing
a krinkly purple skirt (and white panties)
that opened and closed for him
all class long, like a naughty morning glory.

Tamara

He is startled by the brimming curve of her ass.
Then he looks at his hands.

His small hands.
And he wants to cry.
And then he takes the roll.

Brenda

Beginning at the clasp of her necklace,
his mouth following her spinal column,
down. And falling, down,

again, and
again.
Then,
his teeth bared,
coursing down
that long curve
to the waistband,
and the ferocious
gnashing.

Les Girls

Oh, that moment, when they bend forward
to sit, some more than others,
as if the weight of their breasts . . .

And then that swing of their hips
when his heart snaps shut.

Their asses at just the right angle
for a private snapshot.
And that is why he never fails
to arrive early for class.

Tamara

Her scarf threaded like a full Nelson
through her arms,
or even (her idea) across her mouth.
She kneeling as he stood behind her.
Oh, behind her.
She with (her idea) her silver spurs on.

Joy

It's a machine that will someday pick up the words of Jesus,
and Sister Adele urges us to pray devoutly and sincerely,
so that the inventor, a Frenchman, may be able
to finish works on this divine idea before his death.

My first reaction is "Just how in the hell
is this guy going to pick out one,
just one voice, and that the voice of Jesus Christ,

out of all the voices in the history of the world?
Just how in the hell?"

And just what were those words I said to Joy
who wore that tight white dress that showed
every curve and rise, fall and twist, uphill
and down, and turn and bend, the North and South,
East and West of her, the creases, crevices,
mounds and angles great geography of her
beautiful seventh-grade body that must
have sent many of the eighth-grade girls
into raging jelousy, that every boy, no matter
if he attends Mass and receives Communion daily,
desires, would lie and steal and cheat for, would
love to touch, undress, to see and I tell her so
though I can't remember the words, the exact words
I use (the reason I still mumble, mutter, stumble
over the words today, which is why I became a writer,
I suppose), and she goes and tells Sister, and
Sister asks me, but those words are locked deep
inside my throat, forgotten forever, words, uttered
ardently as those a man in France hopes crazily
his machine will snatch right out of the air.

Melanie

Oh, those huge melónes, restrained
only by the border
of her top.

For her,
he would cross illegally
into that country.

Tired, poor and hungry.
Among the wretched masses
Yearning.

The Rose

Diana Rivera

The rose you gave me,
young,
forbidden,
here, tipped in water-glass,
flushes petals slightly creased, hooked to
darker crimsons,
flushes thin, small rolled mouths,
tender blood,
flushes silent, thorny leaves.
Rose
I want to eat your petals
fainting into my tongue,
into my living throat,
now, after we have touched the desolation of hills,
you, soft and flowing in this
crowded seat of cityscapes
I bring you into,
and into which you seep like confluencing veins
and you said,
fondling every minute after our farm desertion,
it does not mean . . .
love you brought quietly trembling and assured I was not
looking,
and placed over the public table,
the old, unhappy couple and the silent
rich lovers perched over chairs like tired birds,
and then said nothing,
the brown paper bag resting and breathing between us,
and I opened it,
and I thought it was
a silk rose,
and you looked
at me with disbelief
that I could not believe
it *was* a rose,

closed in November,
no winter over our thousand clouded hands,
and there you sat,
red-eyed with huge dry working hands
without a home since thirteen,
and we were silent
quivering in flesh, and I said,
I know . . .
and the red bud you gave me was already in my mouth,
and the taste was bitter and sweet but mostly sweet,
and it poured tickling my throat,
but we were quiet
and the world was looking, the quiet
complacent lovers were looking,
and the rose was bleeding deep into our throats, and up
into our eyes,
and then you almost said, if you die
of old, poisoned love . . .
because you also heard my eyes
and my pulse splitting open.

Death of the Lady Slipper

Diana Rivera

It came to an end, the rose of his intellect
flew to meet the soul of his emotions.
A crystal clear delusion took hold of his spirit.

His eyes recalled every inch of light,
line, shadow, form,
memorized the skeleton he could see under my skin,
the clitorial crease in the center of my petal,
the oval perfect, tongue-shaped sways
crushed under his footsteps,
before he raped my patch of forest.

Concave forms, soft curves come back—
you once were, I once was, you inside,
my body calling yours, calling,
earth! sky! petal!
I gripping you tight, holding you in, forming one
inner flower.
Not letting go we loved recklessly,
I swam on your body, over your erotic motions,
your face buried in the darkness of the flower inside me,
your earth under and over the crease of my petal.
Having to let me go must be punishment from the gods. Nearby
the beavers carved the totems of death.

Tearing down trees for more sun and grass
the brightness ate me up, dried me up—I
who once thrived in the moist half-shadows,
small, translucent viscosity
so alive in self-intimacy, under pines by the lake.
As I die
others die in a chain of events.

Oh, dear love
dear beauty, regaining for a moment,
lost again for infinity, as the terror
of a broken thought.
Under lakewaters, a revolution of blood and petals.
Her ache was the thrum of a hummingbird
not finding a single culprit.

You extinct, I extinct—
he betrayed her with his intellect.
He took her moisture away, the chilled lapping of leaves
that fanned her,
the flora which gave form to her breath.

Lady slipper,
language of flowers,
divinely conceived spaces
scattered as small graces—
your untouched, virginal cavities
in love with cool, wet earth, orchid moss, humus dreams,
once lived
dispersed in meanders of half-shadowed,
half-lit habitats.

The wet scent of your petals lingers
near the damp darkness of ferns,
where, centered in feeble pistils,
your heart melted,
where your silken silk shriveled
as puckered crepe paper.
Your last breath released, mountains
cry in your absence.
No trees, no leaves survived
the killer sun,
the rational acquisitions of greedy men.

One Woman Turns Her Lips Away

Alberto Alvaro Ríos

This time, she will not go away so simply.
She, this woman, into whose mouth, whose breathings,
He can see: he closes his eyes: she gives him
Tourniquet kisses,
Saving things, her absolute lips the moment
Holding tightly: everything here is hardened.
And he needs them. Loosening means a dying
Suddenly. Laughter
Too this way is furious, holding something
By its edge, like grasping a carp still living
By its stomach, loving to see it struggle,
Wildishly flipping.
He has held the legs of his women carp-like,
Watched them turn so easily on the fingers,
At his hand and mouth, at his legs: at this minute
Each of his fingers
Knows a different woman, knowing the tinge
Incense gives to rooms, a perfume that travel
Gives to things. But she at his laughter laughs louder.
Quick the exotic
Carp, she turns her animal lips all sticky,
Strong like fingers, stronger than his, not letting
Go: she smells him watching her tight skin, hears him
curiously flipping.
One man cannot have her, no husband craving
Her, his wife: for each of his fingers she is giving
Gifts of softer skin to the men she's wanted,
All of them handsome.

The Mouths of Two People

Alberto Alvaro Ríos

She threw her Paraguayan blanket down
on a section of the shore's grasses
and at first perfectly we sat there
in that peculiar kind of wildest comfort,
talking with our mouths in between figs
about what mouths discuss: the sky,
the thumbflick scattered and jagged minnows,
the unkind heat out there beyond the cottonwoods,
but the real heat, the hot of the night
that finds its way into the body
which cannot then be still, be shushed,
this is what our second mouths asked about,
the mouths that are where eyes appear to be,
mouths whose secret lips are subtle lids,
whose words like the wind are barely heard,
these mouths ask about each other's skin,
about what our feet might look like, feel like,
held by the water instead of our shoes,
ask about what holding each other's calves
might feel like, there among the spring reeds
among the figs and the white chocolate
spread over the blanket on which I have eaten
her hair and all the notable parts of her body,
turning back the corduroy and useless cotton,
the zippers and her snaps most singularly placed.
I watch her, too, fill on my hands,
fill on the shape of my legs to the hip,
fill on the curved part of the letter p
that is the top part of a young man's leg.
Wandering on the blanket in the grasses and reeds
we fill each other with our picnic,
tell spiraling lies to make us stay, and stay,
our true mouths saying to each other
how we long to lie together,

to become recognizable fixtures of the sky,
some Orion at which others might easily point
saying how slowly the constellation moves,
how the stars in its skin seem to fit.

Interminable Rhythm

Enrique Pardo

Sometimes I wish it would have been a dream.
I wish the wave we rode never would have met the shore
and instead time would have halted in its tracks
leaving us locked around each other.

You lay before me
head thrown back, chin jutted
eyes closed, lips pursed in a sweet grimace
as your body surrenders to quakes and quivers,
then you laugh silly satisfactions and coyly retreat.
I climb inside you,
our lips feeding symbiotically
our errant hands roaming for a grip.
You lift and spread your legs like butterfly wings,
then my hips begin pounding out a rhythm
our interminable rhythm
and we never awake.

Untitled

Enrique Pardo

Distance from the warmth of your moist nest
rakes me like a phalanx of sharp claws
leaving me susceptible to a distorted perspective
where love yields to discord
harmony to dissonance
and our rhythm is disrupted.

Until you open yourself wide
and let the thirsty nomad in me
drink and swallow you like a healing potion
like a vitamin nectar
I am not spared.

For your tawny triangle
is my source of exultation
yielding me pleasure
promising salvation
and vanishing my fears.

Conquístador

Ana Bárbara Renaud Gonzáles

for Cristóbal Colon and all those who followed

How do you say *"it was love at first sight"*¿
—Dame tus nalgas.
Here we go again. Ok. "It was a kiss from paradise" . . .
 —El paraíso es mío cabrón.
You never teach me the right words.
—There are other ways to say what you ask.
Jálame.
—That's so vulgar.
Jálame la riata then.
—Better. You only ask for the words to sex.
That's not true. I know how to order enchiladas con pollo.
—En el nombre del Padre, el Hijo, y la Santísima Virgen, eres una
mosca muerta.
What have you got against a dead fly¿
—Bala perdida. Mi puto precioso.
More insults. I am just a man. Why can't you believe me¿
—Language, like bullets,
must find the heart.
Our Spanish has been written
in blood
and kisses.
The words must pierce
what the tongue
cannot
caress.

Choking the Chicken

Joe Duran

Don't worry, ese!
I don't choke the chicken all by myself
in the shower anymore.
No, ese!

She lets me choke the chicken
in front of her.

She wants to see it spit and flower
like the wings she never had.
She loves to wipe it off her chin.

Choke the chicken
and you won't be lonely anymore.
Choke the chicken
with your woman there
and you won't believe
how far you can go.

Choke the chicken, ese!
It's okay if it turns red
like the sunset.
After all, we all have to sing
and let the song go.

Choke the chicken, bud!
Just don't let anybody tell you
chickens love to run
with their heads cut off.

We all have to know
when it's time to withdraw,
go sit in the chicken coop
because other cocks want
to choke the chicken too.

Old Man to the Young Man

Joe Duran

When he couldn't love the anger.
When he chased the line in his eyebrows
until it became protection,
then he hated the window that opened
only when he was distracted by
the flower growing out of her cunt,
like a tree that had the answer
to his wet dream—the moisture
he carried between his legs for decades,
until he knew an old man had
to let go of his dreams,
his seizures, her legs
lifted high in the air,
let go of the ass pumping under him,
until he could retrieve his memory
and love again.

When he couldn't fuck her without her
gasping, "Oh God! What are you doing to me?"
When he couldn't stop thrusting
without her answering herself,
"Oh, Jesus! Don't stop! Don't stop!"
And he cried down to her,
"Fuck with your cunt!
Fuck with your cunt!"
He gasped and his tongue hung out of his mouth
with the quickening pace of it.
And she lifted herself higher on the bed,
his ass rising to elevate what they were doing,
his thighs slapping loudly against her
as he pulled her hair and they collapsed together,
his vibration inside her spilling as if
someone had opened a river he couldn't cross.

When he woke with the shadows on the ceiling
getting closer to his naked chest,

her gentle sleep showed him how love was
the thing he needed to survive the encounter
with the old man who told him never
be taken away by something he can't keep.
He loved her and missed her and gave her
the world without communion or sin,
gave her the years to become the old woman
he loved when he was the old man.

Nombre

Paul Arturo Cabral Jr.

I closed my eyes as my face contorted. I pounded away at her fast. I had started out slowly, but I thought, I don't even know this bitch, so who cares? I could hear the music playing loudly, but muffled, from behind the door. I glanced down at her.

"What's your name again?" I asked between breaths.

"Stella," she replied, in one long, deep breath, as she squeezed her tits together, tighter.

Her tits felt strange against me. They were smooth and soft, but also firm and hard. They were warm as I slid in and out between them. The Vaseline made that easy. My face was squirming to match my feelings, or whatever it's called when you're about to cum.

I noticed her eyes were on my dick the whole time. It was kind of unnerving. I never had done it like this before, but she said it was the best way not to get AIDS or pregnant.

I pushed faster and faster. I felt hot. The sweat on my forehead slowly dripped down my face. My back was moist, as was my whole body. This is a weird position, I thought. I could hear people passing by, down the hall, to use the rest room.

I looked down at her again. Her eyes were still on my dick. She must get off on watching guys like this because I'm sure this position didn't make her feel as good as it did me.

"I'm gonna cum," I said hurriedly.

Her eyes remained fixed on their moving target.

I closed my eyes and pushed faster and faster and faster. I accidentally bit my tongue.

The milky, white semen squirted out onto her, splashing her across the face. I kept pushing. More came out. Her eyes didn't move except for a few blinks here and there. I stopped, exhausted.

I stretched my arms out to rest on the wall that was in front of me.

"Are you done?" she asked as I leaned forward, catching my breath.

"Yeah," I replied.

"Then can you get off me so I can get cleaned up?"

I rolled off her and lay down on the bed. She got up, grabbed a towel from the floor and wiped herself off. I stared at her. My hardness was completely gone. I noticed a couple of hairs on her nipples. They were blonde. Her pussy hair was nonexistent. She must shave, I thought, but when I was on her I didn't feel any stubble. The hair on her head was black, obviously dyed.

I watched her get dressed. I remained naked. She slipped her black dress on over her head and down to her body. She wiggled into it, bent down and pulled her black underwear up to her hips. The music blasted louder than ever from behind the door. The crowd noise was at a low roar.

She walked over to the dresser and stared into the mirror. She began fixing her hair and adding makeup to her face. Her lips moved to the song that was playing. The song was a remix of Chaka Khan's "I'm Every Woman." Her hips shook back and forth to the beat. Looking into the mirror, she saw me. Her blue eyes stabbed into me.

"Aren't you gonna get dressed?" she asked.

"I'm just resting," I answered blankly.

A dash of blush and a pucker of lipstick later she turned around.

"Well, I'm going back out there," she said. "Are you gonna stay here?"

"I'll be out in a few," I said.

"Okay. Well, it was nice meeting you. Maybe we can get together again sometime," she said with a small grin.

I nodded in fake agreement.

She walked up to the bed toward my feet. She bent down and kissed the head of my limp, cum-covered dick, leaving some red lipstick on it. She gently wiped her lips, careful not to smear the fresh, ruby red lipstick.

"Bye," she said as she grabbed her tiny, black purse.

She walked over to the door and flung it open. The music flew in. There was a long line forming out in the hallway for the rest room. As she walked out, several people looked in. They saw me lying on the bed, naked. The cum on me was drying up. Stella closed the door behind her. The music was, again, muffled. I stared up at the ceiling. I noticed, in the corner, there was a long, dirty cobweb hanging down. I should get a broom and wipe it, I thought. I heard a knocking at the door.

"Who is it?" I asked.

"It's me, eh," answered the voice behind the door.

"Come on in."

The door opened up and in walked Ben. The music followed him. More people looked in and saw me.

"What're you doin'?" Ben asked me as he closed the door. His eyes stared at my nakedness.

I shrugged my shoulders. "Just kicking back."

"Mano, the party's getting packed."

"Oh yeah?"

"Yeah. There's all kinds'a people out there."

I nodded my head in approval.

Ben's eyes traced my body up and down.

He paused and then asked, "Who were you with?"

He knew me pretty well.

"Um, just some chick named Stella."

"That ugly, wanna-be Mexican bitch with the black, dyed hair?" he asked sarcastically.

"She's not ugly," I defended.

"Yeah, well she's not that pretty either," he countered as he sat down on the bed beside me.

I brought my hands up to and under my head, using them as a pillow. I continued staring up at the ceiling. The web dangled above me, slowly moving to the changing air current. The song that was playing was one of my favorites. My lips moved along with the lyrics.

"You need a tan, eh," stated Ben, staring at my chest.

"I know," I answered quietly, beneath my breath. "I got that farmer tan right now."

Ben's eyes looked down at my dick.

"It's not that bad," he said. "And you got some dry cum on your dick." He pointed with his finger and got very close to my dick.

I looked down at myself.

"I should take a shower," I stated.

I could feel Ben staring at me.

"Man, I'm fuckin' jealous of you."

I looked at him curiously as I wrinkled my brow.

"Look at you. Your stomach is flat and cut. Your chest is hard and tight, and you're slim and toned. But you're not a big muscle-bound dude like those bodybuilders, aay. I wish I was more like that."

I stared at Ben quietly for a second.

"You *are* like that," I answered in a low, puzzled voice.

"Yeah, but not as good as you."

The muffled music made me want to go out and dance. The song that was playing was an old seventies hit, "Macho Man."

"I mean, look at me. I'm not as good as you."

Ben stood up, grabbed his sweater from the bottom and pulled it up to his neck, revealing his bare chest and stomach. He wasn't wearing an undershirt.

I stared at him. He had a lot of pubic hair that started up in a line from beneath his pants and ended at his belly button. His nipples were large, about the size of a half-dollar coin, dark brown and with hair around them. The rest of his chest and stomach had a thin layer of hair that was barely visible, unless you were very close-up like me. Ben was very lean and very muscular; for him to say he was jealous of me was just plain stupid.

I noticed a bulge beginning to appear beneath Ben's pants.

"Ben, you look fine. I don't know why you think you have to be jealous of me."

Ben played with the dark bush of hair around his belly button.

I stared at him, lost in thought. I never really noticed how good-looking Ben was. And I was right, Ben had no reason to be jealous of me. If anything, I probably should be jealous of him.

Ben's bulge grew larger, but he didn't try to hide it. I felt myself beginning to get hard too.

"I fucked her between the tits," I said quickly.

"What?" asked Ben as he suddenly put his sweater down.

"Yeah. She said she liked it like that."

"What a weird bitch," he said noncaringly.

"I've never done it like that before. But I kinda enjoyed it. Shit, just thinking about it is making me get hard again."

Ben looked down at me. My dick started to rise.

"I'm gonna go take a shower. Are you gonna wait for me or are you gonna go out there?" I asked as I stood up with a semi–hard-on.

"I'll wait for you here, aay," he answered as he lay back on the bed. His hardness was completely obvious, as was mine.

"I'll be out in a few," I said.

The muffled music was loud. The buzz of the crowd was getting louder.

I walked into the rest room that was inside the bedroom. I closed the door a little, leaving it open just a crack. I turned the faucets of the shower and the water came pouring down. I stepped into the glass telephone booth–size box. The water poured over me, cleansing my body. My hardness went away.

I stayed in for several minutes, relaxing, letting the water massage my body, before finally washing myself. I reached over for the shampoo, but the shelf was empty. I peered out over to the sink and there it sat, on top. I slid open the glass door and walked out to get it. The water dripped from my body and splashed onto the floor. I heard faint moaning-like sounds out in the bedroom. I peeked through the open crack of the door.

Ben lay on the bed, on his back, with his legs over the edge, planted firmly on the ground. His pants were open and he held his dick in his left hand. It was hard. He was rubbing it up and down, fast. I stared at him for several seconds. I noticed he was a bit bigger than me. I felt myself getting hard again.

I grabbed a towel and wrapped it around my waist, loosely. I pushed open the door. Ben stopped abruptly. He pulled his underwear up, making the elastic strip slap against his flat, hairy, muscular belly. He sat up quickly. Laughter came in from behind the door.

"You should probably wait out in the party," I said stoically.

Ben adjusted his pants clumsily and headed toward the door. As he opened it, the crowd looked in. They saw Ben pulling his zipper up and me standing naked, wet, with a towel around my waist. I went back to the shower.

Showered and dressed in a black, tight pullover sweater and a pair of equally tight jeans, I finally decided I looked okay. I opened up the door and there, leaning on it, stood a girl waiting in line for the rest room. She almost fell back. The music thundered loudly.

"Whoops! I'm sorry. I didn't know you were there," I apologized almost sincerely.

"Oh, that's okay," she said sluggishly.

Her brown eyes were a bloodshot red and her breath stank of too much tequila.

"That's a long line you're waiting in," I said matter-of-factly.

"Yeah, well when you gotta go, you know¿" she rebutted with a drunken, swerved smile.

"You can use the one in my room if you want. There's no line." I smiled a little too fakely.

"Thanks," she slurred back, no questions asked.

We walked back into the room and I closed the door on the party. The music muffled its way in again.

"Do you live here¿" she asked carefully.

"It's my party," I stated.

"Really? Then why aren't you out there?"

"I was going out there now."

She smiled. "Excuse me while I use the rest room."

I nodded as I sat down on the bed.

A few minutes and a flush later, she came back out.

"What a relief," she said, refreshed.

"What's your name?" I asked, still sitting down on the bed.

"Jesse."

I smiled.

"Let's go out to the party," she said as her body teetered toward balance.

I stared up at her. She was very pretty. Short, cropped, black hair, much like my own. Her eyes were brown, about five foot six, very slim, nice round tits, tight ass, smooth brown skin. Not bad, I thought.

"Have you ever been tit-fucked?" I asked seriously.

"What?" she questioned, unsure of herself or of what I said.

"Has a guy . . . ever . . . fucked . . . you . . . between . . . your . . . tits?" I repeated blankly, stressing each word slowly.

She stared at me. "Have you ever been fucked up the ass?"

I grinned as my dick stirred beneath my jeans.

She walked up to me and knelt between my legs. I didn't move. She unbuckled my belt and undid the buttons to my jeans. She grabbed the pants and pulled them down to my knees. She did the same with my underwear.

My dick hung limply at first, not knowing whether to get hard or not. She touched it with her hands. It came to life.

Several seconds passed and it was sticking straight up. I stared down at myself as she played with it. I moaned lowly.

She seemed fascinated. She played with it, but it was more as if she was exploring, studying.

"Does that feel good?" she asked seductively as she rubbed it slowly, looking up at my face. Her eyes were extremely red and low. The smell of tequila floated up around my nose.

I nodded.

My eyes were wide open, watching her every move. I wanted to stretch my legs out.

"Lean back," she said, pushing me at my chest.

I lay down on the bed.

She threw my pants and underwear completely off, leaving my

socks and shoes on, and my sweater. I pulled the sweater and T-shirt up to my neck. She spread my legs wide open and knelt closer, between me. I stretched my legs out.

Her hands went back to my dick. She rubbed it with her right hand, up and down, slowly. With her left hand I felt her playing with my balls.

A few seconds later her left hand went lower and suddenly I felt her thrust a finger up into my asshole, hard. My eyes bulged open, but I didn't move. There was pain, but not bad. She paused. She wiggled her finger inside of me. I felt strange. I moaned as she giggled to herself.

She proceeded to finger-fuck me, shoving her finger in and out, slowly and hard. I had done this same thing to girls, but in their pussies. This had never, ever been done to me. I felt strange.

My chest and back were getting soaked with sweat. My breathing grew rapid. I couldn't move, but I didn't try to.

Jesse giggled to herself.

I moaned out loudly. Is this how girls feel, or fags? I thought. God help me, but I'm losing it.

"Are you gonna cum yet?" asked Jesse.

I didn't answer. She pushed in and out, in and out. I felt strange.

Just then the door opened up abruptly. It was Ben. We looked up at him in surprise. He stepped into the room and stared back at us for a second before realizing to close the door on what was going on. The line for the rest room, outside, seemed to care less about us. The music roared along with the crowd.

Jesse pulled her finger out of me. I shot. It was a lot, even more than with Stella, and with more intensity. It came all the way up to my chest and neck. Some got on my sweater.

Ben watched the cum shoot out of my dick.

"I'm sorry," said Jesse, apologizing as she stood up.

Ben didn't say a word.

Jesse rushed over to the rest room. I heard the sink turn on. I stared up at the cobweb in the ceiling. It was hanging by a tiny thread. Ben still didn't say a word and I was too embarrassed to say anything myself. I felt strange.

Jesse came out, walked over to the door and left without saying a word. Ben watched her leave. For some reason, I couldn't hear the music anymore, but I knew it was still playing.

I sat up abruptly with a strange, nauseated feeling. Ben stared at my nakedness as I rushed to the rest room.

I lifted the toilet seat and quickly spilled my guts out into the water. It splashed loudly. I don't remember what I had eaten, or if I had eaten anything, but everything came out orange. I threw up again and again and again.

After pretty much throwing up everything I had in my body, I still had a few dry heaves left in me. I gagged until even the saliva in my mouth was completely exhausted.

Regaining my composure, I went over to the sink to wash my face, as well as my dick. I took off my sweater and T-shirt. The clean water felt good against me. I looked around for some underwear or shorts lying on the floor. Nothing. I grabbed a towel and wrapped it around my waist. I went out to face Ben. My shoes and socks were still on.

The truth is gonna hurt, I thought.

I stepped into the room, but it was empty. He was gone.

The crowd roared strongly and loud. The music played violently. The song that was playing sucked. I looked up at the ceiling. No longer attached, the cobweb slowly floated down to the ground.

I got dressed and went out to the party.

from Crazy in Los Nueces

Leo Romero

I

Chopo kept pestering me for weeks: When was I going to take his sister out again? She had been pestering him to find out, and she had too much respect to knock at my door to find out. She had even stopped coming over to see Chopo. She was still living with her parents, so Chopo would see her two or three times a week when he'd stop by to eat or deliver his dirty laundry.

I didn't have an answer. Actually the date with his sister hadn't been the fiasco it seemed it would be when I showed up for her without a car. She couldn't make up her mind whether to go out with me or not until her mother opened the door behind her and scolded her for standing there with a strange boy where all the neighbors could see her. That catapulted her away from the house, and it took me a few steps to catch up to her. Before I knew it, we were at a small neighborhood park. As it got darker, Adela began to relax. I hadn't intended to kiss her on the first date, but before I knew it we were kissing passionately. As I looked back later, I could see how she was in full control but making it seem like I was initiating things. When we were holding hands, I had the slightly uneasy feeling that it hadn't been my idea to do it even though I was the one who had reached out and taken her hand. And when our bodies were pressing against each other, her back against a small wall in a dark part of the park, I could see that I was the one doing the pressing, pushing my chest against her, rubbing my thighs against her, parting her thighs with my leg, but I felt the same uneasiness I had felt when we were holding hands. I had the uncomfortable feeling that she was fully in control of everything. Our embracing quickly led to passionate kissing. She surprised me by putting her hand down my pants, but I quickly followed her example and had my hand up her dress and down her panties. She kept murmuring how hard I was, which struck me as an interesting contrast to what I was thinking, how soft and slippery wet she was— and so fast! It was all a new experience for me for a first date. With Fabiola it had taken several dates before she let me even give her a little kiss, and then she had turned her lips away so that my kiss landed on her cheek, a pale, bony cheek.

"So wet there," Adela moaned as she moved her buttocks against the hardness of the wall. I murmured my approval as I felt how slopping wet my fingers were as they slid around under her panties. With my other hand I was feeling the folds of her fat but not caring that she was fat. It was a new experience feeling the folds of fat, like feeling a breast, I thought—Fabiola didn't have an ounce of fat. And then she unzipped my pants and lowered them, and pulled my hardened penis out of my shorts and held on to it. The whole time I was looking around worried, wondering if anyone was seeing us, and worrying that someone might suddenly bump into us. But, too, I was caught up in the heat of our passion, which was much hotter than the hot night, which was still hovering at 100 degrees. The heat of the night, of the desert night, felt soft and lubricating, like the wetness where my fingers were rubbing. She moaned and her knees gave way, but I was pressing her against the wall, so she stayed standing. "Your hardness," she kept murmuring, "your hardness," and then she tried to direct my penis into her. But I pulled away as the tip touched her softness. I regained my control when certain thoughts flashed through my mind. I suddenly saw what that hot night could lead to, that passion. She'd get pregnant and we'd have to get married. I had seen it happen to a few of my friends in Burque. I thought of them stuck with squealing brats, with mortgages, stuck and not able to leave Burque. That doused my fire. She couldn't understand what had happened, how the spell had been broken. She was hotter than the night. She could have scratched my face, she was getting so angry. Insulted. But I was thinking of brats, of mortgages, of a life come to an end. I didn't want anything to do with that, no matter how soft and wet she was. I thought of Fabiola. It was Fabiola I loved, even though I had fled from her and hadn't told her where I had gone.

Later that night when I was home by myself, I had to admit that Adela's warm—actually almost burning hot—lubricating soft-ness, what my fingers felt, was better than anything I had ever felt with Fabiola. And Adela's kisses were by far more promiscuous, more juicy, more freely given, more impassioned.

Fabiola was freezingly cold in comparison. It took months of going out with her before she even allowed me to suck her breasts. That was something she seemed to thoroughly enjoy, but she very seldom let me kiss her and suck her breasts as well. Kissing was something she did grudgingly. And with time, when I tried to kiss her, she'd direct my lips to her breasts. And I was strictly forbidden from touching her below the waist. Except for that one night when we decided to get married—that is, she decided. Then she decided we should have intercourse as a way of finalizing our agreement. But she hardly got wet, and I found it painful entering her, and she just lay there, not touching me, averting her face when I tried to kiss her. After a short time I pulled out of her—before coming.

She gave me an accusing look for not coming in her. She wanted to get pregnant so we would have to get married. It would be another thing to scandalize her family about. But I couldn't do it, just like I couldn't do it with Adela, but for totally different reasons. At the time, I would have loved to have gotten Fabiola pregnant so she would have had to get married to me, but her coldness while we were having sex frightened me. I put on my shorts and pants and sat at the edge of the bed and looked at her naked in bed, and I felt a tremendous amount of love for her, but she returned my look of love with a look of utter contempt. Her body still as a board. I could see then that there was no way we would ever get married.

With Adela the passion was there but I didn't love her. With Fabiola it was a love as if from afar, to be looked at with longing but impossible to reach. Fabiola sometimes reminded me of a large block of white marble, gleaming and beautiful to look at, but cold to the touch, unyielding, without feelings. And who knows, maybe if I wasn't still getting over Fabiola, maybe I would have knocked up Adela and my fate would have been sealed. My love for Fabiola was fraught with pain, but it saved me a life with Adela, and for that I am eternally grateful. Not that Adela was so terrible, but it would have been devastating to me to have been stuck with a wife and children at that point in my life. I was hardly able to take care of myself and I was going to be responsible for other people¿!

II

Fall! The best time of the year. Even in Los Nueces. It had cooled off greatly. Though "cooled off" might give the wrong impression. What I mean is, it wasn't anywhere near as hot as it had been, so, cooled off. But the nights were definitely cooler. You could see the pecans ripe on the pecan trees around town, and many pecans already littering the ground. There was a gigantic pecan farm on the road to Anthony. I had passed through it those early weeks I was in Los Nueces when Ramon was always inviting me to go with him to Morenito's, that small adobe bar in Anthony.

On the first trip down to Morenito's, I hadn't expected that we'd be driving through a gigantic pecan farm, really a forest. Ramon hadn't thought to mention it; he had driven through it countless times, and he hardly gave it a thought. But to me it conjured images of fairy tales I had read or heard when I was very young, of dark forests where there were trolls under bridges, and little isolated houses where evil old women lived who looked for opportunities to lure small children into their ovens. And wolves that talked and such things. It felt like an enchanted place to me, the way we kept driving but still the leafy trees seemed endless, spreading far away into a darkness of trunks, and limbs, and deep shadows. Also the way they had been planted so that they were in rows added to the enchanted quality. An unnaturalness in how orderly they were, but for long stretches no sign of people, an eerie leafy darkness and silence. But beautiful in how unexpected it was, a forest, its dark shadows and shade, and the desert at its border! Even though when you were in the forest, the desert seemed like it could be hundreds of miles away. And when you drove out of the forest of pecan trees, and there was the desert—the pecan tree forest seemed to me the more astonishing.

It had been the beginning of the summer since I had last been through there with Ramon. But with Dilia having her car, that was one of the first places I wanted her to see—*I* wanted to see it again! Before that, though, there was that night, that first night she stayed with me. We sat at the kitchen table and drank our Cokes. She placed her hand on the table, and I reached over and touched it. I left my hand on top of hers, and we looked at each other, and then I pulled my chair closer to her, and we kissed, and we stood up and embraced and continued to kiss. And as we kept kissing, our hands making timid explorations, I backed Dilia a few steps and we tumbled onto the bed.

Dilia was extremely passionate with her kissing, and, too, with fondling. This surprised me because when we had kissed in the alley in Burque there had been no passion, no fire, and hardly any fondling. What I remembered about it was that it had been fun, the polite kissing of two strangers trying not to go too far, playing safe, no special attraction, just a little fling. Shorly after tumbling onto the bed we were naked, embracing; and the fall breezes entering through the open windows also embraced and caressed our naked bodies with their satiny coolness. It had started getting cooler as soon as the sun had set. And our nakedness was hidden in the protective darkness of the night.

I was thankful that Chopo was out of town for a few days and that he wouldn't be knocking on the door disturbing the wonderful time we were having, savoring each other's lips, caressing bellies and hips; she had pert breasts that I sucked, and I thrilled at the delicate touch of her hand around my enlarged penis and thrilled at the way her fingertips stroked my sensitive balls. We pressed against each other, massaged buttocks and thighs, stroked arms, caressed and kissed necks and shoulders. We explored and kissed and caressed seemingly everywhere. And this went on for a long time until finally I thought, It's time. I parted her legs and tried to enter. But immediately she turned away roughly, her parted legs clamped tight as I fell to her side. She was lying with her back to me, and I was shocked to hear her sobbing.

For a while I didn't know what to say. I was dismayed, angry, but also concerned for Dilia because of her crying. What could possibly have happened, I thought, to ruin such a perfect time?

"Didn't you want to?" I finally said, thinking in amazement of the intimacy we had shared in bed, thinking of our naked bodies still in the bed, thinking of where our hands and lips had been. She didn't say anything but continued to sob. I stared at the dark ceiling for what seemed to be a long time. Finally I asked, "What's the matter?"

And Dilia showly turned her body towards me. In the darkness I could barely make out her features. At least she's stopped crying, I thought.

"You'll have to be patient with me," she whispered. "I've been a nun all these years."

That floored me. What could I say to that? I thought of my limp penis and wondered if it'd ever get hard again in her presence. And I contemplated what she said: that she had been a nun all these years. And that I would have to be patient. We were quiet in bed for a long time, our naked bodies just inches apart, and I kept wondering, What have I gotten myself into?

Ms. X

Enrique Fernandez

Her nipples were so beautiful they made me cry. Perhaps still are. I'll never know.

Discretion dictates I keep her name out of this, although perhaps it's much too obvious; after all, she had the most beautiful nipples in the history of the cinema, and her directors used that beauty deliberately and well. Who can forget the scene when after an afternoon rain shower her nipples show through her wet cotton shirt like some precious pentimento and drive the male protagonist, who is already head over heels in love with her, to dizziness? Drove me too. If I said more about that scene her identity would be obvious, so I'll describe it no more.

I'll just call her Ms. X.

Why be so reticent about identifying an actress who in more than one film was willing to bare her breasts? It's not her nudity that I am unwilling to revel in; not at all—I have reveled in it and will again every time I see her films. It's something else, something slightly bittersweet and sad. Something between us. You see, one day I met Ms. X.

It was in a foreign city, on a warm afternoon—although there was no rain—and at an outdoor party. I knew she would be there, and with very little effort I managed to sit right next to Ms. X. Was my heart beating fast? Perhaps. Did I think of or try to look at her sweet, dizzying nipples? No. I looked at her face.

If the perfect soft pink that tipped her breasts in those movies—serious movies in which her sex appeal was used to work out deep themes and artful arguments—was unequaled in beauty, the same could be said of her face. Her visage was both angelic and sensual, like what one finds in the paintings of . . . again, that would reveal her. Like what one finds in the paintings of the old master who best captured the angelic and sexual beauty of women. Her body—and I might as well deal with her whole physicality—was gently shaped, curved and lithe, sexual enough but so harmonious that no one would ever indulge in that male grossness of singling out one protruding part of it for some typically carnivorous delectation.

But haven't I done this already? Didn't I start out speaking of her nipples? Ah, yes, her nipples I said, but not her breasts.

When men dissect women in our imagination or in the sexual conversation that is part of our camaraderie, we consider tits and asses as if they were pieces of meat. Women, some women, maybe most women, object. It's grossness, as I just called it. But men are gross: dense, thick, animal.

Still, Ms. X, who on the screen often pushed me into an erotic abyss, was not a woman that provoked such thinking. The angel face, the quietude of her cuves, channeled male attention toward a closer look, a more disciplined objectification of her body. Not the totality of the breasts, for example, but the detail of her nipples. Her breasts were beautiful, let me make that clear. Small but present, and dipping gently, almost sagging. Almost: what Ms. X provoked was a self-conscious eroticism; delighting in her, I had to examine what delighted me, had to notice how a breast that sagged somewhat was more enticing than one that stuck out like a projectile.

It doesn't take much study to know that male attraction to female breasts is linked in some way to the primary function of suckling; that we long to kiss them, nuzzle them, bite them and, yes, suck on them as a way of returning to some early bliss. The big breast of American pop erotica is a metaphor for the full breast of the lactating mother. But it's the gently sagging breast that is really alluring, for there the metaphor is subtle, and the more direct, but quieter, reference is to the breast *after* lactation, the breast of the woman who has known childbirth, who is no longer a callow maiden but a caring mother. And if the woman, like Ms. X, has the body of a maiden and the breasts of a new mother . . . ah!

Yet it's nipples I started talking about, and nipples is what a baby's mouth is full of before it learns to talk. Again, the American pop fascination with the big breast may be the fixation of a deprivation. Bottle-fed for the past few generations, American babies have seen the big breast but not enjoyed the sweetness of the milky nipple. The big breast of pop imagination is seen from a certain distance; the nipple at nursing time is all extreme close-up, like everything in sex will be later. Thus, color and specially texture are all.

Dark nipples and big nipples are intoxicating, like deep black rivers that lure us to dive in and never come out, to drown so we can live in some underwater kingdom. But small pink nipples, like Ms. X's, are soothing and blissful and forgiving. Heaven. *Paradiso.*

I'm only talking here of male attraction to women's bodies. I can say nothing of women's attractions other than why women don't ravage each other is beyond me. Of course, some of them do.

Sitting next to Ms. X on that sunny afternoon, I could not think of heaven or of nipples. I could only think of time. The time elapsed between the date of her famous films and the date of our meeting, the time relentless and capricious.

How many years? Fifteen? More? Enough.

Her face was unlined, but it was no longer sensually angelic. It was angular. Ms. X had kept her maidenly figure, but, as it usually happens, at the expense of the slight roundness of her oval face, the babykiss puff of her cheeks, the fullness of her mouth. So profound was the change, this angular thinning of her face, that if I hadn't known a priori this woman was Ms. X, it would have taken me some time to recognize her—she who was so often the object of my enamored gaze in the darkness of the theaters.

Don't think she was not beautiful. Oh no. Again, had I not known who she was, I would have been enchanted to find myself sitting next to such an attractive woman . . . my age. In our forties.

Men age better than women, we often hear. Nonsense. We age the same. Charm by charm, Ms. X outranked me by far. And why shouldn't she, one of the great beauties of our time, outrank me, one of the great nobodies of our time? It's just that we place a higher value on women's beauty and that men are blissfully unself-conscious. We get old and rickety and ugly, but most of the time—God be blessed for this gift of blindness—we don't even notice. Not long ago I looked to see if my passport was still valid. It still was, but I wasn't. That is, the picture that stared at me was that of a young man, while a Polaroid snapshot taken a few days ago on the day of my fiftieth birthday was that of a gray-bearded, weary-faced, somewhat heavyset man well into middle age.

No thought of *my* encroaching old age crossed my mind as I sat next to Ms. X that afternoon halfway between the picture that's still stuck to my passport and the Polaroid of my half-century. On the contrary, I sat next to her feeling the shock of the thirty-year-old who first savored her cinematographic image, now confronting how time had changed her.

In my shock, and numbed by the amnesia of male arrogance, I never stopped to think how she saw *me*. I had come here to see her, I was sitting next to her. In the murky depths of my desire I had thought, what if she fancies me, what if my movie fantasy were to come true, what if I were to—dare I wish that?—have an affair with her, make love to an angel, touch my lips to her nipples. Oh death!

But no. Next to her, I didn't fantasize. Somewhere in my brain, though, a predatory maleness must have been working, for I remember quite well figuring out that she was without any escort, alone in a foreign city I knew and she didn't. I also noticed she was as self-conscious of her fading looks as I was unself-conscious of mine, which hadn't actually faded but simply deteriorated. At one moment she said, to whom I am not sure, to the whole company at the table, which, I suppose, included me: "Yesterday morning I looked absolutely fabulous. I went for a walk feeling really beautiful. And there was no one there to see me!" And then she laughed.

I said no more than a handful of small-talk words to her that afternoon and she—this would be clear soon enough—paid very little attention to me. There was a bunch of movie people at the table, some famous, some not, but clearly I was the least important—and glamorous—person there.

We were staying at the same hotel, a fact that had fueled my fantasies before that meeting but now meant nothing. Oh, it wasn't that I felt superior to her. Not at all. I simply couldn't get over the disparity between the two women, the one I'd just met and that one that flashed in the loop of imaginary celluloid that ran inside my brain.

Next day we ran into each other in the elevator, headed for our respective hotel rooms. We had both been wearing sunglasses on the previous afternoon, which is to say we were eye-masked, as in some Venetian costume ball. Now we stood, even closer than at the table, and looked into each other's eyes barefaced. I reminded her how we had met the day before at the luncheon. She looked at me and said, "Oh, yes. I didn't recognize you right away because yesterday you were wearing sunglasses." Somewhere inside I was saying: and I didn't recognize you yesterday because you looked older than the woman I fell in love with when she came in from the rain, her nipples showing through the wet cotton. Of course, I said nothing like that. Instead, I was noticing something amazing. She was looking at me. Looking at me. At me.

The way a woman looks at a man.

Oh, she was beautiful. Had I just seen her for the first time, I would have thought, what a gorgeous woman the fates have thrown in my path, she alone, I alone, here in a foreign city I know and she doesn't, what joy. I don't crave Lolitas, honest. I recognize, admire and, yes, desire the beauty of women my age. And I'm no matinee idol. This was one of the most attractive and definitely the most glamorous woman I had ever had a chance with. Not to mention that I had been in love with her already for the past decade and a half.

It's not that she was an older woman than the one I loved. It's that she was *another* woman. And I couldn't shake that, not the age but the difference, albeit a difference brought on by age. Cruel, cruel lens; cruel, cruel screen. They steal our hearts and leave us nothing.

The floors passed by. I blushed at her gaze and said God knows what. My floor came up. I walked out of the elevator and watched the door close as she soared up to her room.

Haikus for My Honey

Cecilia Rodríguez Milanés

1

A tingling roughness
dark and deep or closely cropped
boy, I miss your beard

2

Green-brown or khaki
sensitive, piercing or blank
enigmatic eyes

3

Long, lean, hard, shapely
your sweeps and snaps thrill me so
move those legs this way

4

Candle-glow softens
angles though in darkness your
heat generates light

5

Tenderness at the
fingertips or your tongue, sweet
slick; this, no, that's it

Aurora

Rafael Castillo

Blake is taking a shower. The room is hot and steamy, cloud-thick, the vapors clinging to the windowpanes, his silhouette a hazy apparition behind a vinyl shower curtain. The water gushes from the showerhead, slamming against his back. He hears the faint creak of the bathroom door. Who could it be? he wonders.

He turns and sees a blurry figure behind the curtain. Is it Claudia? Before he can call out her name, he hears Boom! Boom! Boom! It happens so fast. He feels a red-hot poker jabbing his chest three times; suddenly, he is falling, in slow motion, frame by frame. Clinging to the shower curtain, Blake passes out: water pounding his face, his skull blocking the drain.

"Oh my God!" a woman screams.

Blake falls into a peaceful slumber against a background of flute music as tranquil as the distant hum of ocean waves crashing against a craggy shoreline. But the flute music? What had Aurora called it? *Prélude à L'Après midi d'un Faune.* Oh yes, the faun, its song. He couldn't remember the composer or pronounce the French title of the tone poem. It didn't matter, really; only the music was important.

The flute tune traveled rhythmically in a sweet beat that made him numb to the outside world. It was bewitching. The sirenlike melody summoned him to peek through the blinds of his bedroom window facing the backyard at Aurora's house. She was probably inside playing her flute, he thought. And if Aurora was there, she would be likely naked on her crimson silk-sheeted bed: sitting by her canopied poster bed, combing her long ebony hair, gazing out her window and placing down the comb as she rasied the flute to her lips, blowing tunes that drifted across the field, lullabies over daffodils, traveling across acres of wild daisies, until they came floating gently into his bedroom, piercing the tranquillity of his sleep.

It was his lover's call.

* * *

Blake peered longingly at the forbidden, just as Actaeon had done thousands of years before him when he stared too long at Artemis taking her bath near a stream. Blake had been watching Aurora furtively from his window, stealing long glances when she'd sit in the sun-draped afternoons, in her white cotton dress, among the towering oaks and cypresses and willows in the backyard swing, playing her flute. He believed in destiny, and felt they had been marked for each other.

He knew what he had to do.

The walk was a good five acres of easy strolling across a grassy meadow before one reached the dwelling where Aurora lived.

Blake walked quietly, gently, trying to go unwatched and ease his way behind the large oaks surrounding her house. He would move furtively, like a child playing hide-and-go-seek, hoping to see unseen, hoping to observe Aurora from afar. But Aurora was too much of a woman for Blake, for she was linked mythologically to an ancient pulse and knew his every move. Between acres of yellow daisies and honeysuckle, she knew the well-beaten path that he would cross.

From where he was standing, behind a large tree, Aurora looked almost ethereal. She had a notebook in hand.

She had already started a fire in an empty oil drum. She stood near the open flame and began tearing pages from her journal, tossing them into the fiery tongue, watching them shrivel up like waxen figures, and then turning her head slightly upward, looking at the blue wisps spiraling to the sky. Then she'd fix her gaze at the fire for a long while, staring vacantly, lost to another time, that time as well lost to her.

Why didn't he leave when I told him to? she thought, looking at the burning pages. She stared solemnly at the smoke, disappointed that life had not turned out as planned, that words, both elusive and intimate, had betrayed her.

Aurora had warned her lover of his perilous fate, but he was one to mock apparitions, phantoms, déjà vu, anything supernatural as pure fantasy. She was a curandera, a sorceress who had, in her dreams, taught the craft to Circe and Calypso; she was a New Age healer and a channeler who believed in the transparency of life, the cyclical myth of Eternal Return; in fact, she was sure she had lived a thousand years ago as the wife of King Agamemnon, and before that as one of the lovers of King David. She even believed she had been the ill-fated Malinche who had brought havoc and despair to King Moctesuma.

Nevertheless Blake relished her myths, and more so it was her idyllic lovemaking that spellbound him. In their passion, he was all the more enamored, awash in the scent of the primordial sea. She was intoxicatingly delightful, so romantically alluring; no woman had ravished him as she, and so Blake was mesmerized by her dark beauty, her enchantment, her tales of misguided kings, deluded queens, and fabled cities.

Everything was in the journal: every nuance of intimacy, every utterance of hope, every lie. Sooner or later, it would come crashing down like an avalanche. And Aurora, feeling old, feeling heartless— sensing that behind the veneer of life was some obscure and unfulfilled wish—felt something eluding her.

Blake was now a bit closer.

At first, from afar, he thought she was burning trash, until it became apparent she was tossing pages from her journal, like withering dead leaves, into the makeshift incinerator. She was standing there, reading for the last minute some recorded passage of time preserved for her eyes, and then wistfully, as a woman who understands her fate, slitting the pages from the Book of Life and hurling them away into the inferno as though angry or upset.

But was she?

He stood watching her, gazing, wondering if it was a coquettish smile that he saw? A grin, perhaps? Or worse, an aloof contentment in watching the pages curl in fiery resolve? Was she taking cynical pleasure in seeing the pages wither into an inky cinder—all the unstated and unbreathed syllables lost in a fiery holocaust?

It was all too calm, too precise, too funerary. The bluish smoke bellowed upwards, hovering momentarily above her, then vanishing into the sky.

Blake kept looking, quite intrigued, wondering about the fight they had had only a week ago. What possible truth could be so shattering that it deserved purging by fire? He thought about it, thinking of his youth when, at one time, he too had burnt the love letters given to him by a married woman who had conveniently ended their affair because the woman's husband had found her out; he was fascinated by the thought of someone being so compelled toward destruction. Word after word went into the incinerator, the flames licking the sky.

She was even burning photographs, tossing them into the drum along with the other material as though they deserved the same destiny. She stared intently at the flames, mesmerized, her hands moving sensuously about her body, caressing her breasts, her eyes lost to a distant past.

Blake was fascinated by the way the breeze blew her raven tresses one way, by the shape of her aristocratic nose, by the flush of her cheeks, and even by her slender, fragile neck. He sensed a choreography about the whole affair, a spectral figure moving deftly around the drum like some fire-dance ballet. It was the way she was tearing out the pages that alerted him to the oddity of it all, because it was so erotic: she'd stare at the fiery oil drum for a long time, as if in silent prayer, and then begin her manner of separating the soul from the dark notebook.

Aurora watched her diary entries catch fire and thought about her lover, Blake, the man whose flattery, whose poetry, and whose flowers she'd known immediately as her destiny. She watched the pages ignite and it gave her both pity and sorrow in discovering, after all, that all things came to an end. It was inevitable, she had told herself, because, in becoming possessive, she had transgressed beyond their implicit boundaries. There were times when Blake had told her to leave him unmarked, for he feared the wrath of his wife; but Aurora, tempestuously aroused, had disregarded his warnings, branded him with her affections.

She could not help herself. She wanted him. She desired him. He was a man shaped to perfection from her repressed dark secrets and erotic dreams. A gypsy fortune-teller had told her that the man of her dreams would have a special sign, perhaps even special powers. And Blake *was* special. He was a freak of nature, a man whose chest bore three prophetic areolas.

And Aurora, during a moment of intimacy, had called them "a third brother to a pair of twins." She was so enthalled by Blake, believing, foolishly, that he would leave his wife.

"You know that's impossible," Blake told her.

"You must, please . . . ," Aurora pleaded.

"I can't. You know I can't."

"And me?"

"Me?" he repeated. "You knew from the beginning."

A long stare and a lingered pause, a lull so pregnant with hope. He smiled at Aurora and said simply: "A fulfillment." *Fulfillment.* Three syllables that struck terror, that confirmed her suspicions, for she refused to believe that Blake had seen her merely as a toy of his dreams.

The fire from the oil drum was burning words that had once quivered her flesh, and that now sent shivers up her body as she remembered every single utterance her lover had ever murmured when he'd touched her or caressed her. It was painful for Aurora to remember the joy the words rekindled because, whenever she read them aloud, she'd remember the feel of his coarse hands, the warmth of his skin against her own, the wet tip of his tongue in her ear. The trembling, engulfing sensation that shook her vulva. She even remembered the whispering and the maddening frenzy that turned her eyes white with ecstasy.

"Yes, Blake, I'm free," she whispered.

But she could never free herself from him because, just when she'd say it was over, Blake would begin flattering her once more, her defenses dissolving; and then—when he'd tell her of the story of two condemned lovers, Paolo and Francesca, lost in the fiery tempest of Hell's Second Circle—they'd end up in Aurora's large bed, entwined like two trees, mighty and gnarled.

Even though she said one thing, her heart always betrayed something else. Yet Aurora was weak, suspended in perpetual orgy; she felt the heaviness of losing part of her past, of burning a moment from her blissful memory that claimed him, if only briefly. She knew it was wrong, but she couldn't stop her fantasies from plunging her deeper into their affair.

Aurora had preserved her feelings on paper, describing in sensuous detail the muscular curvature of his thighs, the scent of his perspiration, the gleamy allure of his sinewy back as he lay on her crimson bed, exhausted and breathing, like a strong creature at rest. And as he lay sleeping, Aurora would stare longingly for minutes, wondering how much longer the joy would last.

One day Blake caught her scribbling in a black notebook. She was unaware that he had been watching her when she thought he had been asleep.

"Why?" he asked her.

Aurora, looking surprised, smiled and said, "Why what, darling?"

For her, it was the most natural thing in the world.

"Don't insult me. You know!"

"Oh," she said. "It's nothing. Don't worry, no one will read this."

A long gulf separated them. Blake stared morosely at her. He knew someday Aurora would betray him. And Aurora lay on the large bed searching for the proper words to put him at ease. "I can read it . . . later, when I'm alone. I can think of you, darling," she said, smiling, her large dark pupils staring into his chestnut eyes. And Blake believed her only too well.

Aurora had written about their affair with relish. She'd study his moves, like an artist studied a model, marking the twists of the body here and the thrusts of his movements there, moaning softly each time he entered her and feeling the tide coursing through her veins like wave upon wave; her head bloated with blood, her throat thickening in response to the undulating rhythm of their motion, rocking forward and backward, suspending time, until the moment when eyes met eyes, making the gorged slithering element flow like a tributary into a vast ocean.

But one day, strange things began happening. Little things. Whenever she'd give him a little love mark here, or try to nibble his ear there, Blake would become agitated. Angry. Other times, he'd make love to her hastily, almost routinely, as if his body was there but his mind somewhere else.

And then she saw it—the inevitable.

"Lust is your fatal flaw," she wrote distressingly in her diary. She had seen a curious red aura surrounding his body; it was the foreboding strangeness of that aura that alarmed her of things to come, of a great body of water turning into a red sea. But she couldn't unravel its murky meaning.

When she heard a twig snap, Aurora knew someone was watching her.

"Who's there?" she uttered.

But Blake, standing beside her, was an uninvited guest bearing witness to the ceremony Aurora was performing. A breeze picked up and the smoke from the oil drum drifted off. She had her back to him as Blake moved behind her.

She felt an uneasy sensation of coldness gripping her waist, her arms; her legs quivered uncontrollably. It was both strange and frightful, for Aurora knew that many things in nature were invisible to the naked eye. And then Aurora began to weep; a shudder swept over her and the pages from her journal became clear as Blake looked over her shoulder and read: "August 14. Blake and I went down to the beach and searched for seashells. He said he'd never leave me, but somehow I know he is not telling me the truth; I can sense it. How much longer can I take it whenever these small joys become less and less; I don't know, because I'm beginning to feel that I'm losing him."

Aurora was sure someone was watching her.

"Blake," she muttered, breaking the silence. "Is it you?"

She shook her head and then said, "Oh, God. Dear Blake, why did it have to be you?"

Blake moved back.

From the treetops, through a gap in the tree branches, Blake saw her. She looked dispirited, as a person without a will, as if the soul was about to disembark from her body. Going inside the house through the back porch door, she came out with another notebook.

"Look, Blake. I have it here in my hands, see? I'm going to burn it as I said I would. See, I'm keeping my promise. I loved you, darling. I love you still."

She tore off a sheaf of paper from the black notebook and, crumbling it, tossed it into the fiery oil drum.

"Aurrorraa," Blake tried to say with her.

The words brushed against her like a chilly sea breeze. Aurora turned and stared into the vacant lot across from her house. Towering gnarled trees loomed menacingly, like giants with desperate arms raised to the heavens. A crow, flying across the graying sky, perched atop one of the branches.

Blake tried to speak with her once more. "Aurora," he shouted. He found it strange that she did not beckon to his call. He was sure Aurora was ignoring him. Something was amiss. Why wouldn't Aurora hear him, he thought. And then a dark thought slithered into him. The dream, that terrible dream. . . .

It was the photo Aurora was burning that made him realize something was wrong. It was no dream, he thought. It happened, he remembered as he was showering that morning, unaware that Aurora was making her way into his house, quite angry; and she thinking it was Claudia.

Aurora walked the long distance between their houses, thinking, carrying her father's revolver, wearing a white dress, disguising the anger and resentment she felt toward Claudia. Aurora looking at the small white-stucco house with its open screen door, thinking, *If you won't leave him, then I'll decide your fate. You're not going to keep us apart. He will thank me; he will.* Aurora moving closer to destiny, clutching the revolver like a mother holding a baby, moving toward a dark cliff.

Aurora stared hypnotically at the dancing fire, increasing and receding at will. The crackling embers almost whispering, "You did it, Aurora, did it," as she stared at the pages engulfed in flames, thinking back to that deadly moment when she walked through the honeysuckle fields, past the gnarled trees, toward the unlocked screen door. Aurora walking through the living room looking at the pieces of Victorian furniture, the photo of the loving couple on the fireplace mantel and hearing the nervous tick-tock-tick-tock of the hallway grandfather clock timing her movement toward the hissing bathroom shower.

Everything is quiet, except the tick-tock-tick-tock of the grandfather clock. The door to the library room is open, with the study lamp casting a curious glow on an opened book; to the left is an old sewing machine, the tread spool like a black orchid bulb. Past the king-size bedroom, where Claudia and Blake make love, is the bathroom. Aurora can hear the hissing of the shower nozzle. She lifts the revolver and cocks the trigger and opens the door.

It is cloudy, like a foggy morning.

She is breathing heavily. Now is the perfect time to remove the last obstacle of their life. The room is vaporous, steam fogging the windows and rising from the tub while her victim, standing in a shroud of mist, is unaware that death looms seconds away.

She sees the outline of a figure in the shower. She thinks it is Claudia. Pointing the revolver like an accusatory finger, her head turned away, eyes squinting, she fires three times. Boom! Boom! Boom! The silhouette stumbles, taking down the curtain with it. There is a gurgling noise. The shower nozzle slamming water against the collapsed torso wrapped around a vinyl curtain. His eyes open, his mouth agape. To her horror, it is Blake. A black bile rises from the pit of her stomach, a feeling of heavy doom followed by a demure arousal of destiny.

Aurora screams: "Oh my God!"

Looking at the frightful body, his skull blocking the drain and the rising water turning crimson, she closes his eyes.

The clock strikes seven.

The murky figure and the creaking of the bathroom door is the last thing he hears just before Aurora fires three bullets into his chest. From a distance, Blake hears a cry, "Oh my God." But the words are muffled; he is moving through a swirling white tunnel. A hand submerges him into the water-filled tub, flooding his bullet-ridden lungs. After this, she pumps three bullets into the frame of the grandfather clock because the chime frightens her.

It was fall, when most of the trees have shed their leaves, making them writhingly skeletal, like wrinkled old things, that Blake looked up to the sky and thought he had seen a ladder. Almost weightless. It was suspended in midair. And then, almost miraculously, Blake floated toward it, past the treetops, above the stratosphere, until he could see the vaporous mist that made up the heavens and look down at the glorious quilt-work of earth, the zigzagging borders and the curious antlike race of humanity struggling to satiate its petty desires.

On his journey upward, Blake thought he had seen the sky about to seal itself, large clouds stirring into a darkening vacuum, blocking the light. But he couldn't climb without Aurora. Not now, perhaps never.

Blake was even imagining the pull of the rotating earth, its axis between what is now and forever, hurling him into the unsalvageable past mingled with the horrible present, denying him the unforeseeable future. He knew that creatures of habit never abndoned their familiar surroundings, and watching Aurora burn the remnants of their past made him aware that passion existed in the present, the past, and the future.

And she, looking at the trees, the wind caressing her dark tresses, answered, "I am here, my love, my Blake."

There, standing near the fiery pit, looking at the dark smoke burning her past and present, Aurora cradled her father's revolver. The tick-tock-tick-tock of the incessant clock reverberating with memories of the act.

A loud bang scattered a flock of crows perched on some twisted oaks.

Aurora closed her eyes, feeling her heart go heavy, knowing that what she had done would never be sanctioned by God. Aware of her destiny, she knew, like the winding down of her heartbeat, the opening and closing of ventricles, that Blake would be waiting for her on the other side.

Raisins

Lorna Dee Cervantes

Raisins are my currency
to date—slightly seedy,
prickled as my nipples,
black as pubis, colored
as my opened eyelids.
I tongue you
fricatives into vowels.
I suck you
to the scabs
you were, forbidden
fruit. Reminders.
Never mind
the way I found you
deserted in the depot
stall. No matter
how this small red box
was once a child's.
Lost wonder, you're
the gift of grace
swept up off
the bathroom floor.
You're my only food
today, the day I left
you, paper husband,
widowed name.
Our final meal
was sweet, you
hovered over me,
an empty package,
beating blades
to froth, teething
me the way I like it,
both lips bit and shriveled
as our last fuck you.
You are black with rust

and will restore my blood.
You're my prize of faith,
stave against starve.
I eat it. Grateful
for the brief exchange.
Twenty eight tips
of fate. Three good sweats
they soaked in sun
as you now soak
my spit, sweet as acid, damp as rot.
This hunger, as your
memory, feeds
by chance.

Le Petit Mal

Lorna Dee Cervantes

after Neruda

Love, if I die
how do I explain it?
Birds harbor mites
between their breasts

and who knows it?
Who speaks the dark
secret of secretive
dark arbors? Were I a bird

I would be a feather
of a bird, as light
as ash upon your gone
brow, the furrow of lisp

over the fur of your
lips. I would take
my advantage of you,
beetle my legs between

yours. Do all lonesome
penance before the sentence
of your name. Say special
grace to your hope

chest, quake before
thin mountains of
rivering, feathering,
full now, a waking

bird, my murmuring heart, my quiver and arrow;
my shot—I'm shot
full of you. Dead.

On the Poet Coming of Age

Lorna Dee Cervantes

for Jim Harrison

there was this poet
                                with a wandering eye
                        he was cool
I was a street kid
            a moving   sheet of ice
                    a floe   a cipher
no moon
            the street lamps aired a golding
    sulfur   my skin
                    gilded
            and the satin   skirt   I was naked
under
                    swept mooned shells
            of light through the glassed asphalt

seventeen   and nobody's girl
            96 pounds of bad
                        burning
                                the midnight
                                        barrio

                        oil   lit
                            a ticking flint
        he sat at the Five Star bar   reading
                Rupert Brooke   or Lowell
            how
                    little now
                            I remember
                    just the smoked pool of light
        how he
                    (not the half-blind poet   but the other
                                    almost man)
                    sat
                            squinting at the leaves
        of verse   I recall
                                        how he cradled the stump
                            in the pouch
                                    of his denim   but not
                his name or the face
                    just a beauty   the blank
                                backlit page
                            my bustless boldness
        never replaced   or ever
                            recaptured
                                how I leaned
                        on
                the bar stool
                                    radiating and   irradiating
                            the sullen drunks
                            the demeaning mouths
            a field   a force   there
                    parroting passages of Baudelaire
                                Rimbaud
                                Vallejo
                                youth
                    remembering   youth
            in   those   years   I   owned
                            whatever I touched
                            whatever I said
        he was another hemisphere   a continent   divided
                by a man   made canal   no side
                    could claim

he was a poet   from the midwest
          he'd come
                    to read Brooke
                                   or Lowell
          at the U   which I knew   was a lie
                    the jolt
that woke his flesh
                         was not the fire
                                      bird
     hand-painted on satin
nor my wild flight
                    of hair
                                        but the English
I spoke
               the enunciated
                                   unexpected
Gold   I said
          and made a date for the Greyhound
                    knowing he'd go
                              cruising for a better   lay
               but when money
                    and beauty failed
                                             to pay
     I took him & his wall-eyed friend
          back to my condemned   Victorian
     there are these ships   see   you can   sail
               without   course
an expanse of ocean crossed on a dare
          choice isn't limited
               to Sartre and Simone
               it's a game   the poor play
                                        at wit's end
it was a game
out   guessing   out   reciting
out   smarting   the   legitimate
               and the boy I took to bed
                         was
                                   sexed
when he undressed
          my defeated city
     he took what could have been a fist

                    from his pocket
                                        the stump
            glowing milk in the smoking light
                    his gnawed-off paw
when I touched it he was soft
                                thin
                        a woman
            in a man a girl could love
he put it out of sight
                                If thine hand offend thee . . .
and with a tenderness for an absence
I both felt   and did not
        I made him   rise
                                swell   cliff
                                        sail
                        Fucking poets
he breathed in the candle dark
                        as I tunneled
                        in all ways
                        that can be
                            taken
                        whispered
                multi   pieced
                lean as pricked goose meat
in the morning
the poet left by cab
I walked the boy to the bus
barefoot through the glass
pissed winoed streets   the other
            left a poem about Mexicans
                                    depots
                                    and the sullen poor
                    all gone
I read it and researched
my 17 hungered years in the mirror
            and I dare it to say it
                                I am a poet

Isla Mujeres

Lorna Dee Cervantes

pa'Javier

There's an arch in your heart,
a deserted landscape languors
steeped in the weight of the sea.
Waiting. Enough of the coral
sand, white elephant sheen,
my pelvis pressed between the pages
of your knees. In the cavity
wind blows through, that part
of you that never stays
like the fixed portions of a blown
through past, I can not change
an absence that is
a space, a whistle-whittled
pain, or ever wish it. Just long
Mayan paths to trace, my indigenous
toes starched with salt, my Purépecha
spine erect, ignorant of your long gone
sex. My brown dog stirs, agitates,
displays. I think I'm a part of you
but it's only celestial, nothing
reflecting the blue. If you were
a man like a rock you could fill,
stave, remember: how our poverty
sticks, how a spirit saves, how frank
the powers are in the ancient
sprays, the perfumed rock, a ruined
sun and the devil wind; a matrimony.

Buttocks

Ricardo Castillo

Woman also has her behind divided in two.
But it's beyond doubt that buttocks of a woman
are incomparably better than those of a man,
they've more life, more happiness, they're pure imagination;
they're more important than both the sun and gold
they're a basic commodity inflation doesn't affect,
a birthday cake on your birthday,
a blessing of mother nature,
the origin of poetry and scandal.

Translated by Enrique Lamadrid

Bogota Transfer

Hector Manjarrez

I should have, yes, I should have drunk your blood
and bitten your clit for one blind and silent moment
before we exhausted ourselves, long before we bathed.
Now your almost muscular body,
grotesquely white, red cunt
and red hair, is so immaculate,
tan quant a soi
like mine. It is certain
that I gave you almost nothing. That you gave me
the revival of an old abortion is so moving
that I cry for not becoming sentimental
like your city.

Today you had no mercy, nor I any rage.
The plane leaves tomorrow
and we didn't have another moment
to play our games with each other,
in our feigned mortal leaps
I castle my king;
your proud queen is going to fly away.

Translated by E. A. Mares

The Tongue Is Mightier Than the Sword

Magdalena Gómez

Swimming through his sea of language
he rises with a pearl
drops it in my ear
I become his fool

"ay dios
ay dios
ay dios"

yes, yes, there is a God
he moans and grabs the sheets
digs his head deep into the pillow
asks if I mind
that all he does is lie there

I meet his question with a laugh
let him wonder at the meaning
he digs his feet into the quilt
life is too short to wonder
second guess
question the meaning of laughter

he plays the game much better than I
I run circles around his nipples with my tongue
those little cherry pits
I own them
but he's moaning
and I'm not

my tongue becomes Columbus
and discovers what has always been there

I raise the flags of my eyes
to see his silent mouthing

"ay dios
ay dios
ay dios"

yes, yes, there is a God
I drown in a storm of sweat
dizzy from the wind of moans
I am the conquering hero

he sleeps deeply, undisturbed
beside me
I spend the night awake, alone

my ship sinking beneath the weight
of pearls.

Delirium

Magdalena Gómez

His hand squeezes
for the milk I cannot give
between my legs he searches
for the will to live

within my mouth he seeks
the words that will replace
the silences of childhood
that kept him in his place

inside my eyes he roams
finding no way out
he seeks the light of truth
to soothe his burning doubt

among my fingers and my toes
he plays among the flowers
singing loves me
      love me not
his game goes on for hours

with his hands upon my belly
his face between my thighs
he devours as he rises
in a powerful disguise

his hand around his penis
he inhales and sticks it in
he doesn't breathe again
until he comes
to his senses

Paura Has No Cunt

Francisco Hernandez

Paura has no cunt: she has a voracious mollusk between
her legs, a throbbing coral, a fruit that perfumes my
insides and the breath of sharks.
They say she was beautiful as a child. That her hair was a
lighthouse on stormy nights, that her tongue saved more
than one scurvied crew.
Certain tones of her skin can unravel nets.
Her nipples point out the ones who will perish by drowning.
In her profound ass cormorants make their nest.
She is the prize that mutilated harpooners, demented
divers, and topmastmen dream of.
Her frigid back dangles from her neck. And her effigy
pecks at my abandoned lips.

Translated by Enrique Lamadrid

from Sweat Song

Jim Cortinas

She was naked except for the leg warmers. Kiko watched her take the cup of ice and tilt it over her hard, sweating breasts. Her nipples seemed to jump and stand as the crushed ice fell out of the cup and dripped down her tight, muscular chest. Kiko's eyes bugged out as she squatted over the weights on the floor in front of her. She placed both hands on the bar and lifted. As the heavy bells came up to her stomach, Kiko saw her pussy lips open and breathe with the tension. He couldn't believe it and stumbled on the treadmill. He tried to grab the railing on either side, but fell off the running belt and hit the floor hard with his ass. He shook his head and looked up. She set the weights back down on the mat, her bending motion opening her taut thighs, the mound of wet hair hanging its silhouette against the light of the mirrors, a small bush he wished he could reach out to and pick. She moved down and froze over the bar.

She lifted herself up on the tip of her strong toes, spread her hips wider unil Kiko had another great view. He couldn't believe what she was doing! She lowered herself down on the bar gently, making sure her pussy lips wrapped themselves around the bar! Her back glistened with sweat. She arched her back and brought her squatting hips down harder on the bar. Kiko heard her low gasp. Her pussy lips kissed the bar and Kiko wished it was his bar. No way, he thought. She pivoted on her toes, turned toward him, and pointed her nipples at him. She shook her blonde hair, which was pulled back and tied in a bun. She finally stood up and walked toward Kiko, who was still sitting on the floor.

For the first time, he was glad he had the first shift at the club. He usually opened at five-thirty A.M. for the early customers, but this morning he'd arrived at five A.M. to find her waiting. She didn't say much to him. He had never seen her before, but she told him she had just gotten a new membership, had an early job, and needed to get in and work out early. Before he knew it, she had emerged from the women's locker room with nothing on except those incredible neon pink leg warmers! He gently leaned back on the floor as she stood over him and messed his hair with one hand. She slapped his hand away when he tried to touch her. She moved closer and pressed her wet crotch onto his face. Kiko couldn't breathe. He did the best he could when he found the lips of her pussy and started flicking his tongue in there.

She shivered, giggled, and tousled his hair with both hands. She pressed his face harder against her and let him lick her until she was snaking her legs all over his head. They fell back on the floor and she sat on his face. Kiko was having a hard time breathing and managed to come up for air a couple of times before the close-up of this delicious treat covered his nose and eyes again. She fell forward on her extended arms and swiveled around his face, trying to keep his tongue inside her. She cried out and gasped and heaved. Before he could protect himself, she reached back and grabbed his stiff cock, which had been fighting to burst through his tight gym shorts. She squeezed hard and he jumped.

She flew off him and rolled laughing on the carpet. He lay there gasping, her juice running down his cheeks. He wiped his face with his hands and looked over at her. What now? Kiko wondered. This had never happened before. He looked at his watch, which said five-thirty. Time to open! There were always four or five early customers waiting for him to unlock the front door. He quickly sat up and peered across the empty gym toward the glass doors. Two men were getting out of their cars!

"Jesus! You better get dressed," he told her as he got up and ran to the front counter. "It's over," he said loudly. "Time to open."

He bent over to get the door key from under the counter. When he stood up, he turned to see she was not in the front room. He hoped she'd made it to the women's room before the men spotted her through the glass. Kiko wiped the sweat from his face with a towel, straightened his T-shirt, made sure the lump in his shorts had gone down, then went to open for the day.

The two men entered, checked their membership cards at the counter, and did their usual routine. Within ten minutes, four more men and women came in. Before Kiko knew it, it was six o'clock and he had not seen any sign of the blonde. He couldn't just walk into the women's room and look for her. He had to wait until Janet, the other morning employee, came in at six-thirty.

When Janet arrived, he made up a story to her about a woman feeling sick and running into the bathroom. He asked her if she would go look and described the blonde to her. Janet came back several mintues later to tell him there was no one around who fit her description. By then, the gym was full. Forty or fifty people huffed and puffed or quietly worked out on dozens of different contraptions and weights.

Kiko walked around the room several times. Once, he went and stood near the women's room. When he made sure there was no one getting dressed or showering in there, he quickly ran in and made a fast inspection of the tiled room. It was empty. His sneakers squeaked on the floor as he stopped suddenly in front of an open locker. Customers were usually careful about their belongings and brought locks for their possessions.

Kiko looked down at the open cabinet and stared at the pair of pink leg warmers. He picked one up and held it to his nose. He could smell the blonde's pussy on it. The thought made him hard, but was suddenly cut off when a woman came into the room.

A very fat, slow, middle-aged woman in a one-piece blue bathing suit stopped in her tracks when she saw him standing there, the leg warmer in his face, the obvious hard-on spearing through his pants. She made an odd noise through her nose and scowled at him.

"You work here?" she asked in a loud voice.

"Yeah." Kiko could barely contain himself.

He threw the leg warmer back into the lockers, slammed it shut with a thundering crash, and quickly sped past the huffing intruder, whom he noticed was drenched in sweat. He smiled, slipped on a wet patch of tiles, caught himself against the wall, and disappeared around the corner.

A Red Bikini Dream

Max Martínez

The dream always begins the same way. It is midmorning. A muggy day, hot, humid. In the distance loom the Berkshires, green and dark and bulky. The sky is a cloudless powder blue. From the base of the sundeck, a wide stretch of green grass slopes. The patch of green holds its line against the tangled weeds and taunting foliage of the forest. There is something, someone, she doesn't know which, in the penumbra just at the edge of the forest. It, he, waits.

She is doing her ironing, nude except for a pair of red bikini underpants, the thin diaphanous material of which spreads tautly over her rounded buttocks. Her shoulder-length hair is pinned up on top of her head in a loose, precarious pile that allows the rare hushed breezes sweeping down from the mountains to cool and refresh her neck. There are beads of sweat on her forehead, on her arms, and in the valley between her breasts.

As she does her ironing, she is expecting something, someone. She is impatient for it, him, to come into the light. She can feel a presence in the forest. She turns several times to peer beyond the trees, into the shadows. A branch on a tree beside the house sways and creaks. A bush shudders as a small bird darts into the air.

She resumes her ironing with a shrug of her shoulders. A tremor shoots through her body. In the rapid movement, her hair comes loose, cascading to rest upon her shoulders. It won't be long. The presence in the forest is in motion. She can feel it, him. A cold flush begins at the back of her legs, moves up through the vulnerable flesh of her inner thighs, courses upward to concentrate itself between her shoulder blades at the base of her neck. Her hair feels stiff and heavy, burdensome and nagging.

Something, someone, is coming now. She is afraid, expectant, impatient, filled with longing, desire. Her arms itch under the skin. A riptide of anticipation swells in her throat. She is eager. She wants to turn and look, to face who it is. She knows what he has come for. She will not turn. Her lips part, glazed with saliva, trembling. She knows it is a man from the way he disturbs the air around her. She has been waiting for him for a long time. She sets the iron to rest on a metal disc. She wants to let him know she is glad he has come, that she is ready for him, that she wants him. She wants to signal that she will not resist, that her submission is complete, total. Her words congeal, she turns to stone.

She can sense him lifting his right foot, dark, brown, with a calloused underside; she feels the steps to the sundeck bend under the pressure of his weight. He is on the sundeck, moving lithely, gently like a zephyr, until he is so close to her that she can feel his breath, warm and moist on her back. It feels like the hushed breezes that sweep down from the mountains. His hands brush her shoulders and glide down her upper arms.

Suddenly the full length of his naked body is touching hers. His hands descend to her forearms, wrists, caress her slender fingers, stopping to explore and gently press each fingertip, fingertip by fingertip.

His hands drop, as though he has carelessly tossed them away. They come to rest on her tanned, muscular thighs. He presses closer to her, the curve of her back perfectly congruent with the swell of his chest and belly. His hands follow the round shape of her thighs and meet and begin an upward sweep to where the red bikini underpants start to flare in opposite directions, up and over her hips. His touch ignites each nerve in the soft flesh at the sides of her belly. He traces the curve of each rib and he stops, finally, under her arms.

His hands move forward, cleaving to the line where the skin of her breasts becomes soft and loose. Each thumb brushes lightly along the parabola of her breasts. Catlike, he lands upon her nipples, perches voluptuously until they become distended, hard, erupting with life. A long, slow, guttural moan surges upward and escapes as a whimper through her parted lips as she shudders, shakes, and struggles to maintain control. He draws her body against his fluid, forceful, entreating sinew. He pinions her forearms. His face is in her hair, lost in its tangles and shadows, searching for her, creeping toward her.

The man's hands move downward, away from the twin beacons of her nipples. He laces his fingers as his hands meet on the soft plain of her belly, a belly barren and fallow. She can feel the pressure build just above her pelvis. She tenses as he slides in and hooks his thumbs on the elastic waistband of her red bikini underpants. In one long slow movement his hands go lower, dragging the thin material over the round mounds of her buttocks. The red bikini underpants become stuck, resist, at the juncture of her legs where the plump flesh of her inner thighs is pressed together. The elastic cloth begins to stretch as he lowers them over the smooth skin of her eggshell brown thighs. She shifts her weight to one leg and then quickly shifts it to the other. The red bikini underpants snap loose and become bunched in a wrinkled lump between her lower thighs.

He has broken through the tangled veil of her hair. She feels the stubble of his beard on her shoulder blade, rasping along the ridge of her spine, down to the pockmark at her tailbone, over the swell of her buttocks. He stoops to roll the red bikini underpants over her knees, down her bulky calves, and then they drop of their own weight down into a vanquished pile around her ankles.

She lifts one leg up to pull them over the heel. With her free foot she pins them to the sundeck while she pulls them off her other foot. Meanwhile, the stubbled cheek rasps against her neck once more, nudging her earlobes. His hands swoop and flutter in front of her. Her nipples jut forward to meet the talons of his fingers. They squeeze, mash, press, lift, balance, hold, and knead her breasts. Another shudder and she leans all the way to press her back against his hairy chest. Her mouth is agape, her eyes are closed, her hands are balled into dampened fists.

His erect penis slithers, snakelike and inquisitive, cold and hard and flat into the crevice of her buttocks. He rocks her to and fro. There is an icy chill, goose bumps, radiating over the round plump flesh of her buttocks. His hands on her hips push her body away from his. The cold, erect penis meanders over the hump of her buttocks. She can feel the engorged, pulsating veins of his penis, serpents in relief upon the snake.

The ironing board tilts over, teetering precariously for an instant before it crashes down on the sundeck. The iron and the metal disc topple along with it. She, too, has gone over, tilting forward, but the man restrains her and draws her back to him. In the brief separation of their bodies, the man's stiff cold organ slides over her swelling buttocks, never losing touch of her. As he draws her back to him, the penis snuggles, chill and wet against the puckered button of her anus.

She is desperate to touch, to feel, to consume his flesh as she explores him with the palms of her hands. She reaches behind to anchor herself on his muscular thighs. As she gains purchase, he touches her elbows, forces them forward. His hands are on the flat of her back bending her over until she can see her distorted face on the stainless steel metal disc where the iron rested. His bare foot taps one ankle bone, then the other, and she parts her legs as far apart as they can go.

The flat of his hand, fingers spread apart, bridges the mounds of her behind and slides down, fingers coming together as they reach into the thatch of her pubic hair. There, in the moist tangle of wiry hair, he spreads her flesh apart, a pale, pink, milky grotto. She can smell her own musk. He pulls her to him.

She has her hands on her knees, her hair dangling sweetly over the sides of her face. She is waiting, expectant, longing, eager. She feels his ice-cold member, rigid and unyielding, shove into the gaping mouth of her parted flesh. She waits for the warm moist receptacle of her body to overcome the unrelenting ice cold of his penis. He goes no farther than the insertion inside the threshold. She waits and he waits. She can feel no other part of him. If he had a body, she can no longer be sure, it is gone, irrelevant, superfluous. All she can feel is the cold, steely feel of the organ, poised for further intrusion.

The shaft of cold begins to move up into the liquid passage of her body. It is a long slow insertion that seems to never end, that spreads out ice-cold tentacles whose suction draws forth sensations she has never before experienced. The cold slithering insertion continues, ballooning inside her body. She has reached the limits of her capacity. Her skin, every bit of her skin, is stretched, tingling at the point of imminent rupture.

If she could, she would beg for surcease, a pause in the insertion while her body accepts the intrusion of the ice-cold organ, while it becomes a part of her and she a part of it. If she could. She is past rational thought. She is past the point where she can heed the admonitions of her body, the unthought thoughts of care and prevention and caution, the knowledge primeval that there is danger beyond the body's limit.

She orgasms. At the instant of her orgasm, the shaft of cold loses its material presence to become immanent. There is not a cell in her body insensitive to her orgasmic release. A joyous, wondrous conjunction of biological expression, singing, in clear and precious tones, the song of itself. At this moment, in this place, the universe is present, in a cell, in her body, in the forest, in the mountains, in the sky. She has but to touch herself for the rippling throes of orgasm to begin again.

The steady hissing of the car's air conditioner lulled Carrie Rasmussen into a floating, dreamlike trance. The road was West Texas flat, two hundred miles beyond San Antonio, with nary a tree, nary a hill in sight. Not a town to break the monotony of the endless miles. For all the terrain varied, she might have been standing still. The instrument panel of the rental car indicated the speed at which she moved, the miles she had traveled, the fuel consumed. For nearly an hour, she had not met any cars coming toward her, and neither had she seen a car in the rearview mirror. She used the edges of her consciousness to keep the car in the proper lane, staying within her allocated space through the opaque prism of her trance.

Carrie had been driving since six in the morning. She spent the night in a high-rise hotel on the outskirts of San Antonio, adjacent to Interstate 10. At dawn she was awakened by a perfunctory call, as she had instructed. Through the plate-glass window, she saw streaks of orange and yellow splashed delicately over the horizon. She had wondered if it were daylight in Boston. While she waited for the parking lot valet to bring round the car, she felt the thick, oppressive, wet air of morning. Within minutes she had bypassed the headlights of pre–rush hour traffic and was enjoying the Hill Country at sunrise. By noon, after a breakfast of egg and muffin at a fast food restaurant and several stops for coffee, she'd gone through Junction. Past Fort Stockton, she drove along a route that was sere and indifferent, inhospitable and forbidding.

It was nearing two o'clock in the afternoon. The sun was directly overhead, so hot that it blistered the roof of the car, straining the air conditioner. Carrie thought it might be time to stop and rest, wait for the cool of the evening before pushing on. Her joints were stiff, her eyes felt like tiny pinpoints inside a wad of cotton. A dull ache of hunger settled into the pit of her stomach. She wanted a brisk, pelting shower, a nap, and some food.

If she could rest and be on the road again by six or seven in the evening, she could easily make Las Vegas by dawn. She had planned the trip carefully, methodically, in the plodding way she had, leaving no detail to chance. She had allowed for an occasional excursus, to take a scenic route, a detour to see things she might never again have the opportunity to see. Thus far the trip had been direct, without a moment lost to whimsy. Even though she might plan for it, it was not in her nature to give in to it.

Her cigarettes were on the plush velour passenger seat on top of the road map. She lit one and picked up the map. It was a trip booklet prepared by an auto club in Boston. As she studied the map, she darted glances to the road out of a corner of her eye. With tentative eyes, she traced the road she had traveled since six o'clock in the morning, following the green Magic Marker arrows to locate her present position. Seven full hours of driving. She calculated a rough estimate of ten miles to the next town. It would have to do. She tossed the map aside and fixed her eyes on the road again. In a matter of minutes, the town appeared as a shimmering mirage in a basin surrounded by low-slung hills. Once she was on flat ground, the hills seemed to hide themselves in the purple distance.

Flat, one-story buildings flanked the blacktop gash that cut through the town. The older, wooden ones had the false fronts of the Old West. White, ashlike sand partially covered over the asphalt as the desert tried to reclaim the part of itself that lay beneath the trespass of civilization. Before she entered the town proper, Carrie had scanned both strips of buildings for a place to stay. She noticed the hotel immediately but was put off by the false front, which leaned to one side as if the roof had partly caved in. Nevertheless, assuming that she had no other choice, she turned into one of the angled parking lanes. She kept the motor running as she looked the hotel over.

The large picture windows on either side of the entrance to the hotel appeared to have a film of grime at least a century old. There was a half-moon scar, curving from top to bottom on one of the windows. Carried become discouraged and apprehensive at the alternative of driving farther on before finding a clean enough, decent place to rest. She turned her head away from the hotel, toward the western end of town. Her spirits lifted a little when she saw the sign that announced a motel. She threw the car in reverse and headed in the direction of the motel. She crossed her fingers for luck.

Carrie Rasmussen sped through town in a few seconds. The motel was built at an angle to the main street, removed from the cluster of town buildings, seated upon a mound of sandy soil, solitary and diffident. Behind the motel, the crisply clean blacktop with its bold yellow center strip beckoned to El Paso.

She turned into the motel driveway, stopping on the concrete floor of a carport. In front of her, in the thick plate-glass window Carrie could see full extension of the main street in reflection, with its gray sun-bleached ribbon of asphalt. The heat rising from the powdery white sand shimmered in the reflection.

Carrie opened the door to admit a gust of searing heat into the air-conditioned interior of the car. She had been breathing treated air for hours. The furnace blast of desert heat blistered her arms, neck, and cheeks. She shivered slightly at the sudden change in climate, becoming acclimated to it in a matter of seconds, and then she found it unbearable not more than a few seconds after that.

Inside the motel lobby, the heat was as unbearable as it was outside, with the added irritation of a musty, stifling smell. A young girl, about seventeen, lay on a beach towel next to a rickety coffee table in the narrow reception area. She lay on her stomach, wore jeans and a swimsuit top which was untied in back. A pancake-size rim of breast squeezed out from her rib cage. Her forearms were stacked on top of each other, her head resting on them. When the girl heard the door open, she lifted her head to get a good look at Carrie Rasmussen.

"Hello. Do you want a room?" the girl asked, desultorily.

Carrie did not immediately respond. She remained just inside the door, clutching her purse at waist level. The hours of driving, the road fatigue, made it difficult for her to speak. She removed her sunglasses, tilted her head, and ran her fingers through her hair.

The girl lifted up on her arms as if she were going to do a push-up, and in a quick motion swung around to a sitting position, her legs crossed Indian-fashion. The loose swimsuit top bunched between her breasts with their plum-sized nipples pointing in opposite directions. Her jeans were unbuttoned at the waist. The girl had massive breasts that drooped flabbily down to her thin waist. She was not in the least embarrassed that Carrie watched her as she tucked each breast into the swimsuit top, which was much too small for the formidable task expected of it. The girl leaned forward to tie the straps into a bow in back.

The girl wobbled unsteadily as she got to her feet.

"Check-in card's right on the counter, ma'am," the girl said. Her bleached blond hair fell thick and smooth along the sides of her face. "You fill it out. I have to go potty. I'll be right back. Okay?"

As she walked away, Carrie noticed the girl's buttocks, disproportionately large and heart-shaped. She would be a very fat girl were it not for the thin waist.

The mephitis of the lobby reminded her of putrescent diapers. Her forehead began to perspire, her forearms felt clammy. Carrie filled in her name on the card, her home address in Boston, and left the space blank that asked how long she intended to stay.

The young girl came back with her hair brushed and pinned with two pink butterfly barrettes. There was a reddish glow on her cheeks, forehead, and nose from the scrubbing she'd given her face.

She'd put on a blue gingham western-cut shirt that had mother-of-pearl buttons. She had not bothered to tuck the shirt into her jeans.

Carrie Rasmussen pushed the check-in card toward the young clerk. She'd taken out her clutch purse, which lay on the counter between her hands.

"How long are you going to stay?" asked the young girl.

"Just long enough for a shower and a quick nap," answered Carrie.

"Yeah, I thought so. We get lots like that, here," the girl said. "Overnights is mostly what we get. Truckers'll come in, sometimes, you know, take a bath, sleep a little. Then they hassle with us. They think they shouldn't have to pay for a full day if they're here for just a few hours. They just took a bath, they think. What's a bath? It ain't worth twenty-seven fifty. They think."

The girl made some notations on the bottom of the check-in slip. Her tongue spilled over her lower lip as she concentrated on separating the two pieces.

"Cash or charge?" she asked.

Carrie took a charge card from one of the plastic pockets of her clutch purse. It was the card she had designated for travel expenses.

The girl's massive breasts swayed ponderously when she slid the embosser grip back and forth over Carrie's credit card. The girl stapled the charge slip to the check-in card and slipped them into a drawer in the cash register. She handed Carrie her charge card.

"You sign the charge ticket when you check out," the girl explained.

"I can sign the charge now," said Carrie.

"Sorry," the girl said. "My daddy's rules. You have to sign it when you check out. Just drive your car straight ahead from where you are and you'll come to the room. The air conditioner works pretty good in that room. About half of them, the units, are broke—including the one in here, darn it! Daddy says if we can stick it out the rest of this year, you know, we'll be able to move out of California. I can't wait. I'd sure like to go surfing."

The young girl smiled generously and clasped her hands in front of her, hunching her shoulders. Carrie returned a thin smile before going outside to the car.

From the trunk of the car, she retrieved a medium-sized suitcase in which she had packed clothes for the journey and a makeup kit. Inside her room, the air was thick and mildewed, trapped and unmoved for what seemed to be months. A shaft of sunlight pierced the center of the room. Dust motes lingered in midair. In the brief minutes that she had surrendered the car's air conditioner, Carrie Rasmussen had perspired heavily. There was a sizable sweat stain, which she deplored, on her blouse. She felt her underthings clinging and clammy, uncomfortable on her damp skin.

Carrie placed her bags near a dresser, beside a scuffed chair. She sighed deeply and lay fully clothed on top of one of the two beds in the room. The bedspread was cheap and rough. She sighed in disgust, closed her eyes to keep from looking at the rust-colored water stains on the ceiling. After a little while, sighing deeply again, she sat up to undo the straps of her sandals. While she sat up, she removed her blouse, which she examined, frowned over, and tossed on the floor beside the bags. She unhooked her brassiere but did not remove it. She unbuttoned her trousers and pulled down the side zipper. She took several deep breaths, and then she bent forward. Doubled over, she pushed her hair over her head to allow the back of her neck to breathe.

The air conditioner was a wall unit stuck high into the wall as close to the ceiling as possible. A number of the plastic slats were missing from the filter cover. Carrie walked under it, stood on tiptoe to flip the on switch, but nothing happened. The thick power cord dangled beside the outlet. She cursed softly and stopped to plug it in. Instantly the air conditioner began to roar. In a few more seconds, it settled into its operating speed, alternately rattling and purring in a gentle roar.

She came back to the side of the bed, where she began to remove her trousers. When they were bunched at her ankles, she pulled off one leg and then the other, after which she kicked them toward the suitcases. She removed her brassiere and tossed it after the trousers. She pulled at the red bikini underpants to let some air in. The noise of the air conditioner became less annoyingly insistent, as if wearing itself out, settling into a soft, almost reassuring purr. Carrie Rasmussen closed her eyes and lay on the bed to rest a few minutes before her shower.

After she'd lain in bed for nearly fifteen minutes, the room still had not cooled. She tossed and turned, shifted her body belly up to belly down, without finding a position comfortable enough to keep still. The feeling of anxiousness would not subside. She convinced herself that she was tired from driving all day. There was more to it, but Carrie had resolved not to think about it. She needed a hot bath, a good solid hour of soaking in warm water.

She got up from the bed, walked to the dresser, where she'd placed her purse and cigarettes. She lit one and looked at herself in the dresser mirror. She stepped back to get a good look at herself. The image was too close, the perspective all wrong. She stepped back farther until she touched the foot of the bed. She cradled an elbow in her right hand, the cigarette inserted between two fingers, inches from her mouth. She felt the claustrophobia of the room drawing in on her.

Carrie Rasmussen had reached an ageless maturity in her mid-twenties which, aided by a carefully annotated carriage, would last her for at least another decade. Her shoulders were too wide, bony; her breasts were a mite too small, but still round, if softer perhaps than she would have liked. They had developed rapidly while she was a teenager and had remained unchanged ever since. The rest of her body, from her waist down, was well-rounded and firm. There was just a slight forward swell to her body which no amount of exercise had been able to flatten.

Carrie didn't want to watch herself. She turned, paced between the beds toward the wall, flicking on the bedlamp before retracing her steps. A brief, inadvertent glimpse into the mirror revealed her image with the light behind her. She appeared as a blur, the sharp outlines of her body effaced, ghostly, indistinct from the furniture in the room. Only the red bikini underpants stood out. Back at the dresser, she picked up the ashtray to carry with her and began to pace. After fifteen years, she'd started to smoke again. When she felt the heat of the cigarette ember on her fingers, she stubbed it out impatiently. She tossed the ashtray back on the dresser, purposely avoiding the image of herself in the mirror.

Carrie placed the suitcase on top of the chair and the makeup kit atop the dresser. The pack of cigarettes was empty. She wadded it up to toss in the wastebasket and remembered that she'd opened it the night before, right after dinner. She was smoking too much. She threw open the suitcase and took another pack from the carton that lay diagonally over the neatly folded clothes. She opened the fresh pack of cigarettes, withdrew one, but did not light it. Instead, leaving the cigarette dangling from her parted lips, she took out a change of clothing.

The air conditioner still had not dissolved the sultry oppressiveness of the room.

Carrie removed her underwear, wadding it up, feeling it warm and damp. She plucked from the suitcase a white plastic garbage bag in which she stored her dirty clothes. She dropped in her panties, picked up the remainder of her clothing from the floor. She debated whether she might stand to wear the trousers again, decided no, and stuffed them into the bag as well. The cigarette in her mouth was wet. She pulled it from her mouth, frowned, broke it in half, tossed it in the wastebasket. She picked up the pack of cigarettes, along with her lighter. She'd have a leisurely smoke in the tub.

As she headed for the bathroom, she stopped suddenly, turned, a flush of apprehension piercing through her body. It was the presence of the unseen man who came to her in dreams. She heard the whirr of the air conditioner behind her, saw the shabbiness of the room. She had felt someone in the room, she was sure of it. Carrie leaned against the door jamb, pressed the back of her head against the wood, closed her eyes. She waited. Her blood began to race, her heart beat faster, there was a tingle in her fingertips, goose bumps streaked along her arms and thighs. Just as suddenly as she felt it, the presence disappeared. Everything became still and quiet in the room, the palpable silence broken only by the sputtering whirr of the air conditioner. She wanted to draw the dream into her waking life.

Knowing it was not to be, Carrie placed a bag containing toilet articles, cigarettes and lighter on top of the toilet tank. She stooped over to open the hot water tap of the tub. While she waited, as was her habit before stepping into the bathtub, she first brushed her teeth, keeping her face close to the running water. The water was hot but not steaming, as she liked it. The mechanism to stop the tub from draining did not work. She compressed her lips to express her dissatisfaction, tried the shower, and was relieved when the water began to gush overhead.

Under the shower tap, she stood still, feet slightly apart, letting the jet of water pelt her back. She closed her eyes tightly until she no longer felt the pinpricks of the water. She saw herself standing before an ironing board wearing a pair of red bikini underpants. The image was sharp and clear before her. She felt her nipples become erect and she crossed her hands over her breasts. She drew her shoulders forward, dropped her chin against her chest. She squeezed her breasts until she felt pain. Nothing happened. Slowly, she lowered her hands, uncrossing them, drawing them apart, lowering them farther, then recrossing them one on top of the other, pressing in the soft flesh of her lower belly. She lowered them still farther, on the crest of her Mound of Venus, into the thick thatch of pubic hair. Nothing happened.

She finished her shower quickly, briskly toweled herself dry, wrapped herself in the damp towel, tucking it high up under her arms. When she came out of the bathroom, the air in the room had cooled considerably. Along with the change in temperature, she could smell the stronger stench of the stale air circulating. The initial nausea gave way to the feeling of claustrophobia.

She felt penned in, swept up by an overpowering urge to leave the room, to get out in the open. She took several deep breaths before she set the suitcase on the floor and sat in the chair facing the mirror on the dresser. The anxiety went away and she relaxed a little. She lit a cigarette. The ends of her wet hair, resting on her shoulders, felt cold and alien.

Carrie leaned closer to the mirror for a better look at her face. The reflection of her face revealed a line or two that she was certain had not been there when she left Boston. She was tired from the trip and from the strain of her disintegrating life. She consoled herself in the knowledge that she would get used to things eventually. Maybe then, she told herself, the lines will go away.

Thus reassured, she settled back in the chair. She leaned over to retrieve a hairbrush with a silver handle from the suitcase. She began to brush her wet hair. After each pass, she snapped it in the air to shake away the accumulated water. As if a sudden thought had occurred to her, she stopped and began to tap the handle of the silver hairbrush rhythmically on the Formica top of the dresser. She lowered her eyes, exhaled noisily, became pensive. She abruptly tossed the brush away. It fell with a jarring clatter. She drew deeply from her cigarette, held her breath, mashed the butt forcefully into the ashtray.

The muscles on either side of her mouth tightened into sharply defined dimples. She pulled on the ends of the towel and let it fall into a pile around her waist. She brushed the towel off her thighs. She stared directly into the mirror with a look that was defiant, unapologetic. She pressed her hands, fingers fanned out, flat against each breast. Pressing forcefully, she shoved her hands toward each other and then she separated her thumb and forefinger to allow her nipples to burst forth. She squeezed each nipple until it swelled, became purplish-black and hard. She inclined her head, puckered her lips, and blew soft, warm air to one and then the other.

She let go of her breasts abruptly and began to scratch the upper line of her damp pubic hair. Slowly she dragged the silver hairbrush along the dresser top and dropped it into her lap. The bristle side dug into her thighs. Carrie jammed the handle of it between her legs and squeezed her thighs tightly. She raised her leg, drew it over the other, and leaned back against the chair, her weight resting on one buttock.

Careful to avoid her reflection in the mirror, she got up to move to the bed. Before doing so, she took a pair of red bikini panties from the suitcase and hurriedly put them on. She stripped the bed of its covers and lay down in the center of it. The sheet underneath was stiff and warm, a pleasant contrast to the cool air now circulating in the room. She stretched out her arms perpendicular to her sides. Her hands, in one of which she held the hairbrush, overlapped the edge of the bed.

She touched the tip of the hairbrush handle to her right breast, gently, without pressure. She brought her left hand between her legs, applied a little pressure, and held it there. She closed her eyes lightly and began to imagine the Berkshire zephyrs delicately brushing over her body. The image was so vivid she could feel the two-by-fours of the sundeck under her bare feet. There was a warm glow on her shoulders from the sun. She was completely relaxed, feeling a persistent tingling between her thighs.

Carrie laid the silver hairbrush on her belly and began to brush the tips of her fingers over her breasts, tracing the contours, drawing geometric shapes. She closed her eyes tightly and before too long, fleetingly, she sensed the presence of the naked man in the darkness of the forest, moving on bare feet toward her. She could see his feet moving, his hands swinging at his side. She'd dreamt it so many times, she knew its rhythms and movements, and its turns. The beginning of it, its overtures of desire and longing, of anticipation and mounting sexual intensity—these she could duplicate.

It was never the same as the dream, though. However perfectly she could re-create the dream, her consciousness was superimposed over it, willing it to happen. She could linger for long moments of those sensations in the dream that brought her the most intense pleasure. Suddenly, much too soon, she would become conscious that she was manipulating herself, that she was not dreaming at all.

In the end, she could never re-create the dream or its effects. No amount of self-stimulation brought the feeling of completeness that she felt upon waking.

She pulled on her nipples, twirling them and then pressing down on them, as in her fantasy she sensed the man coming closer to the edge of the forest. She pressed her eyes down tightly, as if the effort itself would draw the naked man out of the dark and onto her waiting body. She put her knees together and sallied her hips on the bed. She had a sense, palpable and urgent, that the man was watching her, taking in each thing she did, but that he would not come forward, that he chose in fact to remain at the edge of the forest, in the dark, watching. The things she did to herself, under his watchful eye, she did for him. She sought his approval, imagined his arousal, stiff and angled up from his belly.

Her nerves, her energy, her entire existence began to concentrate in the region of her pubic hair. Beneath the thick and curly sprout, pressed in by her bikini underpants, she felt the loose flesh at the entrance to her vagina become wet, puffed, and throbbing. The imagined man became a vague idea, losing shape and vitality, fading. He became effaced, beyond her ability to draw his tactile presence to the moment she created. She grabbed the hairbrush and gently tapped her pelvic bone. A flush, as if released by the tapping, spread through her body, making her aware of how cold the room had become.

She let go of the hairbrush, leaving it on the flat of her lower belly, feeling the pressure of its weight. She strained with all her might, arched the small of her back, compressed her sphincter, lifted her hips, drew her lips tightly over her teeth. Carrie tensed suddenly, as if a jolt of electricity had passed through her body. She shot her legs forward, pointing her toes so they became parallel to the bed. A great wondrous tremor, erupting from the chasm of unfulfilled yearning, rumbled over the planes and contours of her body, rolling in wave after wave. Her entire body became covered in a film of perspiration.

Carrie felt herself levitate, suspended from the pull of the earth-bound life she led. Tense, taut, like a wire pulled between two points, there was the hum of atoms in chaos, pulling willy-nilly to restore their deviated orbits.

She rolled the red bikini underpants midway down her thighs, after which she grabbed the silver brush by the square bed of its bristles and applied the handle of it to her Mound of Venus. A long, low, groaning moan began deep in her chest. The sound of it came up as a whimper, catlike and tenuous, like a fire engine siren drawing near. She took the hairbrush in both of her hands, pressing the flat of it against the swelling she felt in her belly. She felt the bristles prick her palm as she slid the brush farther down. She turned it a little, aiming the handle forward and over her Mound of Venus. She slid the silver tip along the viscous parting of her body.

When she felt it coming, she hunched her shoulders together, threw her arms wide, gripped the sides of the bed. She popped suddenly. She expelled a series of gasps that carried abrupt, jerking moans along with them. These were followed by short, brief tremors that she was unable to control. She raised her legs a little, the brush pinioned by the taut muscles of her thighs.

She was able to summon forth the pleasurable sensations for several more minutes before they stopped altogether and she collapsed, exhausted, breathing heavily, enjoying the feel of clean perspiration over her body. Carrie curled up her legs, rolled over on her side, keeping her hands clasped between her legs. Her mouth was open, dry. Gradually her eyelids were too heavy to hold up. They were leadlike, turning the hazy sunlit room into complete darkness. In a few seconds, following a series of pained whimpers, she was soundly asleep.

Carrie awoke several hours later, cold and sore from having slept without shifting position. The air conditioner hummed steadily. The room felt like an icebox. She had slept uncovered. Her cheeks and her neck felt swollen, numb. She rolled her legs over the side of the bed, placing her elbows on her knees, holding her head in her hands. Carrie felt stiff and sluggish as she waited for her head to clear. She finally managed to get up on her feet and, in the movement of a sleepwalker, she raised up her underpants. She was able to walk, if a bit wobbly, to the bathroom, where she splashed water on her face. She brushed her teeth quickly. When she came out of the bathroom, the chill in the room felt good, especially against her damp face. She curled strands of wet hair over her ears.

She felt sapped and listless. Her face in the mirror was numb and deeply lined with sleep. Her eyes bulged in a pink film with a latticework of red veins. She wanted to sleep more, a lot more. The skin of her body felt clammy. She returned to the bed, covering herself snugly, curling up. She struggled against the sleep that was already settling in over her. She had not planned for this at all. She made one last effort to rise, but the movements were in her mind, as if she were at some distance, observing. In a matter of seconds, Carrie Rasmussen was sound asleep again. When she next awoke, it was dark outside. She dressed quickly and went out to eat.

Sand Jack's had a brightly lit neon sign that blinked on and off in front. From where she stood in the driveway to the motel, she could see a naked lightbulb stuck over the entrance. To the left side of the entrance, there was a dirt-encrusted picture window. About a half dozen vehicles, mostly pickup trucks, were parked in the gravel lot. There was no need for the car. She began to cross the road, finding the absence of any traffic disconcerting. She walked over cautiously, nevertheless feeling in her bones the premonition of a speeding truck bearing down on her, that it would come upon her so suddenly that she'd be unable to get out of the way in time.

The voices of Dwight Yoakum and Buck Owens on the jukebox, singing "The Streets of Bakersfield," met her as she opened the door. To her left was a small eating area, four tables, on which reposed napkin dispensers, salt and pepper shakers, plastic-covered menus, bottles of ketchup and hot sauce, ashtrays. Carrie selected one of the tables. She brought out her cigarettes and lighter, lit one, and placed the package, lighter over it, in front of the napkin dispenser.

On the other side of Sand Jack's were more tables where men in hats and cowboy clothes sat. There was a small U-shaped bar to separate the two areas. No one sat at the bar. At the far end of the room was the jukebox, blaring a hard rock and roll number by Hank Williams, Jr, "If You Don't Like Hank Williams, You Can Kiss Our Ass!" The men concentrated their attention on a game of pool.

She waited a long time before a waitress, who had been inside the kitchen area, came to her. The waitress carried a gallon can of ketchup under one arm and a funnel in her hand.

"Hello, dearie," said the waitress, "where did you come from?"

"Are you closing?" asked Carrie.

"Just about," the waitress said. "We were just putting up everything. If you're hungry, we won't turn you away. Can't make no money turning away hungry people, I always say. I'm sure the cook'll rustle up something for you."

Carrie bit her fingernail as she began to read the menu. Nothing seemed to quite stir her appetite. The elderly waitress recognized Carrie's reluctance to settle on anything and recommended a chopped sirloin steak because it was just about all they had left that was either fresh or out of the freezer. Carrie gave her assent, grateful that the choice was taken away from her. She asked for a beer while she waited. The waitress brought her beer right away. It was wrapped in sandwich paper. The waitress placed it alongside a small glass and slid the salt shaker beside them.

"I'll be right out with your salad," she said, and waddled away through the swinging door into the kitchen.

Carrie had no sooner finished the salad, coated with a vinegary Thousand Island dressing, than the waitress came out again, gliding gracefully for so large a woman, with a plate held over her head. The steak turned out to be an oversized, overcooked hamburger, drowned in a gravy that was thick and lumpy, streaked with blackened pan drippings and black flecks of pepper. It was capped with a mound of translucent, mushy onions. Next to it was a pile of thick french-fried potatoes, broad and bulky like railroad ties. Carrie pushed aside as much of the gravy as was possible and all of the onions. The coating of gravy remaining on the meat was more like a salty film. On a green plastic basket were four diagonally sliced pieces of Texas toast. She liked the Texas toast, as she had never seen a slice of bread quite so thick.

The salty, pungent taste of the sirloin was attenuated by the odd aftertaste of the beer. She found that if she followed each bite with a sip of beer, the food went down without making her gag. Still, Carrie was hungry, which made things easier. She ate and drank quickly, since there was no one to talk to. She felt rushed, wanting to hurry, even though she had decided not to push on after all. She would wait until morning to get going.

The waitress came back, toweling her arms dry. Strands of hair had escaped their pinning and were plastered on her forehead. She was short of breath.

"Did you want another beer, honey?" she asked.

Carrie said, "Yes, please," on impulse.

The Mexican wore jeans and a black T-shirt under his denim jacket. The black gimme cap on his head carried a Jack Daniel's advertisement. His pectoral muscles were pronounced, effeminate, under the T-shirt. Upon entering Sand Jack's, he walked immediately to the right, past the empty bar, where he made the rounds, shaking hands, stopping briefly to converse with each man present. When he had finished, he took a stool at the bar, spreading out his arms over it. He kibitzed good-naturedly with the pool players, who were in no mood to talk to anyone. He walked over to the eating area, where he took a table next to Carrie.

He appeared to be thirty, although given his Indian features, he might have been five years younger or older. His lips were full and fleshy. As he sat down, an incipient beer belly insinuated itself over his lap. The waitress had seen him enter and without his having to order, brought him a plate similar to the one she had brought to Carrie.

"You want a beer with that?" the waitress asked.

"Does a bear shit on a sand dune?" he said, already beginning to pour salt and ketchup on the french fries.

"There ain't any bears around here, and you know it," said the waitress.

He caught Carrie observing him and tipped the gimme cap to her. He grinned and winked, as if to say he was kidding with the waitress. Carrie turned her head away quickly, embarrassed to have been caught staring. She poured the last of the beer bottle in the glass.

"Could you stand to have another beer, if I bought you one?" the Mexican asked Carrie Rasmussen.

Carrie assented, surprised at herself for doing so. The waitress frowned when the Mexican sent her back for another beer. He leaned over.

"Listen, I hate to eat by myself. What say, I join you. Or, you join me." He smiled with large, square teeth, saluting her with the beer bottle before upending it over his open mouth. He did not touch his lips to the bottle as he poured straight into his gullet.

"Why don't I join you," said Carrie. "I'm already finished and you've just begun to eat."

"That's real nice of you. Come on over," he said, pulling out a chair for her.

The Mexican swallowed the morsel he chewed, wiped his hands with a paper napkin, told her his nane, and stretched out his hand across the table. Carrie reached out her hand and told him her name.

"Passing through?" he said, pleasantly, cutting the entire sirloin in neat little squares.

"I stopped for some rest this afternoon. I had planned to be on the road after a couple of hours, but I guess I overslept," said Carrie.

The waitress brought Carrie's beer.

"Put that on my bill," said the Mexican.

"Thanks," said Carrie.

"You must be at the motel, 'cross the way," he said.

"Yes, I am," said Carrie, a little uncomfortable.

He speared a square of meat and a tangle of onions into his mouth. A gobbet of gravy dripped onto his chin. He wiped it away before beginning to chew. He look at her intently.

"Reason I mention it, your car's not parked out front," he said.

"I see," she said.

"Truck drivers, truck drivers'll think they can make the stretch between Houston and El Paso, one haul. Takes a lot of amphetamines to do it. They end up here, sack out for the night, sometimes. Interstate's the best thing ever happened to this town. Brought it back to life, I would say."

"What do people do here?" Carrie asked.

"A little of everything. You name it, somebody does it. Ranching. Roughnecking. There's a couple that has a winery. Out there in the desert. How 'bout that? A vineyard out where even the lizards can't make a living."

"I wouldn't expect it. Is it true?" said Carrie.

"Why would I lie?" said the Mexican, and he winked at her, grinning broadly.

Carrie drank her beer, nodded a few times as he made conversation, asked her questions. Otherwise, she kept her part of the conversation to a minimum.

All of a sudden, the thoughts that flashed across her mind caused a nausea to overtake her. The reason she'd accepted his invitation became clear to her. The Mexican took it calmly when she gathered her check and picked up her purse.

"I should be going," she said, having a difficult time geting her things together.

"I have a jug of whiskey in my truck," he said, raising an eyebrow to ask the question. His meaning unmistakable, his smile inviting.

"You're married," she said, unsure of herself, softening, indicating the wedding band on his finger.

"So are you," he said, aiming a shake of his head at her ring finger. "That makes us even, doesn't it?"

She had aroused an interest in the Mexican, an interest which was flattering and which went against everything she had known in her life. In the life she left behind her in Boston, men made passes which they knew, expected, would be rebuffed. The Mexican's offer was not flirtation. It was a proposition, clear and simple, and he waited for her answer.

She was in the middle of the desert, among people she would not see again. She liked the anonymity of the moment, the fact that she did not know this man, the fact that she could ask him to stay afterward, or that she could ask him to go away. It was all up to her.

The decision she made was swift, out of character, irrevocable.

"I'm in room nine," she said, feeling flushed, her adrenaline flowing. "Give me a few minutes."

"You bet," he said, upending the beer bottle, flashing a smile.

The Mexican pushed his unfinished plate of food away and ordered another beer. No one on the other side of Sand Jack's had paid any attention to them. Carrie paid her check and walked out quickly.

At the motel, Carrie undressed quickly, leaving on the pair of red bikini underpants. There was no time for a shower. Instead, she dusted herself liberally with scented powder, rubbing away its white splotches into her pubic hair. She stood in front of the dresser mirror, lit a cigarette, inhaled deeply. She had left the door ajar, decided it wasn't safe, and turned the dead bolt. She waited with her back pressed against it.

The Mexican knocked softly on the door. She could feel the vibrations of his knock on her back. She reached behind to twist the dead bolt. The door creaked discreetly when the Mexican pushed it aside. She had walked to the dresser to extinguish the second cigarette.

The Mexican walked in, saw Carrie, her back to him, wearing only her red bikini underpants. He carried a full pint of whiskey. He closed the door behind him and removed his denim jacket, dropping it on the floor. As he walked up to her, he drew the shirttail out of his trousers.

The Mexican drew up close to Carrie. Without preamble, he began to kiss the slope of her neck. His breath reeked of the whiskey. Carrie felt his taut chest through the T-shirt pressed snugly against her back. The rough material of his jeans brushed against the back of her thighs.

"All of it," said Carrie, a tremor in her voice.

"What!" said the Mexican.

"Take off all your clothes," said Carrie. "Hurry!"

The Mexican placed the whiskey bottle on the dresser. He began to remove his clothes, as she had ordered. The cigarette she had extinguished flared up again in the ashtray. She mashed it again and picked up the bottle. She drank deeply, feeling the burn of it as it streaked down inside her body, leaving a warm glow in its wake. She dropped her arms to her side.

She heard the Mexican behind her, pulling and jerking on his boots, then on his tight trousers. He came up behind her, bringing both hands round to the swell of her belly. His heaving chest pressed smooth and firm, tight against her shoulder blades. He began a gentle, rocking motion, pivoting on the balls of his feet. His hard penis mashed across her buttocks, his lubricating fluids sopping into the thin material of her panties, becoming a moist spot the size of a quarter. After fondling her liquid breasts for a moment, he put his hands on her shoulders and tried to turn her to face him.

"No, don't," she said. "Don't look at me."

"What the hell is this?" he asked, irritated.

"Please," she moaned, "do as I ask."

She took one of his hands and brought it to the waistband of her red bikini underpants. He began to roll them downward, using the flat of his hands, until they took a ropelike shape. He bent down to pull them over her knees, but she stopped him.

"Leave them like that," she said, touching his shoulder.

She spread her legs as far as she could, stretching taut the red material. Then, she bent over.

"Do you want it in the ass?" asked the Mexican, misunderstanding her intent. "Is that the way you want it? Up the ass, hunh?"

He took his erect peter and began to make poking, humping motions with it into her anus. He reached down between her legs and ran two fingertips along the crevice of her wet pussy. Carrie shuddered at his touch. The Mexican moved away a little, and began to moisten the puckered button with her own juices. He guided the tip of his dick against her ass and pressed in.

"No, don't," said Carrie in a wounded voice.

"You want it this way, don't you?" said the Mexican, soothingly, cooing, as if trying to coax her into it. "Isn't this the way you want it?"

Carrie twisted sideways to reach around and guide him to the aperture below. Once their bodies were in accord, she placed her hands on her knees and waited as he penetrated the lubricated folds of her flesh and began the slow, on-again, off-again, measured insertion. He remained immobile, his hands on her hips, rocking her to and fro.

When he had impaled her to the hilt, he began to withdraw, slowly, stopping every second or so, until he came perilously close to slipping out of her entirely. He draped himself over her back, his cheek resting on her spine, as he inched back in, gently, slowly. He repeated the rocking movement several times. Carrie's thigh muscles became taut, coiling. The Mexican kept up a steady, rhythmic push-me, pull-you; his hands came up from underneath to massage her swaying breasts.

He increased the pace of his thrusts, spreading wide her buttocks to probe deeper, wanting to touch a part of her that seemed beyond reach. He raised himself from her back, pushing her away with the heel of his hands, drawing back with the tips of his fingers hooked over her hips. The Mexican threw his legs apart and pushed up on the balls of his feet. He glanced between their bodies and he placed his hand flat over her tailbone, his thumb going into the cleft between her buttocks, digging inside her anus.

He began a series of jerking grunts, inhaling noisily through his pursed lips. His strokes became shorter, hardly an inch in length, coming in swift, pistonlike thrusts. His ramming into her pounded the bones of her butt against his thighs. He shifted the position of his feet on the floor to keep from getting a cramp.

The Mexican groaned long and painfully, and drew her buttocks to him for one last time and he held them against him. She felt the shudders of his orgasm and reached between them to take his balls in her hand. When she touched him, a second orgasmic spasm went through his body and he jerked himself into her some more.

Carrie felt the final involuntary throbbing of his penis inside her body. He was finished. He continued to hold on to her tightly, relaxing a little at a time until his penis shriveled and the force of gravity yanked it out of her. She remained bent over, her hands on her knees, until she felt the chill of his ejaculate rolling out of her and down her thigh.

* * *

Carrie took a step away from the Mexican and drew up the red bikini underpants. He leaned against the dresser, head thrown back, catching his breath. There were beads of perspiration mingled with the hair on his chest. He reached out a hand to her, grinning.

"That was something," he gasped, looking into her eyes for confirmation.

"Get dressed," Carrie snapped.

"This isn't all there is, you know," said the Mexican, shaking his limp dick. "Let's get in bed. This little fucker will be ready to go again in no time."

"I said, get dressed and get out," said Carrie, firmly.

She went into the bathroom, taking her cigarettes, closing the door behind her. She pulled her underpants down around her ankles and sat on the toilet. Her vagina was tender, smeared with her and the Mexican's emissions. She wiped herself carefully, urinated, lit a cigarette. She remained seated on the toilet, elbows on her knees, while she smoked an entire cigarette. Afterward, she kicked away the panties, got into the shower under water as hot as she could stand.

The Mexican was not sure she really wanted him to leave. His vanity told him she couldn't possibly mean it. She'd feel differently once she came out of the bathroom. They had hardly spoken to each other. When he heard the groan of the shower running, he shrugged, gathered up his whiskey and left. He wasn't sure that what he had was a story he would want to tell.

Carrie spent a good twenty minutes in the shower, scrubbing away unsuccessfully at her indiscretion. She felt she had violated a personal code, a standard of decency, which had governed her entire adult life. She had second thoughts about having fucked the man. It was what she had wanted to do, no doubt there, but nevertheless it was a stupid and dangerous thing to do.

She opened the bathroom door an inch or two, apprehensive that he still might be in the room. She breathed a sigh of relief when she saw that the Mexican was gone. The red bikini underpants were on the yellowed floor tiles. She picked them up to stuff them in the plastic bag.

She came out of the bathroom, hair wrapped in a towel. She checked the door and flipped the dead bolt on it. She slipped into the teddy she used to sleep in. She had intended to brush her hair but she felt tired, slightly hung over from the three beers, unable to comply with habits from what seemed to be a long time ago.

Carrie turned off all the lights and threw herself on the bed, lying there in the dark, her eyes open.

It had not turned out the way she had expected it would. The Mexican had played his part, perhaps a little too well. He had been sure of movement, swift to complete his pleasure. She was angered by the single-minded method of his fucking. Of course, it wasn't his fault. The terms of the encounter, had they expressed them, made each responsible for the taking of what there was to take.

What she had expected, what she wanted, not the Mexican, and not any other man, could provide. Carrie recalled every movement and sensation of the encounter. His lips on her shoulders, the hair of his chest against her back. None of these bore any resemblance to the dream. His penis, thick and bulky, did not have the clean, cool feel of the male presence in her dreams. The ridiculous, grotesque pounding he'd given her, lost in his own private sport, had little to compare with the even, smooth entry that she wanted. She had not even had an orgasm. She touched herself, and as quickly as she did, she stopped. There was little point to it, she told herself, and gradually drifted into a troubled sleep.

At one o'clock in the afternoon, Carrie awoke, groggy and stiff from too much sleep. She was cross with herself because of the time. As she prepared for the day's travel, the Mexican was already becoming a remnant of a past which she did not think she would ever want to resurrect. The sooner she left, the better.

She finished with her makeup, selected a light spaghetti-strap summer dress with a built-in bra for the drive. Thin-strapped sandals completed the outfit. She surveyed the room to make sure she left nothing behind. As she stepped out into the heat of the day, the sun was white-hot, glaring. She put on her dark glasses.

Carrie drove the car to the front desk, leaving the engine and the air conditioner running. She was checked out of the motel by a red-faced man who bore a puffed resemblance to the girl who had checked her in. The man with the drunkard's florid face smiled timidly and told her he appreciated her business.

Carrie drove to the gas station next to Sand Jack's. In fading blue lettering against the whitewash, it advertised groceries, beer, and hunting gear. She stopped beside a pair of rusting pumps. As she stepped down from the car a dust devil came up suddenly and flared her skirt.

She asked the lone attendant inside to fill up the car. While he went outside, she selected some cheese, a plastic tube of braunschweiger, and a box of Ritz crackers. Not much of a breakfast, she told herself. Carrie took a cheap cooler from a white pyramid in the center of the store. She put it on the counter, went back to the coolers for a six-pack of beer, which she dropped in the cooler. The attendant returned and began to total the items on the counter. She asked him to spread a bag of ice over the beer.

She left the town behind her in a matter of seconds. The desert spread itself out before the hood of the car, coming steadily closer, yet remaining just beyond reach as if it were teasing her. The car had an automatic cruise control mechanism, which Carrie set for fifty-five miles an hour. The car briefly lurched forward before it settled on the designated speed. She bent her right leg under her left, and leaned back to relax in the plush velvet seat.

The car cruised steadily, heaving occasionally to cleave to the rolling grade of the road. She ate a little of the food, which she washed down with one of the beers. She became fuflly awake, bright-eyed and alert.

She had driven for a good fifty miles before she tried the radio. Among the hiss and crackling, she tuned in one country-western station after another, a few hard rock and roll. Disgusted, she shut it off.

At three-thirty in the afternoon, she went past another town that appeared as if out of nowhere in the desert. On the outskirts, she noted the arched entrance to a development of tract homes, Land o' Lotus. It was a momentary respite in the bleakness of the desert, and no sooner did it appear than the terrain became flat and monotonous again.

The road was a newly constructed, stark, black ribbon. A gleaming yellow, broken stripe went along the middle and parallel white lines bordered both edges. The road shot straight ahead until its pinpoint disappeared far into the horizon.

As far off as Carrie Rasmussen could see, there was not another vehicle in sight. She steered the car with a long, manicured finger on the wheel, concentrating on staying in her lane as a way to prevent road hypnosis. The beer had given her a slight, sudden headache.

Then, the left rear tire blew.

At first she thought it might be a shift in the grade of the road that made the car swerve abruptly. It became more difficult to steer, forcing her to grip the wheel as it became stiff and unforgiving. She realized it couldn't be the road, as it was smoothly paved and even. She tapped the brake pedal to release the cruise control and allowed the car to show on its own. The rumble beneath the car, as if someone were spanking it, confirmed her suspicions.

The car began to slow rapidly, and as it did so, it started to swerve more stubbornly, whipsawing. Carrie Rasmussen used all of her strength to keep a grip on the steering wheel. She managed to keep the car under control.

She waited until the car slowed considerably, moving along with a noisy thumping. When she felt it was safe, she pulled over onto the glistening white gravel shoulder. Her body shook as the car rolled to a stop. She opened the driver's door and was struck by a thick gust of hot desert wind. The sun reflected by the white gravel made her squint. As she stepped out of the car, another gust of wind ballooned the skirt of her dress over her thighs. She had but to glance to the left rear tire to confirm that it was flat.

Her mouth felt dry and uncomfortable.

"Fuck!" she said, aloud, angrily.

She looked back at the road she had traveled and saw not a vehicle moving. Neither was any vehicle coming from the direction in which she was going. Carrie scanned the horizon east and west in an involuntary plea for help. She gathered up her wits, reminded herself that there couldn't be much to changing a tire, even though she'd never changed one before.

She went back to the front seat of the car, sat down sideways, kept the door open, her feet on the ground. The engine idled and she noticed the noisy rush of conditioned air roaring out of the vents. She kept her feet on the ground. She reached behind her for the cigarettes on the adjacent seat. Carrie felt no great urgency to change the tire. She refused to be pressured by this small crisis.

She did feel the urge for another beer. Prudence told her to change the tire first. However, to change the tire, she would have to change clothes first. Her resolve to wait before having the beer lasted for only a few minutes. She'd drink the beer, and, maybe, while she drank it, someone might come along. She reached into the ice chest for a can of beer and popped it open.

She took a sip of the beer and looked across the road to a small ravine beyond which sand dunes began, white and plump like goose bumps on the landscape. She remembered Chubby

Johnson, the archetypal prospector of the movies, leading his mule over grass-speckled sand dunes. I wonder what that noise is, he would say, scratching his scraggly beard. While the audience shouted at the screen, Don't go there, fool! Chubby Johnson would go behind a sand dune. A flying saucer would rise out of a cloud of dust, leaving in its wake the ashen outlines of Chubby Johnson and his faithful mule. Or, maybe he had his flesh sucked right off his bones by a giant tarantula, she couldn't remember exactly.

Carrie smiled thinly and took a long draught of the beer.

A little more of the beer to go before the can was empty. There was no telling when someone might come along, and if they did, they probably wouldn't stop. She was going to change the tire herself—there didn't seem to be an alternative. There was a pair of jeans and an old T-shirt in the suitcase. She finished the beer and tossed the empty can over the roof of the car into the sand and weeds. She made a plan. Change clothes, have another beer, change the tire, have another beer, hit the road.

She went around to the other side of the car and got into the backseat from the passenger side. She opened the suitcase beside her. The jeans were rolled into a tube right on top. Carrie unzipped the dress in back and raised up to slide the skirt of it over her hips. As she did so, she banged her knuckles on the car's roof as she brought the dress over her head.

"Goddamn it!" she said. After a pause, during which she sucked on her knuckle, she repeated, "Goddamn it, goddamn it, goddamn it!"

She dropped the dress on the floorboard and unrolled the jeans. Getting into them in the backseat was troublesome at first and finally impossible. She looked through the tinted windows again in both directions for traffic. Seeing none, Carrie got out of the car. She wore only her red bikini underpants and the sandals.

She folded the dress carefully, packed it neatly in the suitcase. The few minutes in the sun caused her to perspire profusely. She wiped her brow. The scorching sun burned her bare skin. One of her bare breasts touched the metal of the door frame, searing it, and she cursed. Hurriedly, she stepped into her jeans and as quickly she put on the T-shirt.

Dressed for the job, her confidence was renewed, she felt more in control of things. She took another beer, popped open the top. She leaned back in the seat to cool. When she'd finished the beer and tossed the empty away, Carrie went around to the rear of the car. She could not open the trunk without the keys, which were in the ignition as the car idled.

She retrieved the keys, and opened the trunk to a momentary panic: She did not see a spare tire. She figured it must be under the imitation carpeting of the trunk. This she peeled to one side to reveal a crisp new tire. She bent over, pressed both of her hands to the tire, expecting it to be firm and plump. Carrie Rasmussen simply sighed in resignation when she discovered that the spare was flat, too.

Her arms felt damp and clammy. Her forehead was thoroughly wet. A bead of perspiration trickled down her cheek and dropped into a crease in her neck. A gust of warm desert air blew a strand of her hair, matting it to her dampened face. With miles and miles of Texas desert all around her, she slammed shut the trunk lid.

She came around to the driver's side of the car and got in. She started the engine and turned on the air conditioner full blast. What the hell, she thought, the gas tank needle still indicated close to a half tank. In a few mintues, the temperature inside the car became comfortable. She lowered the window an inch to keep the gas fumes from being trapped inside the car. She opened another beer.

"Shit!" said Carrie Rasmussen. She finished the beer, tossing the empty can among some dry twigs that sprouted out of the sand.

She opened another beer, held it high up, tipped it in salute to an imaginary self just beyond the windshield. The imaginary figure sat, naked except for a pair of red bikini underpants, on the hot metal of the car's hood. She leaned against the car seat, flipping on the emergency blinkers, just in case someone drove by and might not otherwise notice she had a flat tire.

The trailer rig zooming by made Carrie jump up in the seat. The driver had seen her upending the beer can and had pulled the cord of the truck's horn, leaving a trailing sound that reminded her of the foghorns in Boston harbor. He had not stopped or even slowed. Carrie quickly opened the door and leaning out of the car, she waved to the driver. Again, she heard the horn. She kept watching the rig as it became a speck on the horizon and disappeared.

The rush of alcohol made her feel flushed and hot. A bloated feeling pushed against her bladder. Of course, she thought, that had to be next. Carrie walked around the hood of the car, opened the passenger door to shield her from an unlikely coming car. Facing the road she had traveled, she lowered her clothing to urinate. When she finished, she kicked dry sand over it. Back in the car, she opened another beer, brought her face to the air conditioner vent and let the stiff, cold air rush over her.

Carrie Rasmussen, drowsy from an alcoholic haze, insulated from outside sounds, did not notice the pickup truck that pulled up in back of the car. She had slumped deep into the seat. The radio was on and she was tapping her fingers on the steering wheel in time to the music, her eyes closed. The man's knuckles rapping on the window startled her. She turned her head, her eyes opened wide.

"Got trouble?" he asked, the sound of his voice muffled. It was a soft, friendly voice, accompanied by a deferential smile.

"Where did you come from?" Carrie said.

"I saw your lights flashing, ma'am. You have a tire looks flat. Can I help?" he said.

Carrie took her time before she gave her answer. She drew farther into the car, gazing into the man's face.

"Yes, please. Thank you," said Carrie, after a long interval.

Out of a corner of her eye, Carrie saw the man grab the door handle. Frightened, she threw her hand on the padded window ledge, inches away from the lock latch.

"I need your keys, ma'am," said the man.

"My keys? Why?" asked Carrie, apprehensively.

"Get in the trunk. I have to get in the trunk. Spare tire. There's a spare tire in there," he said.

"No, there isn't," said Carrie. "I mean, it's there, but it's flat, too."

"Are you sure? Have you checked?" he said, finding it hard to believe.

"Yes, I checked already."

"Well, do you want me to drive you somewhere to get it fixed?"

"No! I mean, I don't know."

"All right, I understand, ma'am. I'm going up ahead and I'll tell them to come out and give you a hand. Should be a truck from Orange's Garage. Look for an orange truck. I'll tell them you need a tire. I'm just going to check on what size and I'll be on my way."

The man went around to the rear of the car and Carrie Rasmussen began to tremble with fear. The rear door was unlocked. She turned to watch him. All she saw was the man's head going out of sight as he bent down.

He stood up and began to walk toward the pickup. It was a brand-new truck, black with thick red stripes, trimmed in lots of shiny chrome.

She heard the truck's engine kick over and shortly the truck eased up alongside the car. The window on the passenger side went down. He spoke to her without leaning over.

"You sure? You sure you don't want to come into town? Be no trouble. It might be better if you did, ma'am. Could be a while before anyone can come out to fix the tire." His voice was reassuring.

Carrie Rasmussen held up her left hand, palm out to indicate she wanted him to wait. She leaned over to gather up her purse and car keys. She took the remaining pair of beer cans, still yoked in their plastic collars, and brought them with her.

Inside the man's truck it was icy cold. She offered him one of the beers.

"I don't drink, ma'am," he said, throwing the truck in gear and moving off onto the highway.

"I'm sorry about what happened back there," Carrie said, trying to find something appropriate to say. Instead, she sipped the beer.

"That's all right. You were afraid, I guess. Lady lost in the middle of the road. I understand how you feel," he said, his eyes fixed on the road.

"I don't know what came over me," said Carrie. "I appreciate your help very much."

"It never hurts to be careful, ma'am. I always tell my own wife to be very careful every time she goes out. She never goes anywhere but just in town, you understand. Still, you can't be too careful, no matter where it is. You know?"

"I guess I should feel pretty silly."

"No, ma'am. You won't have anything to be afraid of, not anymore," the man said.

*   *   *

When he turned off the black ribbon of highway into a pair of ruts of an old mining road, Carrie Rasmussen turned her head suddenly.

"Where are you going?" asked Carrie, a streak of panic shooting through her. Her nipples pierced through the T-shirt.

"I thought we might stop, before going on into town."

He was polite, his voice soothing.

"What for? What is this? What are you doing?"

"You just behave yourself, that's all."

The man drove over a steep sand dune, with a long flat crest. About two hundred yards farther he stopped the truck in the middle of a wide dry creek bed. He leaned across Carrie to open the glove compartment. The back of his head was inches from her face. She could smell a rancid hair tonic on his hair.

He took out a large hunting knife encased in a scabbard blackened from age and use. Holding it up, close to the windshield, the man unsheathed the knife. The sun glinted off its surface, striking Carrie in the face.

"Get out. I want you to take your clothes off," the man said, still polite, his voice quiet and unhurried.

Carrie Rasmussen began to tremble. She whimpered in tiny liittle squeals. Her lower lip vibrated. She tried several times to open the door until the man became irritated and impatient and yanked it open for her. Carrie stepped down, her foot sinking into the soft hot sand. She closed the door gently.

"Hurry up! Goddamn it!" the man shrieked, beginning to lose control.

She took a few steps toward the front of the trunk. Quickly, she pulled the T-shirt over her head. She turned to face him, holding the garment to shield her breasts. Her eyes were full of tears, her hands trembling against her chin.

The man averted her head, trying not to look at her.

Carrie let go of the T-shirt and began to unbutton the jeans. She wiggled out of them, slowly, tossing them aside into the desert sand. Arms at her side, she stood before him in her red bikini underpants.

All of a sudden, Carrie was no longer afraid. A peacefulness and serenity came over her.

"The rest of it," the man said, his voice hoarse and thick.

Carrie hooked her thumbs on the waistband of the red bikini underpants. She began to turn slowly, giving him her back. Her chest flushed with goose bumps. She felt the presence of something, someone, behind her, moving toward her. She slid the panties over her round buttocks, down her thighs, and stopped at the knees. The figure, someone, something, came closer. She could feel the nearness of its presence. She spread her feet as wide apart as the straining material of the red bikini underpants permitted. She bent over and placed her hands on her knees.

Anytime now. She waited for the feel of cold steel penetrating her body.

Aldebarán

Lilia Barbachano

in memory of Howard Phillips Lovecraft

Losing himself via Alexandria
nimble as a jellyfish
already free from the tethers
of my chained shadow.

Aldebarán releases himself
in a transparent dragonfly
and penetrates the warm and
deepening noon of the orchard.

His presence invades my mind
like a dream behind a dream
a green mirror of chrysalises
boundary between seacoasts.

I feel his ivory tongue
restless forest of mahogany and salt
when he licks he conceals my lips
never really knowing me.

On the edges of thought
I try to seal him in fire
reducing him to white hellebores
breaking him with gentle breaths.

Duel

Marina Fe

All the vague blackness of your swamp
could not swallow me.
Now I have become heavier than water
lighter than your clinging mud.

Though I attempt to drown myself,
if I wanted,
I could not penetrate you,
failing to surround me completely
with your lily breath,
your arms of sand,
not smothering myself in you,
because you begin to dry with time.

Red

Sabina Berman

Yesterday, when desire
released us in passion,
I scratched your shoulder,
and then, under the quivering tree
of your sobs,
I kissed your wound

How will you explain the mark
to your other lovers?

Until our next meeting
your longing for me
will be tinged with hatred

Journal of a Moving Teardrop

Bernardo Galvan

delivered in a cycle of love and the seduction that encompasses
the vibration deposited, lost, regained when the hand opened and
grabbed the limb.

unknown to the galaxy that penetrated the navel of the firstborn
as if it was war to declare homage to the slippery enjoyment, the
kiss fondling the world so it can get off the spine and pretend
there are masks made of flesh, sorrow, the running water escaping
when she took the garden hose and pressed it between her legs,
the surge of power lifting her toward the gate where no one
watched except this mask of flesh.

to a son with no name who will destroy his shame and love with
all honesty and attention, the close manner of wrapping his legs
around the sweating lover as she humbles him, loves him, follows
him home so they can be aware of how many doors they left behind, their final clutchings and pulling of hair, a moment when
nothing was clearly spelled.

basking in the frame upon a tiny object deployed to record the
sins of laughter and doubt before they can cover the scent, the
smell, the slapping of thigh upon thigh inside the thumb, placed
there when they bit their lips and kept moving up and down, in
and out, not knowing there was a sign on the wall, an image on
the screen, a sorrow that gave them more time to love one another without doubt or the extra shove.

furnished with opinion against the cough, wheeze, and illness of
the history of touch.

to ask how the picture was invented to capture one moment inside itself without giving the sleek legs a chance to throw away
the secret of peeling the green transparent hosiery off, the bending
over and flash of dark hair glistening before the man can return
himself to his pants, before he can close his eyes and weep for

the last time he was able to fuck her without giving his life to
the self-imposed will of desire.

memory of how we gain and lose the humid form of what we escaped from without bending over and gently inserting the huge
rubber dildo toward the sunrise.

broken toe swollen to warn the cycles of faith there is going to
be a ride into the grasses that grow north but face south as if the
tear will fall and cover the story of conquest, the escape from the
old friend who told him she took on three guys when she was in
high school, wanting to know what it was like to surrender to
the strength of a meanness so deep, she cried and cried after they
left, but she touched herself down there and told herself it was
going to be okay, it was supposed to teach her how to live in the
world with her ignorance, shame, and the manner of taking over
each and every day set before her.

to keep distance from the sun that lavished rain when it couldn't
see how long it would take for the onion to reveal itself as the object she sat on and swallowed with her cunt like the crystal lights
exposing her painted nipples upon the stage of confusion, the men
collecting bets about which object would fall out first when the
music started.

without a need to keep his cock inside her long after he comes,
her body pinned to the edge of the bed, her ass up in the air, her
legs folded beneath her, the power she will possess to destroy
him building inside her as he rocks himself, sideways slowly,
rocks and pretends he never has to pull out.

without the sweat of the time to envision there could be stairs,
windows, and frames housing the dragon that revolted there, cut
the clouds into charts of moving bodies, humans it took into its
cave to teach them how to cry.

as an oath to the ugliness of the lips, the faithfulness of the
wind, the escape from one book to another where the Japanese
man puts it into his mistress sideways, the two of them hanging onto the headboard as the water lilies rise and fall around
their bed, his enormous cock entering her like the falling trees

of the forest where they were born to copulate, cry, fornicate, cry, switch positions, cry, wipe away the tears, cry, run out of ideas, cry, button themselves, cry, unbutton their tunics, cry, pound their fists on the water lilies as he suddenly rips his timber out of her and sprays the pool with everything he has owned.

without wanting to define what dragon means, which dragon moves, which dragon can change from the expected word of dragon to the unexpected word of *amor, pelado, cochar, chingar*—as if the unexpected foreign language would dry the tears on his face, set him gently back on the bed as the woman in the bright yellow spiked heels enters the room, her bright yellow bikini the only other thing he is blinded by as she moves to the bed, her long black hair falling between her small breasts, the look on her face telling him he is going to breathe the wrong fire from the dragon he has carried on his back.

he entered the place called "the cave" and was shocked that all the *putas* sitting at the bar wore black eyeliner, painted all their fingernails black, and wore black lipstick. It was the scariest adventure of his young life and he couldn't believe it when those black lips gripped his young cock and wouldn't let go. afterwards, he looked in his wallet to see how much money he had left. his two friends had abandoned him, scared by the sight of the ugliest, most menacing *putas* they had ever seen.

toward a more menacing truth that inspires its flames to settle into the core of the earth without wanting to be a part of any superstition or any desire to have her carefully place the tip of the spiked heel against her clit, have her push it gently in, until he sees the tear on her face and knows he has done nothing wrong because she controls everything.

wet phallus rubbing against her cheek, trying to soften but springing hard to the trace of her fingernail over the smooth head she acknowledges with the tip of her tongue, gleaming long phallus rolling across her cheeks like a fresh roll of bread, the dough slowly seeping at the tiniest point, sparkling as she suddenly swallows the whole thing and he jumps, wishing he had been able to tell her the whole story of the crying saint that came down off the altar to punish him for being so alone, for having to be here to let her devour the final memory of where he came from.

as if movement was the most important thing he possessed when he loved so many women that respected him, believed him for a short time before understanding why he had joined them. once, he looked at himself in the bathroom mirror, the scratches on his chest still red and uneasy, and he thought he saw a strange woman standing behind him. of course, there was no one there. he was alone in his apartment. he barely turned sideways and the vision disappeared. he looked at himself again, thought about shaving when the woman appeared behind him again. this time, he thought he felt a sharp finger jab him up the ass. he quickly turned, but there was no one there. he looked down at his hard-on. what was he doing? his lover had left hours ago. he went to the edge of the bathtub, closed his eyes, thought about the time the two of them went to see the infamous "donkey" show in Tijuana, and jerked off quickly. he sprayed the shower wall, grunted his eyes open, then climbed in to stand in a very hot shower that almost scalded him. when he came out, the steam on the mirror looked like the woman he thought he saw standing behind him, at least the outline of her face. he leaned over the sink and traced her profile with his finger. the outline vanished slowly as he dried himself. he got dressed and walked out into the bedroom which was clean, the bed made, not one trace of steam shadowing the objects around the room.

any sign that the lies hidden from the son were actually the means of survival, the acts of a father removing his mask so the tears would not touch its precious black satin, its years of wear and tear in the room of whips more important than the crying son.

the whole story came when he first crossed into Tijuana one night, entered the dirty bar to find dozens of whores waiting in torn booths, staring at him with their black eyes, until he found one, gave her five dollars and fucked her right there in a dark booth at the back of the bar, her heavy ass sitting down on him as she rode him facing away from his cold look.

*   *   *

for the way he was able to hold her, let her cover his cock with the plaster when she claimed she had learned it from a rock and roll groupie who collected plaster casts of famous rock stars—sole reminders of what she had done decades ago. he let her cover him with the messy stuff which took a couple of hours to dry. by then, he was tired and feeling alone, wondering why she even thought about shaving herself down there and doing a cast of her familiar spot. he lay back for a long time and thought of her clitoris as a cemented work of art, a hard-white mold he could take and attempt to fit and compare against other women which allowed him to explore down there. let her do it. let her run the plaster all over herself and make a mess. did she really think this whole groupie thing still worked, years after the madness and frenzy of others who had less to give up than they did? when she removed the mold from his tired cock, he didn't recognize himself in the hardness. it was too thick. it wasn't him. it was another man invading his body to help her freeze her memories and keep them to herself. it wasn't him.

as if movement on the face means the mirror is standing still, capturing every wet hair that comes down the surface of the tense clock to show the couple how time took them away and forced them to lie here and destroy each other. her thighs opened slightly, the barely audible sound of parting skin making him press his left ear against her vulva. could he ever listen? did he know how to hear her flowing? was it possible to take it back, remove his ear from the warmth of the world and place it in the arroyo of tears? it was everything he dreamed of as he heard several sounds that brought him back to the woman beside him as she tightened her legs again, put one finger inside herself and turned to him as if she was done with him forever. she threw her head back on the pillow and smiled. he knew she had discovered everything about him and would not allow him to fuck her until he was able to stand in front of her and masturbate on her stomach, an act she demanded from him for a very long time, a request he has been unable to fulfill because when he gets hard, the sounds he hears in her vulva come back to him and keep him floating on the bed like a strange manner of love that won't go away. then he sees the juices shining over her body, the rings of overflowing cups he held between her legs so he could lift her high above him, bend her over and run his tongue the entire

length of her throbbing ass. it disappears, it becomes him, it decides it is a closeness he finds hard to handle, the growing trail of
water and weeping making him feel self-conscious, getting him to
finally daydream about the time he saw the neighborhood woman
in the apartment across the alley standing by the window, naked.
she looked over and spotted him at his window, but did not
move. she straightened tall and proud at the window, her huge
breasts leaving the room as she slowly raised an arm and gave
him the finger. she mouthed the words "fuck you" at him, then
gently closed her curtains.

appearing in the photograph—the two of them fucking blind, the
pillows and sheets torn around their bodies, the sweat painting
lakes that sparkled in the cheap flash of the camera, exposing him
to the first taste of blackmail that would follow him home, until
he decided to collect these photos and moments at a faster rate,
the second photo revealing how he had inserted the unpeeled banana up her cunt until she whimpered for sweet mercy and
turned to the camera with her frenzy as if she knew all along the
hidden thing was there.

he followed the black woman into the room where her twin sister waited for the two of them. her sister was naked, her body
completely covered in a smooth, ice-blue cream that scented the
room with incredible streams of human urgency and fallen lust.
the first woman turned to him without a word and motioned for
him to close the door behind him. he closed it and watched her
undress like her sister. the water bed rippled as the two of them
sat on it and stared at him. he didn't know what to do, but it
was answered for him when the two women started licking each
other. the one with the blue cream smeared some of it on the
other one's breasts and let her sister lick her own nipples until
they stood above the glow of the cream. he stood there and
watched them angle themselves likes wrestlers, the bed moving
faster with the weight of their struggle. he noticed neither one of
them licked each other between the legs and he thought that was
interesting. he surprised himself because of his lack of an erection,
but didn't have time to think about it when both women lay on
their backs, side by side, and spread their dripping legs wide
apart. he stared at the twin cunts and realized he was going to
kiss both of them. he knelt in front of the waving mattress and

smelled the flavor of four lips as the two sisters waited. he buried his tongue inside one, then another, moving rapidly from one delicious swirl to the second one and back again. before he knew it, the two women were moaning and grimacing in their own style. one came before the other and they embraced each other tightly, held each other like family as he sat back on his legs and watched the two black bodies float away from him and his strangeness.

the orgasm builds and builds. he falls down a deep well where the last wall of the castle waits for him as he thinks he has become a part of her body, the rapid condition of his unstoppable quivering pasting great shadows and shapes over her body. her legs hug his neck and the scarf she wears around her own neck she uses to drape around his head as he comes and comes, the hidden placement of his extension jumping inside her because he can't let go of the fact it is the last time.

"you are not my mother," he whispers to her.

extensions designed from above the bed where a mirror has been mounted so the triangles and postures may serve them both.

extensions oozing from the greased anus where the flower used to belong. extensions frozen from the finger up the smooth ass where the body rotates, the body answering in grunts and sighs, the empty hand digging deeper until it touches the other side of a moving wall.

conditions swallowed like the come that broke the glare of the room and shot farther across the bed than he had ever seen it do before, the target of her mouth moving in the nick of time, refusing to consume the energy of his wisdom because he was too quiet to make her feel at ease.

conditions right for existence when she dances naked and lets him fuck her standing up, the two of them sweating in the candle light, the two of them quiet for hours, not wanting to let on to the truth, her long brown hair stuck between her breasts, her heaving chest rising up and down as he sprung into her, grabbing her by her thin waist, pushing himself into her, fucking her standing up, dancing with her, facing each other, finally breaking the silence by telling each other stories their parents told them, whispering the plots into each other's ears as they fucked. the only time a handcuff was allowed, he wound up on the floor, locked to the bedpost while she went crazy with herself, performing for him like an expert, the wet t-shirt clinging to her sharp breasts, her dance showing him she was not a great dancer. her idea to spend the time in this manner resulted in him shooting all over the place, her wet t-shirt and panties soaked in honey before she put them on, the frozen moment of her standing with her legs spread over his head making him fall back, uncomfortable, his wrist hurting from the cuffs, the whole scene displaced as two or three drops of the brown honey actually rolled off her blue panties and fell accurately on his upturned nose.

delivered to let him write it all down, punish himself by never forgetting how he came here to be respected by those he loved and those who abandoned him. delivered to let him recite the motions and moons he saw when he was too tired, yet still ambitious enough to search for the woman of the turquoise, body-length veil, who once entered his room by mistake, her naked body white under the transparent veil, he tried to sit up, but she ran out, said something in a foreign language he couldn't understand.

he couldn't stop fucking her and she told him not to stop, they rocked back and forth on the bed, the two of them vibrating as if some invisible force was in control, her legs wrapped around his bone-thin back, his sac shaking under his spread ass for anyone who would come up behind them, kneel down eye level to the bed and watch him slide in and out, telling her over and over that he didn't know how to stop fucking, that his body wouldn't slow down, that she had to help him by crying louder, the two of them vibrating as if some invisible force was rocking them, over and over, the hours on the clock whispering that something had to slow them down, some vision or eye movement had to make one or the other finally crash through and break the efficient machine of fucking they had invented only for themselves.

delivered in the delirious aftermath of a frozen farewell where the anger of release becomes a gift for parting and returning. delivered in the mistaken position of holding each of her ankles high in the air as she lay on her back, her legs spread, his fucking pushing them toward the thing they were after, his bended legs underneath his bowed back, her cries and moans meaning something totally different, the way she half rose off the sheets to pronounce his name as she came. delivered with her finally confessing to him that she was going to leave him, not allow him to give her the family they had wanted, her need to fuck him making her stronger, making her decide what was going to happen.

unknown to the girl under the orange lights, the man has been studying her crotch for a long time. he leans forward and grips the edge of the stage while the stupid song comes on again, her physical endurance allowing her to crouch down on her white spiked heels, spread her orange legs in fine balance as she runs her index finger down her crotch, pauses, throws her head into the music, and sucks on the finger. He rises from his stool when the song ends, the first time he gives her a twenty-dollar bill, the last time he enters the stinking place.

basking in the photograph—a young boy fucking a girl, another boy watching with a big hard-on. high school age? college age? independent? years ago? basking in the black and white of personal history there is a young boy in a white t-shirt carrying the girl around the room, her legs wrapped around his waist, the two of them running out of breath as they fall back against the door, fuck in midair, spin around and bounce onto the bed.

furnished with memory, the moving teardrop has made its way down the wrinkles of lost time, crossed the red mark on the skin to glisten with the same motion the last drop of semen oozes out of his dying cock, the transparent trail of its travels kissing its gravity with the slowness of a tongue kiss, a belly button blown with air from her good friend who has taken her place to wipe the secrets from his eyes before he decides he will find her inside the room where eight people are naked and fucking. he would not be able to identify her. she is free and he is not, so he stays with her good friend and shapes the trail of a whimpering resolve, a hidden idea he learned from his father who was the last monk to untie the rope around his waist and puncture the nun from behind. he even told his son the tale of the room with the thick green hanging vines where he fucked several nuns, always bent them over the wooden pews so he could watch them shake up and down with the pleasure of faith and commitment, their tears taking longer to change him than the holy water that trembled slowly in its mounted cups on the wall, his last memory before closing his eyes and letting the flurry of knees, asses, balls, cocks, cunts, mouths, and spurting angels of come decorate his world of talented treason and healthy fucking that developed him into one of the best minds of his powerful generation of men.

from Breath

H. Emilia Paredes

1

Your body, opalescent, moon-trussed flora
opens wealth of firmament, stars
blaze my skin, exhume ghost appetites. Fingers blush and grasp
open and close, as meteoric heat unfurls.

I was alone, astal-shard hurled onto earth's fomenting soil
night air chilled sinew and bone, powerful cold numbed my veins.
I imagined you, flesh and blood, to survive myself
rose petal nipples to greet my kisses, smooth thighs to slip between.

But the hour of illusion has fallen away and I love you.
Body of earth sweet smells, of hair and fingernail, of fervent tongue.
O press of your breasts on my face! O your eyes lucid sienna
green and golden! O the light, heathery tangle of your pubis!
O your sound calling my name!

Body of the woman I love, I survive in your pleasure.
My want, my black despair, my tentative walk
vast *Amazonas* where infinte sorrow continues
and inexorable fatigue continues
and blue flame of moonlight.

5

I speak the dialect
of your heart
hear
my words visible as rain.

In my garden, beneath the sea, I grow
impatiens, mint, and lilies, eager for the tug of your fingers.

And I watch from a distance

the white arch of your wrist, my words
a bouquet held to your breast, more yours than mine.

They stutter and lisp, compose themselves in your grasp
you hear the silence, the unspoken.

No thorns to prick your flesh, only sound of color humid
on dark limbs, bursting and scattering in ripeness.

Before you, they, inhabited the carapace of my heart
accustomed to the moan of my sorrow

they speak what was cut from my tongue my 7th year
words bled in stream burst of first rage, first passion.

But I want you to hear what the petals in my garden say
to the blue moon while you sleep. Do not mistake my words

for autumn winds turning leaves outside your window
embrace me in dreamlike lucidity, whisper them back to me.

You waken all the voices dormant in my throat, sound sexual
as honey bees, hot, amber droplets drip down muted vocal chords
scarred tongue, tastes sudden raw sweetness, says
love me, *compañera,* sing me the sad, E flat minor of my soul.

My words spiral from your pores into cupped hands
a garland of *flores, como tu amor,* say, you are one woman

I am one woman, and we are mortal in a garden of impatiens
mint and lilies, steeped in the wild, wet forever of our love.

6

I remember your eyes that day by the sea
clear, Atlantean green, gilded irises.
Our bed of pampas grass and sand dune
salt taste as mouths succumbed to tide

waves slow and placid spoke truths
pressed into mine, your body

pressed into mine, burning
away the distances between our souls.

The sea, lost in the pupils of your eyes
encompassing cry of gull and hearth
where deepest longings melted into liquid
kisses like embers on my skin.

In this memory
a hundred leagues beneath the sea
I forget I am alone!
Beyond this still sweetness, waves wrest
with the many oceans of your gaze.

8

From my pores, scent of corn silk
after rain and abundant sun.

I, the impetuous one, smoke and fire clearing soil
for new seed. *I know how to lose everything.*

I reach for last kernel of magic, last fear
in the multiplicity of my mind, you are my last desire.

O invisible one!

Hand lights on breast, there a seedling
quavers beneath palm, eager and firm.

Beneath solar plexus murmur of taproot
chest expands, contracts.

Mouth melts upon soft, savory flesh
down silken navel, where heaven began.

O invisible one!

Solitary swale of cornfield, your presence
a subtle ecstasy. At first light, flurry of crows

frightened by glint of sun struck dewy stalks
caw and caw in flight. The earth is opened.

I breathe one, brief forever of you
scent of corn silk, sweet effulgence.

O invisible one!

9

Twilight cups my horizon
sighs of the sea sucking in wave
night spills all over, takes me in her mouth
teethe white and furious, you lick

foam from the shore, say, *I will never leave you*
her water devours the chimera dressed in shadows
salt stings nostrils, one deep breath
before the long journey, no time to say

here, my heart, eat. My passions are hard
desperate things, burning and freezing, sun and moon
rising and setting, I need your earth in my pores
and the island you promise as you swelter and shiver

beneath me. Your voice is mirage covering my nakedness
in flames that would be your kisses, this night humid
electric, *la selva* between our limbs and dreams
this ocean admonishing us to drown a little

limp, pale and blue-lipped, her water seeping
into our lungs, only heart beat sounds doubling as slow
arcing waves, until she spews us out gasping and sobbing
                                                on the shore.

Flash Flesh

Virgil Suarez

When we moved from Miami to Los Angeles, we lived in an apartment building on Marbrisa Street, across from a McDonald's. One day I was sitting on the front stairs of the building, waiting for Julio, my Nicaraguan friend, to get home so we could play catch. The stairs was my favorite spot upon which to sit and look out at the street. Nothing new happening other than the normal occurrences: women sweeping the leaves and dust off their porches, men working under the hoods of their cars.

I sat there gripping and shaping the McGregor glove my father had bought for me at Thrifty's. It would take a while to break into the new leather. Then, out of nowhere, it seemed. A *vato* or *pachuco*, as the people who knew them in the neighborhood called them, came walking down the sidewalk, arm in arm with his girlfriend. It was Sunday so they were sporting their best clothes: he crisply creased chinos, a Pendleton shirt buttoned to the collar, a sparkling belt buckle, and shiny black shoes; she a white, low-cut blouse too short to cover her belly button, cords, and white sandals.

She also wore so much makeup and eye shadow her face looked like a mask. Her hair stood in a curl over her pale forehead, the rest of it spilled over her brown shoulders and the front of her big breasts. Her corduroy pants were tight; tighter in the crotch— so tight I thought of my hand in my glove and how the leather stitches welted against my fingers.

The *vato,* seeing me eyeing him and his girlfriend, walked up to the stairs where I sat and said, "Hey, *ese,* where you from?"

"Cuba," I said.

"A *Cuba-Cubanito,*" he said, and turned to the young woman. "This is my *ruca,* say hello."

"Hello, Ruca," I said, not knowing that *ruca* meant girlfriend.

"Ruca's not my name," she said.

"She's *La Gata de la Trece, ese,*" he said, reaching into his shirt pocket, from which he withdrew a pack of Marlboros. "You want one?" he said, and tapped out a cigarette.

"I don't smoke," I said, and placed the glove on the step between my legs.

"Umm," he said, and lit his cigarette. He acted real suave and let the smoke swirl around his face. He blew the rest in front of me.

It was then I noticed the tear tattoo under his right eye and "*La Vida Loca*" written out in script on his neck. "What you looking at, *ese*؟" he said.

"Nothing," I told him.

"Hey, *pendejo,* how old are you؟"

"He's a kid," she said.

"Twelve," I answered.

"Twelve," he said, and laughed. "That's old enough."

I should have stood up then and gone upstairs to a world more familiar to me, but kept staring at the woman's breasts, at the V of her cleavage, and the soft skin there.

"You have any money؟" he asked.

"No."

"Can you get some؟"

"What for؟" That was the wrong question.

"What for؟ What for؟" he said, then, "Are you insulting my girl, eh؟"

"No," I said.

"If you get a ten," he said, and stopped to put his hand on her breast, "she'll show you something."

"Cut it out," she said, getting his hand away from her breast.

"With *mira,*" he said, and rubbed the tip of his fingers, "with ten dollars, you can see her *panocha.*"

Panocha. I didn't know what that was, but it was clear that it was some part of her anatomy.

I kept hoping someone would come to the rescue, like Julio, but no one did. I was alone on this one.

He started to grab the woman and she kept fending him off. I didn't know how these two could be together, but something kept my attention. He pawed at her flesh, of which I was seeing some.

In one attempt, he pulled down her blouse and grabbed one of her breasts. "See this؟" he said, and smiled. "You see this mark right here؟"

I looked at her flesh. I saw the brown pink of her nipple, then the hickey he pointed to. "I gave her this," he said.

I looked on.

"Stop it, *no chingues,*" she said, slipping her breast back inside her blouse.

"Okay, ese," he said. "You can have her if you give me your glove."

I told him I couldn't do it, my father would kill me.

"INSULT NUMBER THREE," he shouted. "Shit. You keep offending my woman."

I put my foot on the glove.

"*Horale!* Okay," he said. "Tell you what, if you give me the glove, she'll let you see her *panocha.*"

He worked furiously at unbuckling her belt, the cigarette dangling from the corner of his mouth, his hair falling over his eyes.

I was speechless; I didn't know whether to run or shout for help. When he couldn't do it, her pants being too tight, he shoved his hand inside her pants and grabbed her crotch. She screamed and started to hit him with her fists. Suddenly he pulled his hand out. He presented his closed hand to me. "Look here," he said, opening his fingers one by one.

In between his fingers were curly pubic hairs. He picked them one by one and threw them at my face. "*Pendejos, pendejos, pendejos,*" he said. "Perfumed pubic hair. How about it, *pinche cabrón?*"

"Let's go, Victor," she said. "Leave him alone and let's go."

"No," he said. "Can't you see it in his eyes? He likes you."

Victor brought his fingers close to my face again. I froze. With one hand on my shoulder, the hand with the cigarette—I feared he would burn my ears—he held my attention, and touched the tip of my nose with the fingers of the other hand. He rubbed the smell, *her scent,* under my nostril, then touched the tip of my nose. I pulled my head back and he let go. He was smiling and I could see the pink of his tongue behind his dirty teeth.

"Okay, but let's get out of here," she said.

"No, last deal, my friend," he said. Once he was done smoking, he flicked the butt on the floor and crushed it out with his shoe.

The gutted cigarette on the sidewalk blew away with a gust of wind.

"For your glove," he said. "She will pull on your *slinky.*"

"No, *ya vamonos,*" she said.

"How about it, *Cubanito pende-jito?*"

"Gotta go," I said, and stood up.

He tried to grab the glove off my hands but I was quicker than he was. Then, my moving up the stairs with the glove upset him.

"*Horale cabrón,*" he said. "Don't let me catch you around here anymore or I'll kick your ass. If not me, then one of my homeboys."

I walked up and stopped on top of the stairs, turned and looked down one more time. He was saying, ". . . insulted my *ruca,* and I

VIRGIL SUAREZ • 245

don't like that. Nobody insults *La Gata de la Trece* and gets away with it."

I left them both there and hurried to my apartment, opened the door, put the glove down on the sofa, and closed the door behind me. My mother was sewing in the bedroom; my father was napping on the easy chair.

I went to the bathroom and stood by the sink. I closed my eyes and thought of the girl and her flesh. The sweet scent of the perfume came up through my nose, a little faint. Flesh. Soft and brown. Her flesh. Pink nipples. The contour of her belly button, the fuzzy hairs there. Her crotch. I looked into the medicine cabinet mirror and saw my own adolescent face. Punk, I thought. I felt embarrassed and humiliated; and yet excited. Extremely excited at the nagging smell rising in through my nostrils.

I was twelve. I thought about how much longer it would be before I became one acquainted with the flesh of a woman.

from Puentes y Fronteras

Gina Valdés

All days with you
are Sunday in my memory,
and all nights together
will be hallelujah Saturday.

Dark one lovely dark one,
if you don't know I'll teach you,
you'll see that with what you learn
you'll stay awake all night.

How pleasant when it rains
the rain tapping on the roof,
all night we listen
to the rhythm from our bed.

Your guitarist hands
keep on playing and playing,
if you continue playing me
you're going to drive me crazy.

Man of gentle hands
I would give you my heart,
if you would also do in the day
what you do after dark.

You are a wild forest,
blooming, humid and green,
among your branches and rivers
I would like to disappear.

I remember that night
how the moon lighted us
through an open window
a rosebush perfumed us,

to enjoy the fragrance
I kissed your dark body.

I want to see at sunrise
the sun on your dark face
and when night falls
the full moon on your body.

The water is aroused,
all the beach rejoices,
each time you caress me
the moon lights up the rocks.

Moon the full moon,
our skin warms the sand,
the tide rises, rises,
wave after wave breaks.

Moon of the moon sweet moon,
what a pleasant sea night,
your hips with their rhythm
and the waves with their rhyme.

Infinite Wheel of Desire

Gina Valdés

The yoga instructor never looked passionately into her eyes,
embraced her desperately or kissed her with fury. He sat
in front of her in a lotus position and said in a voice that
came from his diaphragm, I want to realize myself with you.

The music professor wanted to tune her ear. He turned off
all of the lights in the room, to improve the acoustics,
and played a tape of fertility music from Indonesia with
which the gods multiply.

I want to make love with you. Tonight. Now, said
the Ramakrishnananda disciple. If tomorrow I pass away
I will leave unfinished business, and be born again and
again in a never-ending wheel of desire.

Blessed the Hungry

Demetria Martínez

A poem for two voices
Setting: two women on a bed.

Older woman:
   A friend,
   A friend was all I wanted
   Tonight for leftovers
   Of turkey and peas,
   Home movies of a trip
   To Jerusalem,
   The twins, asleep,
   My husband abroad on business.
   Business: he intones
   That word as if it were a totem
   Against my loneliness.
   Souvenirs clatter in drawers,
   Chipped, yellow,
   Like teeth.
   Look at the blackened walls,
   We have invented fire in a house
   Where everything is flammable:
   Paper flowers, paper dolls,
   My gold ring.
   We will be incarcerated,
   Like children who light matches
   Beneath beds,
   The parent-killing types,
   We will be incinerated,
   Ashes cast to the wind,
   A curse, a sign.

Younger woman:
   Your tongue journeyed
   Down my spine,
   Like snails I let inch

Up my shins as a child,
Awed by the fleshy wetness.
You kissed my lifelines,
A blessing upon my future.
You spread my thighs,
In the moss found an ember,
You breathed on it,
Coral to red, flames spreading,
Earth tremors, soles to head.
Waters of my birth canal parted
As your tongue moved in me . . .

Older woman:
Stop! A mistake, like vows
Taken in court it can be
Undone, dismissed.
A friend was all I wanted,
Joy was not intended.
The joyful dash across streets
And are hit by cars
Or by a father's fist.
Ice cubes on your thighs
Will erase the marks
Like lies erased at confession.
A mistake, unintended,
The gavel drops,
We are acquitted.

Younger woman:
Down there, down there,
My mother whispered, ashamed,
Cultures where fetuses
And illnesses fester,
Fetid, open wound
Man enter and reenter,
Leaks and reds
On white sheets.
My first bleeding
Came like sudden death.
Each month I wore black,
Widowed, riddled with shame.

I am a virgin again, unbroken,
Brought to by your touch and scent.
Stay at my house this week or more.
We have been friends for years.
I am your sister, brother,
Mother, father.
What joyful hours rising
As lovers.

Joyful women pick themselves up
Off the street and heal
Their own wounds.
The man's tires
Flatten mysteriously in the night.
If you live with me
Our loving will split atoms,
No explosions, just additions,
New constellations
For the world to see.

Older woman:
My family, we are four,
Divisible by two,
If I lost my mind to you
My spouse and twins would be three,
Indivisible as God, a mockery.
I would lose my place
In phone books, church lists,
An outlaw, far from the sweet ache
I felt at seventeen when I took
The gold ring, unquestioning.
Veiled, I could see nothing.
Man, woman, husband, wife:
Such a comforting ordering of parts.
How it fits me.
How it makes for visibility.
I know my place
And will not touch another tree,
Even if the fruit delights,
Curiosity kills paradise.

Younger woman:
     I am not ashamed
     For having tasted,
     At your breast
     My hunger ceased.
     Milk and wine: the body
     Asks so little,
     The mind wills gases, acids,
     Faces unhinged by blasts,
     Designs for doors to stand
     While houses collapse.
     I want no part of such monstrous heat.
     We will generate light
     Like the Ner Tamid before Torah,
     A flame burning in the temple,
     Perpetually.
     I tell you, God is pleased.
     When everywhere men plan wars,
     Our love is a sign,
     An act of piety.

Older woman:
     It is midnight, you must go,
     Better that I sit in this
     Big house alone.
     You speak in brilliant tones,
     You don't know the blacks and whites
     Of children crying at night,
     A husband, who in his own sweet,
     Pained way, gropes for words to say
     I love . . .
     Three lives in my hands,
     Needs to meet,
     Ordinary.
     I am not so proud
     To want differently.
     Tomorrow I wash sheets,
     Skim the news, buy groceries:
     Milk, carrots, chocolate, peas.
     These are the little rituals
     That save me from dark dissolve,

My contribution to peace.
I don't need you, I am strong,
In my own common way
I'll go on and on and on.

Circle of Friends

Ricardo Lopez Masarillo

He dreamed of invasion, finding himself rolling in the yellow liquid of life, the cylinder holding the three of them shining like glass, reflecting round walls that made the three naked bodies roll and glide across its smooth surface. He opened his eyes with a gasp and didn't know where they were, but noticed Chato had a huge hard-on. He looked down at himself. He throbbed with the revelation, the smooth head on his dick redder than usual. But, what was Mona doing here?

She rolled in the yellow water and sat up, her long black hair dripping strings of the stuff, her huge brown breasts exposed to Chato for the first time. He sat there wanting to hide his dick from Chato. Something was going on because Mona beckoned to Chato with her spread legs. Chato looked at him as if asking permission. He couldn't answer yes or no. Whatever had them had stolen their speech. He sat and slid slowly on the wet contours of the slick floor as Chato carefully crawled toward Mona.

He glided a few feet closer to them as Mona suddenly dove for Chato and threw him back. The two of them rolled across the yellow mud and came back toward him. He couldn't believe it because Mona was sitting on Chato, his big thing already stuck in her. He stared and felt a surge of blood power sweep through him as he watched his best friend and girlfriend fuck each other in the yellow ooze. His thing got harder and longer than he had ever seen it. It rose up to his belly button and he thought it was going to spring off his body because of his excitement over Mona doing a great number on Chato. She lifted and fell casually on him and he heard them moan, the first noise he had noticed inside this strange chamber.

Suddenly, a low wave of the yellow stuff pushed him forward and he drew even closer to the fucking friends. He looked again and noticed how deeply Chato was ramming Mona. He thought he would be angry, but the yellow liquid calmed him each time he was going to change the level of his awareness. All three of them were half-swimming and half-floating in this odorless, nonsticky substance. It would just drip off their bodies, not cling or hide

Chato's balls as they slapped under Mona, nor plug her ass and keep him from staring down there at her mighty cunt lips that were spread and straining to hold Chato's thickness.

Mona was going wild and Chato couldn't stop. As he witnessed the woman in his life and his best buddy performing one of the nastiest and wettest fucks he had ever seen, he was caught by surprise when Mona reached behind her and grabbed his dick. She practically pulled him forward to join them. He hesitated as the three of them became one in the yellow sea. He was the first to be able to stand in the shining mass of whatever had caught them. He had swallowed some of it in surpise, but it didn't taste like anything, not even like water.

He tried to balance himself, then was helped by Mona when she reached over and took his dick into her mouth. Chato floated on the yellow water and kept fucking Mona while she hung on to her real lover with her mouth. He didn't know what to think because Chato was grunting loud and clear, his rough cries echoing and bouncing off the finely tuned walls of the cylinder. None of them could talk, but they could still moan and groan.

He quit resisting when he noticed that the yellow liquid that rose to ankle level did not stick to their naked bodies. Mona flicked her tongue in a way that drove him crazy and he grabbed her long, wet hair with his fist. He got into it, the fear of not knowing where they were giving way to the three of them going at it quite freely.

Chato splashed around him and came and came. Mona gasped and let go of her lover, the three of them not knowing exactly what to do next because everything was so slippery around them, waves of the yellow stuff flying into the air as the three fuckers let go. He backed off and came loudly, his spasms and releasing grunts echoing through his brain. His huge wad flew through the soft air of their confinement.

Mona slowed her rhythm down as the three of them stared at his come, which floated in odd shapes throughout the chamber. It didn't fall or spread apart. His own kind of yellow matter floated in the air like flower petals that wouldn't fall. Chato leaned back, a wide grin on his face, the fact he had just fucked his best friend's woman not bothering him at all.

And, it didn't seem to bother her man, because he lowered himself into the warmth of the yellow and relaxed. He wanted to talk, but knew the three of them couldn't speak. He figured the other two could think and have some of the same thoughts and questions he had, but they couldn't mouth any words.

Mona turned on her stomach and swam a few yards away from the two men. He watched her ass stick up above the liquid. She stopped and lay motionless on her stomach, the gentle waves of whatever sustained them lapping over her body, entering and exiting from between her legs.

He didn't act surprised when Chato got up and went to Mona again. This time he joined them right away. He grabbed Mona before Chato could think of anything and drove himself deeply into her from behind. She shook in surprise and he tried to recall the first time he held a mouthful of warm water, then spit it into her cunt when he was down there one night. It was a rush another woman had taught him.

Now, he knelt in the yellow and started pumping away. Chato went to the front, manipulated himself until Mona grabbed him and started sucking him. He pumped and closed his eyes, the woman he loved bobbing on some strange stuff he had never seen before. Where were they? What had happened? He opened his eyes to see Mona's ass shake like jello as he reamed her. She cried out the best she could because she was busy with Chato.

He looked at his best friend and liked him more than ever. He turned his head up to the roof of this cell and noticed a kind of light radiating through the smooth panels high above them. Was there something up there? Had the three of them been abducted by aliens and forced to fuck as an experiment? Chato didn't last long because he fired right away, bending his hairy chest over Mona's head as he sighed and heaved a final time. He pulled out, his thing a red contrast to the yellow liquid that was slowly turning into a comfortable foam.

Chato lay back and grabbed his dick, his friend and Mona watching the whole time. Chato closed his eyes and took his hands away. Mona and her lover kept fucking and fucking. He thought he was going to come, but realized the fact that his friend had already had Mona twice was going to delay his climax. He fucked Mona harder and harder, not knowing why he couldn't stop. He fucked her, twisted her legs around, rested one on his shoulder and entered her again sideways. Mona kept opening and closing her mouth, the long strands of black hair glued to her blinding breasts like maps to wherever the three of them were going to wind up. He thought of this as he fucked and fucked.

Suddenly, one of the radiating panels in the ceiling moved and something fell slowly toward them. It was the only instant he was really frightened. His eyes widened when he saw what was gently falling toward them. He spotted Chato rubbing his eyes. Mona was in a climactic frenzy. He reamed one more time and she went crazy, not noticing the huge transparent dildo, attached to a belt, that splashed near them.

He pulled out and wanted to make sure he wasn't seeing things, but the silent Chato beat him to it. Chato grinned and pulled the transparent dildo out of the liquid. It was a fat dick made of rubber you could see through. Chato flicked it with his fingers, but the sound of his merriment did not come out of his mouth. He watched Chato and pondered the belt that was built into the dildo and the thong under it.

Mona rose from the yellow stuff with great confidence. She wiped the tears from her face, stumbled a bit, and grabbed the translucent dildo from Chato's hands. Before the two men could even guess what was about to happen, Mona slipped into the ass thong and strapped on the belt. She stood straight up with her long dick sticking into the air.

Chato's smile vanished. His best friend witnessed Chato's abrupt loss of balance as the whole cylinder trembled for a few seconds. Chato fell forward. His head was temporarily under the liquid. He came up for air gasping, flailing his arms, trying to move away from Mona as she came around behind him.

His best friend watched this unforeseeable change of events as Mona knelt behind Chato, rubbed some of the yellow liquid on the thick dildo, and speared Chato in the ass. If sound had been allowed in this place, he could have imagined Chato's cries of surprise and pain. Chato's eyes bugged out and his long mustache twitched with the wide open O of his mouth. But, still, none of them could talk.

As he watched Mona slip in deeper, he realized it was going to be okay, but difficult. Mona smiled as she fucked Chato in the ass, the sensation sending all three of them onto a higher plane of sensitivity. Chato shook like a gigged frog as Mona fucked with great confidence and experience. Her lover was deeply moved at the sight of her penetrating his best friend in a sacred way he knew Chato had never accepted before. It meant things were going to be okay between the three of them.

Then, he thought he heard a distant hum that entered his ears and almost hurt. He looked up toward the area of the ceiling that had thrown down the dildo, but couldn't see anything. When he turned back to the butt fuck, he saw Mona eject herself rapidly from the shaking Chato. The motion was like a hunter cleaning out the insides of a slain deer. Chato convulsed and sprang forward into the foam, which kept hardening around them. He landed facedown, his ass red and swollen, his legs trembling with ecstasy.

Mona rose and came toward her lover. He'd never conceived of this. He could accept what was happening to them, was not really surprised that he couldn't figure out where they were, but the idea of his woman fucking him with a see-through rubber dildo was beyond his wildest nightmares. He retreated slowly, wishing he could float high in the tunnel-like air like that first load of cum that had sailed away.

He stared at the slimy cock, which pointed right at him. Mona shook her head to get her hair out of her face and the dildo vibrated in the air like an arrow impacting into a tree. He did not want to believe this, but by believing it, lost his balance as Chato had. He fell back and had no time to right himself, because he found the woman he loved had an unbelievable strength and style she was revealing to him for the first time.

He lay on his back as her hard fingers opened his legs. He was able to shake his head a couple of times, but could not cry out into the void between them because she gracefully violated him. He shook with the hard, cold feeling that something was passing through him. The pain lasted a few seconds, then became a deep, dark pressure that lifted him and gave him the first real knowledge of where the three of them had come from and where they were going by this constant fucking.

Mona fucked him with a solid revenge and deep love. He felt the world slipping back and forth inside him, felt the dildo melt into his stomach and wondered if this was what life was all about. Two seconds of incredible pain were followed by the most intense and incredible feeling of getting fucked he had ever felt. He was simply fucked inside out by this silent, hungry woman who used the transpoarent dildo as if it were an extension of her arm and her complete body.

Mona was his woman, but she was a woman alone, doing what she wanted to both these men. Yet, he wondered why she had to reach this peak with a dick. Why didn't she do this to him with her cunt? Was something wrong here? Did whoever kidnap the three of them decide the lone woman could only take over with a rubber cock of power tied on her body?

He couldn't ponder any more stupid, deep thoughts because

Mona fucked like an artist and covered every inch of his internal knot. She pulled back until only the tip was embedded in his swollen anus. He thought about relief, but she slipped back in real fast. The jolt actually took both of them two feet off the foam. They floated two feet off the yellow clouds, Mona's great dildo stuck inside her man like a love and desperation he had never given her. His legs dangled in the air above them.

Mona held each of his ass cheeks in her open hands as she swiveled and fucked in delight. He managed to open his eyes and meet her smiling, happy face. She was having a great time and knew every move necessary to become the transparent dick and totally drill every notion he had about men and women completely out of his mind and spirit. She twisted, jumped, heaved, rocked, swayed, and screwed with the long thing, completely cleaning him inside out.

He was breathing hard, his rhythms moving toward an incredible, frightening escape of violated fury. He noticed the first signs of sweat on the two of them as trails of it ran down Mona's hardworking chest. She breathed heavily, the look on her face both a mask and the real image of a woman who was not going to get this chance ever again. He wanted to come back down to the yellow, but she wouldn't let him. He let out the most magnificent, silent scream the three of them would never hear. He thought he was going to have a heart attack as he convulsed with the most devastating orgasm. Mona leaped back and released him without mercy. He sputtered backward, both arms flailing the air as he was thrown several yards away from her. Mona had collapsed on her back, her breasts heaving rapidly, the transparent dick standing tall and unforgiving between her exhausted legs.

Then, the three of them heard the sound. It was a loud, shrill whistle that hurt their ears and made them look up. Even Chato pulled his face from out of the yellow mess and gazed with crossed eyes toward the ceiling. The sound stopped and made Mona and her fucked man come back down. The three of them lay back, all of them lost in their own thoughts, naked, tired, and energetic with their predicament.

By the time they woke from several hours of deep sleep, the yellow stuff had turned to a soft layer of bouncy material. He was the first to wake and notice something had changed. There were noises and scrapings going on way above them. The yellow liquid had become a sea of soft pillows. The cylindrical walls glowed with a low blue light. He turned to find Chato's lifeless body being led away by two beautiful, naked women. Mona lay next to him, sleeping. He tried to wave and call out, but the two women, both brown-skinned with short and black curly hair, ignored him. He could not stand up because his entire body was painfully sore.

The women had Chato by each leg. They dragged him across the pillows, his cock tiny and cold, his body hairy in contrast to the women's smooth, tanned look. They pulled Chato toward a distant opening in the far wall. He wanted to cry out to his friend and to wake Mona, but his aching arms were heavy as lead. Chato and his captors disappeared into the wall.

He lay back and wanted to cry, but couldn't bring enough energy into his being to do so. Mona stirred, opened her eyes, and gently rolled into his arms. He gave Chato one last thought as Mona's welcome warmth enveloped him. For the first time since they were trapped, the two lovers held each other, a mute comfort growing between them. Mona yawned, drew her hair off her face with her right hand, and hugged him across his chest. She fell asleep again.

He didn't want to move or wake her. He wondered where they were, had thoughts he'd experienced earlier, until the nightmarish potential of them sent him back to nasty, horny images of the three of them fucking and fucking like there was no tomorrow. He noticed movement on the ceiling, but could barely keep his eyes open. He managed to stay awake long enough to see a door open up there.

For an instant, he thought they were going to throw another dildo down, but the dark panel that slid open made way for two naked angels that lowered themselves through the opening. He stared at the sight of the male and female angels, their brilliant white wings barely moving in the distant height of the chamber. The male angel had an erection larger than Chato could ever come up with. The woman's cunt was shaved and let off a radiance he could feel all the way down.

He held Mona tighter as the two angels slowly descended toward them. As they drew closer, he had to admire their neat appearance, their brown skin, and their freshly cut short hair. Both angels looked athletic and attractive. They smiled with a radiating welcome that almost made him let go of Mona. But he held on tighter when they hovered only ten feet above him and his woman. He waited for the male and female to switch sides, because the angel's huge erection was right above him and the woman's desire hung right above Mona.

He waited for them to switch sides before he could accept their challenge. He nudged Mona in surprise and sudden panic when he realized the angels were not going to switch. They came down closer, the male's enormous thing already leaking a sweet drop onto his chest as they met. The last thing he saw before raising his legs was the way Mona opened her eyes and how the female angel's thighs shivered in response.

Reversible Lovers

Juan Felipe Herrera

Ancestors come first, for me. You must know this.
This is the first thing I'll tell you when we meet this evening
at the tavern or the theatre—your choice.

Spotted. At an angle, in exemplary camouflage.
A tropical pelt of rivery passions. These senses
will be immediate, as you walk up. Your loose breasts.
Stealth and wonder, an inner strength.

The casual evening will drop and then get caught on a prop like a
theatre curtain. A carved stone will tear through our legs—an
ancient Olmec feline mouth, wet then dry and then wet;
remember that archeology course on La Venta, Veracruz, Mexico
where the Mother cultures of this continent emerged?

All that information will be gone now.

Now, all you have is this suit I am wearing.
I thought you would like it, like this—a cinnamon,
a greenish tint at the lapels, reddish frond kerchief
in the breast pocket. The photograph
I give you is an unusual one, I must admit.
But, I'll give it to you anyway. I am stalking; you can see that.
I am roaring yet, only you seem to hear me. This is odd.

Look closer. Examine the insignias
on the well-thought-of apparel.

Fur, brilliant. Velvety dark leaf shapes
inside you,

in the masonry behind me and most of all—
elegance, especially, the hands: flared, opaque.
Then, the mouth; opening a bit, then slowly closing,
carefully, cautiously.

We have not yet talked about love.
There will be a few words as it is accustomed.
Murmurs, uncommon glances. Lost buttons.
The foliage is heavy, a bit overdone.

Look at me open a tiny diamond-shaped pocket mirror.
You know it is a serious matter. All this. So, you walk up,
in a typical daylight into dusk gait, a bit hurried, unclothed
almost dancing. As you come closer, I step forward.

It is a matter of life and death.
Perhaps (only perhaps), all this leads to masks.
Máscaras. Have you ever—truly known me?
I cannot tell.

Does this question go back to Borges' on labyrinths? Any book
will do, actually; any cover with gray mazes or unending fences
where you live unable to ever leave or to ever know anyone
above the basement of dead husbands. Have you looked directly
at me (into me)?

A hint of batwing—a strange cape of sorts, a sugary lapel,
something akimbo in the glance, in the spectacle; listen (again)
to the ventriloquist bull finch, the hat spinning in the air
a-la-Cesar Romero, a Zorro musketeer cap of sorts,
up there in the blue-green. Your hand cups me.

This is facile, too gross—immediately perceptible,
the usual fetish of Western media strips.

I think there is something more personal in all this,
that is, in how to see (me). First, though, you need
to figure what lies between us. What separations?

What distinct approximations? Cousin Amelia, older, plump
without a bra, in polka dot underpants playing hard with me,
south Broadway barrio Logan? Maybe Rolando, just Rolando
with the left hand up against your office table, your silk
open, fourteenth floor.

Then, there is Michael, just Michael too, who plays
basketball on Fridays when you want to go out

lifts weights and says things—good things, like
look Victoria Platero, all I can do is about (he stalls)
seven thirty, ok, after the game—

whadya say, ok,
Victoria, ok?

The open-air. Something (I rarely see)—
the white-greenness of the outdoors.

You usually say I am thinking too much. I think.
Writing mysteries. A detective novel would be best.

A young boy was last seen wearing a pair of old Nikes, blue
sweats without a top heading towards the old Sutro Baths area in
San Francisco (Remember: when we went to the Cliff House to
have a drink overlooking the ocean and you said it was pure
color, the color we never see if we don't hold on to each other.)
He was there, nearby. No one ever found him out. All we have,
at least according to the coroner's report, is a severed head that
was buried back there behind the baths, underneath the network
of brush, wires and soiled orange wax papers. Raped by an ex-
con. He was so alone that evening, they say. Someone was
coaxing him, then so suddenly—dragging him.

A cartoonist does better than a writer, I think.
He works with pouts, you could say he is a master of poutery—
the crazy ceramics of the gut and face when the heart unloosens.
Say, like Andy Garcia (I love cinema, it is so helpful).

He mesmerizes without a target in mind,
an unshakable relationship is always in the making, full of romance,
rosewood; indelible, going towards a powdery rouge
and a little tender knife.

He could be your dark half, you know: the moon lover
that comes out with the night, a bluish guitar from Sonora,
stilled lakes, sage brush.

You never speak of him as a sunny faced singer of morning
breakfasts. If you look closely, you see he doesn't wear the usual

baby blue or pink T-shirts. Iron. Crystal. Silver-ancient coins in a
miniature wooden box suit him better. Do you think so?

Oh, yes and a map. It always leads back to you.
To your deep fragrance, your fevers. Our dark thighs
that splash into each other. A note of debts.

This could be true: like an old jaguar self, I seek (always)
an openness beyond my reach. This is why blood-ties fascinate me.

I am constantly looking for my other (love).
This is why I appear here (and there). For example,
the mirage of a candle-boy: the heart a bluish cream cap on fire.
Now I am at the supermarket or better yet, at the mall
with all of its post X-Mas impressionism.

Let's go there sometime again. So safe and nimble.
No one screams or smolders, they only play
at this intersection of common desires:

Greetings, cards, almost-hellos; when I go there,
I glow. I don't know why. When you pass by.

It happens. The light caves in (to me).
My gestures are slower here.

A tick-tock follows me, a striking beat of differences.
My face against your back, Up, down. Down. You are too aware of me.

Where are my goofy gloves?
My apple turnover hands? And my Simpson's haircut?

Look at him again (even in his beige college suit),
he is drawing you in, there, by the Chaps cologne stand,
way down the aisle next to the watercress ties.

You are bringing him into focus.
He is coming. Ever so slowly, without interruptions
from the commoner's quarters, taking you inside. Yours.

This is a banquet; an Italian passage (yes, Italian),
reddish tiled roofs and exquisite linen on the tables—

golden enameled plates with carp and fishers
in bold yellowish outlines.

A perfume, unrefined; something flowery,
a milky petaled violet, maybe—glassy, skylight.
Breeze. You pick up the light wine and savor the bouquet.
Then you kiss him.

Darling, he says, this is where we shall begin.
We will never leave. Let's forget what has happened.

Please? (The keyword is forget.
But, how can you forget?

There is so much that has been measured, so many little private
repetitions, imagined vignettes, in a word—everything—after so
many years with the silvery haze and that special signature that
you keep in one of your books in the living room, I think—Crane
or Lorca?) Let's.

And then all the bickering about you and me. You look away
repeating the referents—smiling.

The moment is aquamarine, now.
Rolanda comes up—the way he painted women's faces
without knowing who he was really drawing.

You made adjustments here. The matter of art
always goes with the idea of escape and with the violences
of all romantic get-a-ways.

There is a deep forest. Rain. And translucent spiked leaves above
you, palm fronds and the baritone call of the Toucan parrot. This
time the jaguar is not present, only some of his calculated traces;
a wild ray of light cuts in from the shredded sky. Gnarled vines.
Succulents. Over your belly. Coppery rings of old sea shells on
the ground, then a wavy road appears ahead. It is time to walk
through this, you say. Through this relationship. To lay and
caress. The hour and place does not matter anymore. The blurring
of things is paramount, the falling—It is time. Time, you say. Just
a step through the foliage, the speckled stones with hidden

hieroglyphs on the soft side facing the earth. Nothing is as it appears. The nettles could be a leggy star wrapped in cashmere or an argyle ankle swiveling towards the law firm. It is slippery. And the pine cone could be what was said last night; how it was presented, the voice, especially the way the vowels curled when I mentioned your name. The warmth is unraveling and giving things away. Inside. A new subject is coming into being—the blue coiled snake with its silvery side vanishes. The hands are clasped. And breath is poured in and held deeply inside. A candle inside the throat comes up, held up high by your profile blending into the shore. Then, there is a forest. You are constantly through this passage. On every occasion you meet different figures. Tenderness or loss? Where is my daylight calendar? My off-white sports watch with a soprano timer? The one you gave me. Let's. You and me— through the fuzz anointed reeds, the chains of lake fog, wading in your greenish business pants; the water is running down our arms.

The concrete palisade
and the Ferris wheel tumble down to the center of things—
a moment for the city and its lovingness to fade;
at least to dissolve into a half-lens aperture

and leave the spectators with a jagged wash of color and new bridges where once there were only foreboding, solemn skyscrapers—generals of geometry and anguish (remember Lorca?). Two black leather jackets pasted with an eagerness inside the straps. Two red pearls balanced on your whitish breasts. Blackish jeans meant for a fallen queen—for living with forced velocity and laughter. This is where you live and I visit. There is a reeling sound, toothy—connected to the centripetal force of the company office where you often work. They have a jewelry box for the workers, this is new I think. A Cezanne still-life by the water fountain.

The water appears flattened, somehow, inside, as if there are little yellowish sheets of paper sliding through there, occasionally flashing, then fading out, turning to a streak of hard blue at the edge of the water bottle. Emptiness.

In the palisade
there is little room for tardy lovers.

Science. Post-modern theory and
disappearing acts are adored, primary.

He is always on time.
He has been brought up this way
(even if you have been led to believe the contrary,
things contradict this now).

This is why when you go out, he holds on to you.
Let's call it holding, for a moment. Possession
in an arcane term, out of fashion, overrun
with Gothic dreams.

In the palisade
there is a race on the grain slate of boulevards
and quick-pik numbers and fast food boutiques.
In the palisade, I investigate.

Actually, it's an old job that I have had for a long time.
I am kind of a Sherlock Gomez without
an English cap or a fraternity pin. Maybe.

Here is the essence of the matter. Boundaries.
How to get to him since it is all in fantasy-light.
How to reach through the vendors, the crystal palace
(the best marketplace in the world)
and the tap-boot dancers,
nude with their geranium-dotted bandannas?

But, no one is out, really. Every man you see is doomed,
you think, frocked with a wintry whorl of Uptown culture
and a new shaving kit of sorts, the style is insignificant—
what is of import is the little razor scissors held in the fleshy palm,
the adumbrations.

Where is your lover—
back at the Spanish terraced apartment?
Was it Julian? You see how he almost stands
with his cotton-candy in one hand, knock-kneed like in a (Juan)
Wayne western, in leather again.

The color and designs repeat themselves
He points to you and then to the Ferris wheel, way up—circling
    each other;
the clothes pull away inside the steel game box, swiveling in
    absent thought
and gravitation.

Usually she tells me that I get too flowery,
that I am a yes-man and never really come out and say things
    straight out.
What is that supposed to mean? This morning I woke up at four
thirty.
What channel? Comedy. Sex without saliva. Tried it twice, a couple
    of years
ago in a cafe that served hot apple cider with cinnamon sticks.

Trenchcoat, make-up. How about a new act
where I come out very astute, making Roman faces?
Señor Pagliachi. Too serious. That's my problem.

I've been going out with Margaret L.
(I still haven't got her last name right,
kind of sounds German.
She said in Spanish it means light.)

Makes me laugh because she drives a beat-up olive Plymouth.
A 1957 with wax. Requires pure muscle to change gears
not to mention working the steering wheel. She comes to my room
in the back, we strip and shave our bodies, then see-through syrup
pours up, then down.

We see each other early in the morning at a local pastry shoppe
and then we both head out into the smog. Sometimes we meet in
a laundry. I feel suspended most of the time. Not enough seems
to be going on in the plot.

Who's waiting? Not me.
You'll see me working hard most of the day—
there's my theatre workshop (plus jazz piano
with Bob Miranda who can still play Thelonious Monk
with his left hand, easy), Squash and sometimes
just browsing through used bookstores.

We toss and turn.
Her parents refuse to see me
(And I think I thought I was light-skinned!).

Nuts. So, we meet in her tiny studio when it's predictable.
I love the antique furniture in there, especially the round mirror
   above her
dresser, all in an eggplant brownish color. Look up from the floor
naked again, two flame blue spiders, two blue neon stars.

Things are going awry. Margaret said it's time to break up. It's
been eating at me. Because I believe in a God that's pure energy
she said (in a note). She needs a personal God. With hair? Kind
Santa Claus eyes—what? And, get this, she says how can we
raise kids if I believe in a God that's just like an atom bomb?

Nuts.
Nuts.

The lover awakens, appears—after a long drama
in the retina, Technicolor in part, in part blue-black.

Subtractions in the screen that slide before us
as if we were looking up from the belly of a tidal wave,
way up to the glassy gargoyles.
A twisting brocade sucking us in.

Listen: This is all there is—the undulation of our emulsion, a
natural science of seduction, odd-angled praise and dissonance in
this sand-stone light. A dish—yes. And, adjacent, a bowl of ruby
ants with electricity for their offspring that hopscotch through
prismatic wave-lengths of scent (uncanny attractions). His time-
piece (remember?) melts. You expected this and you were correct.
The briefcase spills too. The mirror does not have a silvery back
slate, so you fall in and then face what seems to belong to
another story of cut and paste, chisel and Plexiglas. How to reach
him, you say? A patch of carmine red. He strokes himself. Two
more centimeters and it will all fall in place. Look up again—to
the campanile.

The library hums with books and photographs that fall from the
the fourth floor stacks. A funny prayer erupts. It's uncalled for. A

young man floats above the leaves and neon signs at the cross-walk, he seems to be carrying a papaya and a paperback—a typical anthropology student, of course. Tan backpack, unbridled. Swinging a bit. Biting his lips. Savoring you. Up there, nailed. Against the brilliant bands of cloud. Maybe you think of religious associations—St. John on the Cross (another Juan) peering at you now. He looms and seems to grow larger as you walk up to feel the fabric and loudly he says, finally saying something directly to you, in a neutral voice, with affection, you feel, he says it to you.

Crossfire

Jose Enrique Pardo

You have decided that tomorrow moring you will leave Ibiza, the island of sun-worship and suspended living. You have been staying in a small hamlet on the eastern coast called Santa Eulalia del Rio, about fifteen kilometers from the heart of activity in Ibiza proper. You are well rested and hungry for your last meal. It is eight-thirty on a Sunday evening and you saunter over to Los Dos Amigos (The Two Friends) for a last lenguado con ensalada y patatas washed down with vino blanco seco. Los Dos Amigos is an unpretentious restaurant where the customers bus their own tables while the two amigos take orders, cook and cash in. There are only eight tables, each with four seats, and the traffic of comelones is overflowing the small square room.

You are sitting at a table alone, having already finished your meal, save for the wine. At the table facing you are the women whom you have innocently flirted with throughout. One has short reddish hair, beady gray eyes and a hawkish nose; the other has flowing dark blonde locks framing her luminous gold-green eyes and full senuous lips which she curls around a cigarette. You know that they have noticed you but until now you have lacked the opportunity to approach them. Now a group of eight sunburned Germans want to join your table to another, so you graciously rise, wine bottle and glass in hand, and move over to their table, where you sit abruptly without asking permission. Unsure of what language to speak in, you speak Spanish.

"Me permiten sentarme? (May I sit down?) Le di mi mesa al grupo. (I gave my table to the group.)"

The redhead responds. "No tenias que haberlo hecho. (You needn't have.) Hubieran esperado o ido a otro restaurante. (They would have waited or gone to another restaurant.)"

As you suspected, they are not Spanish, although you have not figured out their origin. You try English, and this time you address the taller one with the piercing ocelot eyes.

"Are you German?"

She laughs snidely, throws back her head and says, "No, we are Dutch." She stretches the last syllable, making a sound like an egg thrown on a griddle.

You remember that the previous day the Dutch soccer team has won the European Cup so you introduce the topic. "Congratulations then, you have won the Cup final."

"Olé!" says the redhead, and gives a thumbs-up sign.

"Are you vacationing here?"

The redhead speaks first again. "I am working here for the season. She is on vacation, just arrived today."

"That's a shame. You arrive and I am leaving. This is my last night." You say this looking straight into her hypnotic eyes.

She frowns upward and shrugs her shoulders as if to say that's the way it goes. By now you've finished your wine and decide to prolong the conversation by ordering another bottle.

"Mas vino?"

They look at each other. "Vale," says the redhead.

As all begin sipping the second bottle you ask their names. Again the redhead speaks first. You begin to notice that she is more interested in capturing your attention. "I'm Cori," she says. You shift your look to the goldilocked hypnotist. You realize she bears a resemblance to Carly Simon, without the buck teeth. "I'm Elen."

Now it's Cori's turn. "You are Spanish?"

"My mother is. I'm American."

Elen asks, "From what part?"

"New York. Ever been there?"

"No. Maybe when I'm sixty-four." She laughs offhandedly at the absurdity of the statement. You gather it's not high on her list of places to see.

"Not interested, ah?"

"Well, yes, but . . . there are many other places I would rather see first." She pronounces the *i* like a *u*.

"Such as?"

"For example, in December I am going to Indonesia. Last year I was in Thailand. Three years before in Ecuador. Next I wish to go to India, but I need a lot of time for it . . . three to four months."

"You love to travel."

"It's the most important thing in life for me." She yawns. "Excuse me, I am very tired."

"Ponte las pilas! (Get charged!)" says Cori, unwilling to let her friend's fatigue curtail her evening. "Now we're going into Ibiza for unas copas. Vienes con nosotros? (Are you coming with us?)"

You have not carried on an extended conversation for a week and you do not really have to leave the following day and you take one more look into Elen's sleepy, but still marvelous eyes, and you figure there is nothing to lose. "Let's go."

Your first stop is in nearby Cala Llonga at a bar called Mister Cairo. It is decorated in an Egyptian motif, awash with white and blue tile. The music blasts and you continue to discuss your different worlds. You find out that Cori has spent her last four summers in Ibiza. She last worked at a tour agency and speaks four languages fluently (Dutch, English, French and Spanish). In October, she returns to Holland, where she'll work as a secretary until the end of spring. Each year she takes on a new job. She has known Elen for seven years. They met while Cori worked as a secretary at the university where Elen was studying psychology. Elen has spent her last three summers with Cori in Ibiza but she confesses to be tiring of it. She does not work during the summer. In Holland, she's employed as a child psychologist counseling children who have been abused, subjected to incest or addicted to drugs. It usually takes her a couple of weeks to wind down after such a stressful daily routine but tonight, on her first night, Cori is pushing her to the limit.

You follow them into Ibiza, where the next stop is a hippie hangout called Akelarre. It sits on a concrete platform in one of the curved streets of old-town Ibiza. Outside its entrance, there are a dozen black, wooden tables with bar stools occupied by various long-haired men and costume-jeweled women sipping watered-down drinks and smoking hashish rolled into tobacco. You order a round of drinks and wonder why the police, who are half a block away, aren't busting the purveyors of the cloud of smoke you are immersed in.

"It's legal," Cori informs you. "You're allowed to have up to four grams for personal consumption. What you can't do is sell it."

Elen is fading fast but Cori is still raring to go. Soon you are joined by an Argentinian named Chacho who, after kissing Cori and Elen hello, drops some hashish on your table and asks Cori to roll un porro. She willingly obliges. The Argentine has been hiding from the authorities since he was busted for growing pot on his farm. He has been expelled by the Spanish authorities for three years and has lost his appeal of the decision. So instead of leaving he has shaved off his beard and cut his hair to travel incognito. Almost a year has elapsed and he has yet to be apprehended. He's waiting for some friends to drive him to the hottest disco on the island, named Ku. He proudly mentions that his three-and-a-half-year-old son is staying with him for the summer. Normally his son lives with his wife in Sweden. She is Scandinavian, the sister of a girl who happens to be in attendance at Akelarre. He points her out to us.

"Where is your son now?" Cori asks.

"He's at the farm with my present companera, who is also taking care of her own two children. Nos turnamos cuidandolos. (We take turns taking care of them.) Sale bien. (It works out well.)"

You ask if the child is going to school yet and feel pretty stupid when he replies.

"No, he attends a day care where supposedly they teach him things. But if it were up to me, I'd rather he travel around with me. After all, what does school teach you . . . nothing. It doesn't make you more prepared to deal with life."

You react with puzzlement. On the other hand you are conditioned to think children need to master the three r's above all else, but in Ibiza, where alternative ways of life are quite the norm, you wonder if Chacho may not have a point. Not wanting to be judgmental, you let the topic drop.

Chacho's friends are signaling their departure so he bids a hasty adios and rushes off. You are certain that you'll never see Chacho again, yet he has left an unforgettable impression on your philosophy.

A half hour later, with Elen barely able to hold her head up, you stroll back to your parked cars. In your best gentlemanly manner you escort the ladies to their car and extend your hand to say good-bye. Instead, they each kiss you in the standard double-cheeked European manner. Elen's second kiss, though, falls on your lips. Before backing out of the parking space Cori says, "I'm really sorry you're leaving tomorrow. I wish you didn't have to go."

You think this through real quick. Is this a proposition? What exactly is she getting at? "Well . . . I don't really have to go but I've already checked out of my hotel. I have nowhere to stay."

"You could stay with us. We have a two-bedroom apartment with two double beds." She pulls a pen and her appointment book out of her purse and starts writing. When she finishes, she tears away the sheet of paper. "This is my number at work. Call me after you check out and I'll give you directions to our house." She hands you the paper. You still haven't agreed to this arrangement but by now it's academic. You know you are going to stay.

"Good night," you say.

They wave back as they cruise down the avenue. You have a feeling they also know you will stay. Life is one big surprise, you tell yourself, as you turn over the ignition.

Cori recites directions over the telephone. "Take the road out to the airport and make the first right after a restaurant called Sa Punta. We're in the house across from the church. See you there at two."

You have three hours to wait. You throw your bags in the trunk and drive to the beach to kill the time.

At two o'clock Elen is stirring from her sleep. As she parades around in her bikini panties, you get your first look at her endless legs, slim, long and flexible like bamboo vines. Cori offers some lunch. You decline. So she fixes herself some toast with pate and Dutch Gouda cheese and washes it down with a newly opened bottle of red wine. You do not refuse the wine. Cori suggests that you drive Elen to the beach, since she has had to return her rental car and is now using a borrowed Mobylette (a no-frills moped) for transportation.

You and Elen drive to Aguas Blancas, one of the most beautiful beaches on the island. Situated on the northeast coast, it is unmarked and inaccessible to tourist buses. Because it is surrounded by cliffs, to reach the beach you must hike down a treacherous, rocky path. You have already been here alone on various occasions and have even befriended a waitress at the beachfront bar. You say hello and walk along the shore to a suitable spot. Although many nudists frequent Aguas Blancas, today they are a minority. Elen pulls off her tank top and reveals her peach-sized breasts with perfect brown nipples. You notice how dark the rest of her skin is, even without exposure to the sun.

"After I'm in the sun for a month I get so dark my eyes look yellow. Most people find it hard to look at them then."

You know you could stare at them without a problem. In fact, by now you're having a hard time keeping your eyes off them.

After some swimming and silent sunning you make your way over to the bar for some beverages. Elen is hungry but the cook has closed up shop. You suggest a short ride to Sant Carlos, a one-horse town which stands valiantly in the way of modernization by forcing the tour buses to bypass its narrow street.

You sit at a plastic outdoor table at the only bar in town and order bite-sized pieces of marinated fish called boquerones. "I guess we can't get real food anywhere," you say as the waiter brings the order.

"We'll just have to drink away our hunger," Elen replies. This girl is right up your alley.

Your conversation ranges from the oppressive demands of Elen's job, which are slowly burning her out, to her divorce from a husband who, unable to accept her lack of domesticity, moved to Japan, where he married a subservient Japanese woman.

"He still writes to me, you know. Says he misses our conversations, but only once in a while. Most of the time he prefers his Japanese maid, who has his dinner waiting for him whenever he arrives from work and refuses to eat until he does. I couldn't handle that."

"I have an eight-year-old daughter who I cook for every day."

"She lives with you?" Astonishment etched in her visage.

"Since her mother and I were divorced . . . six years ago."

"Five years for me. I think it's wonderful what you're doing. You're lucky to have a child. After my divorce I traveled for three months . . . Ecuador and Bolivia. There was an Indian woman who wanted to give me one of her children. The most beautiful little Indian boy. I guess he was about two years old and I thought about it but in the end I decided not to take him. I had a hard time keeping myself together at that point. If it were today I think I would have taken him. I'm getting to the point where I may not be able to have a child of my own."

You nod your head: the female time limit.

"I'm glad I have one but it's an incredible sacrifice. Changes your whole life around. Except that if I were alone I don't know where the hell I'd be right now, maybe underground."

That evening, after you've had a satisfying five-dollar meal and sat over coffee in the plaza watching the flesh parade of tourists, you coax the ladies into an early retreat and head back to the apartment.

Elen heads off to her bedroom complaining about her gelatin-mattressed bed, which relegates her to sleeping in a u shape with her feet and head rising above her submerged torso. You begin to prepare the couch, anticipating that it will be most uncomfortable because it is too small to accommodate the full extension of your legs. You decide to sleep on the cold tile floor instead and begin to arrange the cushions thereon when Cori comes into the room wearing only panties and a sheer nightie.

"You don't have to sleep on the floor. You can sleep on my bed. It's got a board under the mattress. It's very comfortable."

You don't have to think about this decision. Reflexively you agree and slip on a pair of running shorts for decorum. Cori is right. The bed is the most comfortable one you have slept on in the last two weeks. You lie on your back in the far corner next to the windows and stretch your arms along your sides, purposely avoiding any contact with her. By now, Cori has slipped off her nightie and curled under a sheet. You choose not to cover yourself with it so that it will act as a buffer between you. Cori twists and turns frequently and you suspect she is drawing closer to you but before you can confirm this you fall asleep.

In the middle of the night you feel Cori's leg rubbing against yours. You look over at her in the faint predawn light and notice that her eyes are closed tight. She's probably just shifted to that position during her sleep, you tell yourself, and move farther towards the edge of the bed to eliminate the contact and return to sleep.

The next morning over coffee Elen and Cori are having an animated conversation in Dutch rife with giggling and thigh-slapping laughter. Initially you feel as dumb as a sixth-grader in a physics class and allow them their intimacy but then you notice Elen staring at you between chuckles and you begin to think they are joking about you.

"So what is so funny?" you say, unable to remain silent any longer.

They look at each other, then Elen speaks up.

"Cori says you were scared of her last night. That you slept like a cat cuddled up in a corner of the bed with your hands covering your groin." They both laugh. You feel yourself starting to blush.

"I was only trying to be a gentleman. What was I supposed to do?"

Cori unloads a weighty question. "Real men don't run away from women, do they?"

"I don't know what real men do. I just know that I wasn't scared." You cannot help but sound defensive.

"She's just kidding," says Elen. "Of course you were a gentleman. Maybe it was Cori who didn't behave like a lady." She glances over at Cori, who replies with a hands-on-the-hip smirk.

"I'm leaving. I'm going to be late for work."

Cori rushes off and you are left alone with Elen. The weather is not good for the beach. The sky is filled with black clouds and rain is imminent. So you loll over your coffee and spend the rest of the morning reading your books in isolated silence.

At one-fifteen Cori returns for lunch. Anticipating her arrival, you have prepared some cheese sandwiches, but she enters upset over the fact that it is pouring rain and neither one of you has been inclined to pick her up. She is soaked from head to toe in spite of having gotten a ride from a coworker. You open a bottle of wine and drown her anger in it. During lunch, the sun breaks through and, as you are set to drive Cori back to work at three forty-five, the sky is cloudless and azure blue. Elen announces that she is going up to the rooftop terrace to sunbathe. You can either go to the beach alone or come back to the terrace, as you wish.

In record time you're back at the house climbing the stairs to the roof. The door is ajar. You open it slowly and witness Elen lying naked on a beach towel absorbing the sunlight with her Walkman and her sunglasses on. Her gazellelike silhouette stretches out and arches up towards the sun. You make up your mind at that moment that before you go back downstairs you will let her know that you are attracted to her. You walk onto the roof. She notices you and raises herself on her elbows.

"You didn't go to the beach?"

"I missed you too much . . . couldn't have lasted three hours."

"Hah!"

You sit down next to her, pull off your tee shirt and kick off your flip-flops.

"The sun is so hot, it's making me thirsty," she says.

"Do you want some more wine?" You notice she's brought up a glass that is now empty.

"Please."

"I'll bring you some . . . and some cold water too."

You return with the wine and the water. Elen has turned over on her chest, affording you the rear view. Her ass is small but cheeky. Her locks of curly hair form stripes across her back.

"Here you go."

"Thanks."

"Salud," you toast. Elen returns to her position. You take a long look at her lying before you and you cannot refrain from touching her. You start to caress her by running your fingers softly across her back. She seems oblivious to it so you begin to kiss the back of her neck and her ears. Now you get a response. Abruptly, Elen shifts her body around, puts her arms around your neck and pulls you down to her lips, soft, fleshy and anxious.

You spend the next two and a half hours kissing, cuddling and listening to Van Morrison on the Walkman. At several points you work yourselves up to the point of no return but you never cross it because Elen is unsure and halts you. Nevertheless, for you those hours on the terrace are steeped in romance and by seven o'clock when Cori returns you share that bond of intimacy which belongs only to lovers.

You run off to dinner early because Cori knows a hotel in San Antonio (thirty minutes away on the western side of the island) which serves up a cheap all-you-can-eat buffet for five dollars stocked with fresh vegetables. The only vegetables you have eaten in Spain are lettuce and onions, because they come in salad, and potatoes. The Spanish restaurants aren't very big on them and you long to bite into a stalk of fresh broccoli.

As you gorge yourself on vegetables in the sprawling mess hall full of Britons, Cori and Elen conduct their own private conversation in Dutch. You try your best to ignore them but a certain feeling of helplessness attaches every time they do this. Unlike the Romance languages, Dutch is entirely foreign to you so you have no clue as to what they are discussing. From the outdoor patio adjacent to the dining area music filters in. It seems the hotel's activities director is running a modified version of Simon Says, with children being expulsed from the group if they fail to stop dancing when the music is turned off. "You're out!" she yells at the kids as they are eliminated one by one. You also feel left out as you bite into a carrot.

After dinner Cori takes Elen and you to a bar on the water's edge just in time to see the end of the sunset. The view is magnificent, the sea stretching to the horizon, stars popping up like polka dots in the midnight blue sky. You feel relaxed here, sitting alfresco with a woman on either side. There is very sensual saxophone music playing. Elen comments that it is her favorite instrument and you proceed to give her a list of all the great sax records you know. You are entranced by the peacefulness of this setting and if it were up to you you would stay here all night; but now it is Cori who complains of fatigue and after you finish your drink you drive back home.

Miraculously, upon your return Cori gets her second wind. She takes a shower and comes out doused with perfume. Elen is writing a letter to a Dutch friend she will be meeting in Mallorca in a month. She has been distant throughout the evening and you wonder if she will change her attitude and invite you into her bed. You wish she would. Cori bids good night, goes into the bedroom and plays Erik Satie on her boom box. You pick up Hemingway's *For Whom the Bell Tolls* and attempt to read but you cannot concentrate. Seeing Elen still immersed in her writing, you head for Cori's bed.

The room is bathed in candlelight and Cori is naked on the bed, pretending to be asleep. The circumstances have now made it obvious that she is waiting for you to make a move but you decide against it and assume last night's position on the far edge of the bed.

"Please blow out the candles before you fall asleep," she says resignedly.

Immediately you blow out the candles and drift off to sleep.

The next time you awake it is caused by Cori's leg being draped across your thighs. Her hand is scratching at your chest and her lips are kissing your neck. The dawn light is filtering through the windows and you gaze at her through foggy vision. Without a word, she slithers over your body, her nipples rubbing against yours, her mons pressing yours, her feet clamped to yours. She kisses you wildly and deeply and you feel your sex rise excitedly. Like an animal in heat you respond, your blood boiling over, washing away logic and reason. Minutes after, you are locked inside each other rolling on the bed threatening to shatter the board beneath the mattress. After orgasm, you wonder whether the exultations of lust have been heard by Elen in the next room. You hope not but you are too spent to care. The placid postcoital satisfaction envelops you and you fall back asleep.

Soon you are aroused by Cori giving you a goodbye kiss; she's off to work. Afterwards you cannot catch any more z's and decide to start your day. Elen is already up and in bright spirits, seemingly unaware of the morning's earlier event.

"Would you like me to make you some coffee?" she asks.

"I thought you said you weren't domestic. Sure, I'd love some. I've got to go into town to change some money and pick up my boat ticket for tomorrow. Would you like to come with me?"

"Yes, I will go, but I need for you to do me a favor before."

"What is it?"

"Well, now that you are leaving I am going to need some transportation and Cori told me about this place down the road that sells used Mobylettes and . . . I want to buy one. I thought maybe since you speak the language you can help me with the transaction."

"I'd be glad to."

She pours the coffee and you sit across from each other at the dining room table.

"Did you sleep well last night?" she asks in an ambiguous tone halfway between sarcasm and genuine concern. You wonder if you are being set up.

"Yeah, I did. Cori's bed is really comfortable, although I would have preferred sleeping in your uncomfortable bed with your comfortable body."

She smiles mischievously.

You strike up a deal with the Mobylette salesman. Elen will have one in two days and he will buy it back from her at the end of her stay. You run the errands together and although the activity is mundane, the nearness of your departure begins to make every moment you spend with Elen more meaningful.

You have agreed to meet Cori at the apartment in order to go to Las Salinas beach together during her three-hour midday break. You pack up some sandwiches and a bottle of white wine and drive through the salt marshes to this secluded two-kilometer stretch of sand where the beautiful people congregate to display their sculpted, well-oiled bodies.

It's a cool day for the beach and the crowd is sparse. You stretch out your towels on the crest of a sand dune. You uncork the wine and pass the bottle around in hobo fashion. The girls drift off into their usual Dutch chatter but now you are more apprehensive than ever about its nature.

Powerless to steer the flow of the conversation, you ignore them and stretch out on your towel, staring at the dirty gray sky.

After about twenty minutes you notice that the conversation has ceased. The silence is heavy as a giant boulder. You smell trouble and feel parched with anxiety. You want to leave, to be by yourself. It appears that Cori does also because she rises, deposits her belongings in her bag and walks off down the shore. Now you know they have discussed the encounter of the night before and you must prepare yourself to meet your fate.

Words are a precious few until Cori returns to work. Elen sits morosely on the couch, attempting to read. You produce another wine bottle and offer her some. Then you sit next to her on the couch.

"I'm feeling very cynical," she says.

"Oh, that's too bad. Why?"

"You know why."

"Because of what happened last night."

"I can't believe you did that."

"Would you like to hear my side of the story?"

"I don't know if it's going to make any difference."

"It would make a difference to me."

"O.K., go ahead."

"Last night when I went into the room Cori had set up this romantic trap. Candles everywhere, Satie playing on the cassette. She was stretched out in all her glory on the bed, expecting me to succumb to the seduction. I didn't. I went to sleep. The next thing I know I wake up at dawn and she's got her leg draped over me and she's touching me then kissing me and she gets me hot . . . and I couldn't turn back. It's difficult for a man to turn back at that point. A rush of adrenaline seizes you and you have to expend yourself to release it. It's as reflexive as going to the bathroom, as feeding yourself when you're starving. So it happened. It wasn't romantic. It wasn't like being with you. I wanted to be with you but you wouldn't have it. And then it was over. I'm afraid it may have meant more to Cori but if it did she misinterpreted it. If I had truly wanted her I would have made love to her the night before."

You down the entire glass of wine, rise from your seat and pace back and forth across the room.

"I don't understand that about men. Just because a woman touches you you can't walk away?"

"You're not a man. What can I tell you? You have a muscle down there. It gets hard and it must be exercised to relax it. Women don't have that."

"Women get wet. Why couldn't you just get up out of bed or just tell her to stop?"

"I don't know. I suppose I could have."

"But you didn't. You know, I thought you were different. I'm not angry about this. It's already done. I thought you had more self-respect, that you weren't like the ordinary man, but I was wrong. You're full of the same bullshit."

"Well, I'm sorry I let you down. Believe me. I wish it had been you."

She shook her head, filled with consternation. "Maybe it was my fault. Yesterday on the terrace it was so wonderful for me, so special, and I didn't make love to you and maybe I should have. If I had, none of this would have happened."

You stride over to her. She has her head in her hands cowered down over her lap. You take her hands in yours, lift her face up towards you and kiss her tenderly on the lips. At first she resists, but you persist and in one motion slide your arm under her thighs and lift her off the couch. Then you walk into her bedroom and immerse her gently in her spongy bed and dive over her, sinking into her softness. You pour your love into her raging sea, gently but persistently, and a wave builds. She closes her eyes and thrashes her head about wildly until ultimately you both scream in unison as the wave crashes thunderously against the shore, wiping it clean.

As you lie in the afterglow of love, your head resting on her breast, her fingers combing your hair, she says, "You have to promise me one thing now."

"Yes."

"You cannot make love to me again after today. You cannot come into my bed tonight and I will not let you sleep with Cori."

You are back on the living room floor, where you had intended on being since the beginning.

"Why are you punishing me?"

"Because Cori and I go back too long. We are old friends and I would not like her to see us flaunt ourselves in front of her. She's entitled to respect."

You understand respect, in fact you find it admirable. "But it's so cold on that floor," you say. Then you burrow deeper into her chest and take her nipple in your mouth.

"I'll lend you a blanket."

You have come full circle. But for now you hold on tighter, hoping to make time stand still.

Cori arrives with the same stone face she wore when she left. She heads straight for the wine bottle and plops it before her on the table. She sits and lights up a cigarette, exhaling the smoke forcefully. Elen sits across from her at the table and you ten feet away on the couch. Cautiously, Elen starts a conversation. You cannot understand any of it but you know what it is about. As it gathers momentum, the volume and tone of speech become insulting. Back and forth the invectives fly as you sit on the couch twisting your head from one combatant to another as if you were watching a tennis match. The gesticulations increase and there is thigh slapping and fist pounding and at times both of them are yelling so loud that seems impossible for either to be listening to the other. You feel like a fly amidst a pack of elephants. Although they are talking about you, they never once look your way. Finally during one of their breathing breaks, you interrupt.

"I know you're talking about me and I think the least you can do is speak English so that I can be included in the discussion. Now look . . . I don't know where to start but I don't think I'm the only person to blame for this. I mean . . . it takes two to tango." You're staring straight into Cori's eyes. "I went to bed last night and you had made the room all romantic . . . candles, music. You had the whole thing set up. And then I went to sleep, and it pissed you off. So the next thing I know I wake up at dawn and you're all over me, getting me excited, and then we have sex. And now you're going on and on about it like we're Romeo and Juliet. C'mon, you wanted me and you got me; it's that simple. If I'm to blame, which I suppose I am to some extent, then you are also. I didn't have any intention of sleeping with you when I went to sleep but you made sure I did so before I woke up."

"So I am to blame? Why didn't you tell me you wanted to sleep with Elen? Why weren't you just man enough to tell me to stop and get out of the bed? I didn't force you to have sex with me. I thought there were some feelings between us. I didn't know what had gone on between you and Elen."

Elen interrupts. "I am to blame, because I should have told Cori about yesterday. If I had, this wouldn't have happened. I should have just let you sleep with me because I wanted you to, but I didn't."

"Why should it be your fault? Why couldn't he just have stopped it? Your male ego wouldn't let you and it felt too good."

"Is this coming from the same person who said I was scared of her? I'm sorry if you thought there were real deep feelings attached to this; there weren't. But you're no teenager, and you know what a man's going to do when you touch him like you touched me. Don't give me this bullshit about me calmly walking away. If I had, you would've been angrier than a bitch in heat."

"I can't take this. Now you're insulting me on top of everything else." She gets up to go to her room. You grab her by the arm.

"Listen to me!" you demand angrily. "I'm not insulting you, I'm just telling you the truth. Now you can either pout like a little baby about this or just let it go and go on with your life."

"I'm not going anywhere with *you,* that's for sure. I'm going to take a shower and go to bed." She yanks her arm free and stomps off. Elen looks at you as if to say now you've really done it, but you're too livid to care.

"What am I supposed to say except the truth?" You deliver your final statement and sink back into the sofa.

Realizing how upset Cori is by all this, Elen is determined to persuade her to bury the hatchet by all of you going out to dinner together. You have previously extended an invitation and stand by your offer, although you know it will not be a joyous occasion.

After another protracted round of private negotiations, Elen emerges successful from Cori's room and you head off to a paella dinner in Santa Eulalia. Cori proceeds to down so many goblets of wine that her venomous stare degenerates into a cross-eyed intrusion. Elen does her best to keep everything light, joking about the other eaters and devising a comedy routine mocking her cigarette habit, but Cori is not amused. She continues drinking and wearing her stubborn donkey face until you get home. You are feeling so out of place by that time that you begin to debate whether you should head back into Ibiza and sleep in the car. You mention it privately to Elen but she emphatically disagrees. "It's my house too," she says. "You come on upstairs and we'll work it out."

Like a wounded lioness, Cori silently retreats to her bedroom, bidding an abrupt good night. Elen sits at the table, pours another glass of wine and lights up yet another cigarette. By now, she cares little about how much she's smoked and is instead more interested in self-ridicule. You sit down across from her and take her hand in yours.

"Another Marlboro, eh?"

"One more before I go to bed."

"Cori wasn't very cheerful," you say sarcastically.

"It would have been better without her."

"You tried to do the right thing."

"I felt sorry for her, the way she was hurt."

"I didn't imagine she'd take it so hard either."

You rub your thumb along the top of her hand. Her fingers are long and bony, her skin taut like a drum. You look up, searching for her eyes, but she is looking down at your hands.

"As long as we have this time, I just want to tell you that I'm going to miss you very much. That in you I've found a different woman from any other that I've ever met. Uncomplicated, unconcerned with material trappings and secure enough not to have to impress anyone except by being yourself, your unaffected self. I admire you for that."

She looks up now and you think you detect tears starting to cloud her eyes. "Thanks. I'm going to miss you too. But we have to be thankful that we had a chance to meet, even if four days is all we ever spend together. I still believe you are different from most men, and you have taught me about discipline and responsibility. I wish I could have a child like yours, but I don't think it will happen."

"I can help you with that." You say this half in jest because you're not sure you mean it.

"Don't make a promise you cannot keep." She is dead serious. She runs her fingers through her hair and shakes her head. "Ay ay ay."

"What about coming with me tomorrow. Why don't you just come with me."

"It's too soon. I just got here. If it were two or three weeks from now I might go, but right now it's no good. We have to say good-bye. That's just how it goes. You get used to it when you travel a lot. But between us I know we are leaving something that will not die."

She reaches over the table, takes your face in her hands and kisses you blandly.

"Now we must go to bed and in the morning I will go with you to the port to see you off. Remember, you must stay out here or I'll kick you out of my room. I'll get you a pillow and a blanket."

You position the cushions in a T like you did the first night, but now you know they will be your bed. Lying down with all the lights out, you think about Elen in the next room and you sap all your energy keeping your word.

Your wake-up call is the bathroom door being slammed about three feet from your ear. It is Cori, ready to leave for work. You rise, rearrange the cushions on the sofa and head into the bathroom to wash up. When you emerge, she is ready to leave.

"This is good-bye," she says. "I wish you luck and a safe trip." She shakes your hand perfunctorily, as if you are someone she has just met for the first time.

"Good-bye," you say. "I won't keep any bad feelings about what happened between us and I hope in time you won't either."

She nods her head and arches her eyebrows to indicate her understanding, then raises her palm, bidding farewell.

Immediately after Cori steps out, Elen enters the room, already dressed to leave. She makes some coffee without engaging in conversation. You are corraled by ambivalence and anxious to leave the apartment.

"I'm ready to go. Are you?"

"As soon as I finish my coffee. Are you sure you don't want any?"

"I'll have some in town."

While Elen drinks her coffee you take a long analytical look at her for the purpose of helping you remember her after you part. You lose yourself dreaming about what would happen between you if you could prolong your stay. Maybe it would not get any better? Maybe you would discover this was all just a lark? You comfort yourself with this negative assumption but you do not want to believe it.

After the inevitable bureaucratic wrangling at the port, you park your car alongside all the other vehicles to be transported in the hull of the liner and head across the street to a cafe. You sit over coffee and a breakfast pastry and order a sandwich to go for the trip. You pull your camera out of your backpack and photograph Elen close-up. She is embarrassed by the photos and asks you to stop.

"I want to be able to look at you when you're no longer with me."

"And you will need a photo? You cannot just see me in your mind?"

"I guess I can but this way it's easier and more exact. I'll send you a copy."

"I'd prefer one of you."

"As long as you promise not to use it as a dartboard."

You sandwich her hand between both of yours. She smiles consolingly.

"They're starting to load the cars."

You drop enough pesetas to cover the bill on the table and, towing Elen by the hand, walk back to your car. Once seated, you reach over and kiss her passionately, wanting to leave your seal on her heart and mind.

"I'm going to miss you."

"We'll write to each other."

"Maybe I'll visit you in Holland."

"If you wish."

"Will we see the sights or spend all our time in bed?"

"I don't know. See the sights, I guess."

"We'll leave Cori out of it this time."

She does not answer.

The car is approaching the ramp leading into the ship. Once you drive in you will not be allowed off. You lean over and embrace Elen tightly one more time.

"I get off now. Take care of yourself. I'll write to you."

"Bye." She is left standing in the spot next to the passenger door as you run the car up the ramp and into the dark cavity of the ship's hull. The deckhand signals you to the beginning of a new line, guaranteeing that you'll be the last car off. You run upstairs on deck wondering if Elen will be standing by the dock waiting until you shove off. You strain over the rail on the side of the boat alongside the pier and look down. She is standing against a bench by the ticket office, her hand cupped above her eyes as a visor so she can look up into the sun. Your heart is beating faster and faster and a balloon bursts inside your chest. You look down at her, smile and wave your hand. She waves back. For several minutes you are locked in each other's sights. An errant tear falls down your cheek onto your lips and you taste it, salty and warm. You do not have a handkerchief, so you rub your forearm across your eyes and put your sunglasses on. You wonder if Elen is also crying but you are too far away to tell. The ship whistle blows like the sound of a giant cow mooing and the vessel slowly pulls away from the dock. Minutes later, Elen's outline dissolves in the distance and climbs aboard your memory.

Researching Frida Kahlo

Markanthony Alvidrez

I see her entering the Henry Madden Library and my eyes stare at her long white skirt, exposing her calves with every step. She walks past the information desk and computer lab. I follow her.

Her blouse is thin, white, and a red sachet is wrapped around her small waist. Even though the weather is warm, this woman wears a black shawl. It looks hand-woven and she probably did it herself.

She waits for the elevator. I stand behind her, trying to avoid her face, but it's hard. Our eyes collide with an innocent stare. I smile, she doesn't. The elevator doors slide open and we enter. The woman presses the second-floor button.

"Has anybody ever told you how much you look like Frida Kahlo?"

The woman smiles, exposing her white teeth. She extends her small hand. "My name is Frida Kahlo, I'm pleased to meet you."

"My name is Arcello Nunez." I shake her hand. She says her name is Frida Kahlo and I go along with it.

The elevator stops and we walk out. I quickly walk away from her. She grabs a big book from a shelf and sits at a long wooden table facing the elevator. I pretend I'm searching for books, but she keeps catching my eyes staring at her. The woman who calls herself Frida throws her shawl to the floor. Her blouse quickly comes off, showing off her brown breasts. With her fingers she gestures an invitation. I hesitate. Frida stands up and takes off her skirt, then kicks it away from the table. Her thin body is beautiful, brown, and naked. Frida smiles and touches her stomach. She leans back against the table and then lies on top of it.

My crotch bulges and my palms are wet. I stare up at the ceiling and the lights change colors. My eyes find Frida's body again. I walk closer to her.

Streams of pink and blue lights settle on her round breasts. "Lie besides me," she says as she rubs an art book between her legs.

I stare at her body. A body that I've worshipped for years. Since I was in high school, I've masturbated to her pictures and paintings. All that is in the past now. A cold and near past. Frida Kahlo lays on the heavy wooden table and whispers my name.

"Touch me, Arcello."

"People are watching," I say, turning around and realizing the library is empty.

"Take my hand."

I take two steps towards her and kiss her stomach. My lips sink into her softness as her smell floats into my flaring nostrils. Her small fingers run through my hair. Frida's legs spread wide and the book drops to the floor.

"I love you, Frida," I mumble.

She responds by grabbing two fistfuls of my hair. Frida heavy-breathes unlike any woman I've had sex with. She is different. Frida is a legend. Frida is mystical. Frida is an artist. Frida is a communist. Frida has been dead for over forty years.

I kick my shoes off and my socks follow them. The carpet is cool and soft beneath my feet. "Somebody's going to see us," I say. I'm unsure if she hears me. The library is quiet except for the low hum of the air-conditioning system.

Frida sits up and pulls me closer to her. She unbuttons my faded jeans and I pull them down along with my underwear.

"Take your shirt off."

I do as she says. It was logical before to say that I would never get a chance to make love with Frida Kahlo, but here I am, naked, cool, and turned on.

The elevator rings and the second-floor light is on. The doors slide open. We turn to see who's interrupting us, but the elevator is empty.

Frida is still sitting up and she grabs my penis with her right hand. The hand she used to paint with. "Your dick is brown, warm, and hard, Arcello." Her grip is soft, yet firm.

I bend my knees slightly and hold her small face with my large hands. I kiss her lips, feeling her light mustache against my upper lip. Our tongues touch and explore each other. I bend my knees a little more and I start to kiss her neck.

She continues to massage my dick and then stops when I begin to lick her dark brown nipples. My tongue moves as if I were a cat licking himself clean. Her nipples are erect when I begin to suck on them. Her right nipple is first, and then the left.

I wrap my arms around Frida, bringing her body closer. "Oh, Frida," I moan, and repeat it three times, resembling a low-budget stag film. I find myself getting lower and lower until my lips glide across her dark pubic hair. With my two hands I rub her outer thighs. My tongue, a soft instrument, enjoys the woman of Frida.

... updownupdownupdownupdownupdownupdownupdown-
updown ...

My tongue continues its work and my hands reach out for her
small, but round, breasts.

Frida throws her head back and thrusts herself into my face.
She repeats the thrusting about six times and each time my tongue
thrashes faster than the last.

The cool air from the air conditioner is now a warm mist. The
mist gradually becomes thicker, enveloping everything, including
books, tables, studying stalls, and the elevator. It envelops everything except our naked bodies.

"You taste sweet," I say with my head still between her legs.

"How sweet, Arcello?"

"Sweet, sweet like fruit."

"Do I—ahh," she moans. "Do I taste like a banana?"

"You're sweet like a ripe nectarine."

Frida sits straight up again before she wraps her legs around
me. Strands of wet hair sticks to her forehead and below her jaw.
Sweat rolls off into the bushy eyebrows that she's famous for. Frida
puts her arms around my neck and I wrap mine around her sweaty
back. She tells me to pick her up. I listen. When Frida Kahlo tells
you to do something, you do it.

"Lie back on the table—I want to fuck you," she whispers in
my ear.

Still holding her, I lie back. While Frida sits on my stomach,
she grabs between my legs from behind. The library is dark and
quiet. The air-conditioning system no longer hums. The warm mist
gets warmer. Our naked brown bodies glisten with sweat. The pink
and blue lights disappear because they were never there.

Frida lifts her lower self up and then sits back down. I feel
myself in her. My erect cock, the one she calls warm, brown, and
hard, swims inside Frida Kahlo. She slaps her hands against my
chest and then gently pinches my skin. Sweat rolls off her nose and
lands on my torso, mingling with mine. Our fluids become one.
Even our bodies attempt to become one as she violently thrusts
herself.

I place my hands beside her hips and guide her up-down movements. Those movements are met with my own. A rhythm begins.
It's a rhythm that can be found in a Muddy Waters song. The song
is so beautiful, Frida sings along with it.

"I love you, Frida. I want to fuck you forever." I attempt to
keep up with her speed as her up-down thrusts become faster.

She whips her head back three times, her loose hair flying about. Frida lifts her arms above her head. The library echoes with our lovemaking and the walls sweat with our lust. Her breasts bounce with expert control.

I can no longer keep up with Frida's pace. My body is now under direct order of Frida Kahlo as her inner muscles tightly grip my wet cock. Her love is sweet nectarine juice and her lust is paint. My body is a cheap piece of canvas. I'm dry, plain, and I desire her stroke. Frida paints my mind.

. . . she is dressed in a long skirt that was made by her french lover . . . her hair is dark and falls over her shoulders . . . she paints her trademark mustache . . . she paints her trademark eyebrows . . . there is no smile on her face . . . it is grim in thought . . . it is grim in life . . . diego is absent . . . he's off painting a mural on the ass of the world . . . her paintbrushes . . . her paint knives . . . they reach my brain . . . frida rebuilds my lust . . . it's normal and innocent now . . .

She screams out loud. So loud it cuts into the warm mist. Frida's body relaxes and stops moving. The music is over. Silence lingers and floats with the mist.

Before her screams, my internal organs momentarily expanded. They expanded, but they are normal now. I'm still in her, but in more ways than one.

Frida has come before me in physical and mental form. She lifts herself off the table, licks my lips, and then kisses them.

I reach out for her, but my weak arms cannot grab her in time. Frida's beautiful naked body vanishes in the warm and silent mist. The elevator rings, the doors slide open, and Frida Kahlo enters. I pick the art book up from the floor and place it on my wet lap. I can still smell her. The pink and blue lights return. I lift the book to my nose and shut my bloodshot eyes.

The Apple Orchard

Rudolfo Anaya

The last week of school and the warm spring weather made us restless. Pico and Chuerco ditched every chance they got, and when they came to school it was only to bother the girls and upset the teachers, otherwise they played hooky in Duran's apple orchard, the large orchard which lay between the school and our small neighborhood. They smoked cigarettes and looked at *Playboy* magazines, which they stole from their older brothers.

I had stayed with them once, but my father had found out about it and he had been very angry. "It costs money to send you to school," he had said, "so go! Go and learn everything there is to learn! That's the only way to get ahead in this world! Don't play hooky with those tontos, they will never amount to anything!" So I dragged myself to school, which, in spite of the warm spring weather, had one consolation: Miss Brighton. She was the young substitute teacher who had come to replace Mr. Portacles, who had had a nervous breakdown. I had her for first-period English and last-period study hall. The day she arrived I helped her move her supplies and books, so we formed a good friendship. I think I fell in love with her, because I looked forward to her class, and I was sad when she told me she would be with us only these few days until the end of school. Next year she would have a regular job in Santa Fe.

So for a few weeks I was happy, and my fascination with Miss Brighton grew. During study hall I would pretend to read, but most often I would sit and stare over my book at her. When she happened to glance up she would smile at me, and sometimes she came to my desk and asked me what I was reading. She loaned me a few books, and after I read them and told her what I had found in them she was very pleased. Her lips curled in a smile which almost laughed and her bright eyes shone with light. I began to memorize her features, and at night I began to dream of her.

Then on the last day of school Pico and Chueco came up with their crazy idea. It didn't interest me at first, but the truth is I was also filled with curiosity. So I gave in reluctantly.

"It's the only way to become a man," Pico said, as if he really knew what he was talking about.

"Yeah," Chueco agreed, "we've seen it in pictures, but you gotta see the real thing to know what it's like."

"Okay, okay," I said finally, "I'll do it."

That night I stole into my parents' bedroom. I had never done that before. Their bedroom was a place where they could go for privacy, and I was never to interrupt them when they were in there. My father had only told me that once. We were washing his car when unexpectedly he turned to me and said, "When your mother and me are in the bedroom you should never disturb us, understand?" I nodded. I knew that part of their life was shut off to me, and it was to remain a mystery.

Now I felt like a thief as I stood in the dark and saw their dark forms on the bed. My father's arm rested over my mother's hip. I heard his low, peaceful snore and I was relieved that he was asleep. I hurried quickly to her bureau and opened her small vanity box. I knew the small mirror we needed for our purpose lay among the bottles of perfume and nail polish. My hands trembled when I found it. I slipped it into my pocket and left the room quickly.

"Did you get it?" Pico asked the next morning.

We met in the apple orchard where we always met on the way to school. The flowering trees buzzed with honeybees as they swarmed over the thick clusters of white petals. The fragrance reminded me of my mother's vanity case, and for a moment I wondered if I should surrender the mirror to Pico. I had never stolen anything from her before. But it was too late to back out. I took the mirror from my pocket and held it out. For a moment it reflected the light which filtered through the canopy of apple blossoms, then Pico howled and we ran to school.

Miss Brighton was the kindest teacher we knew, so we decided to steal the glue from her room.

"Besides, she likes you," Pico said. "You keep her busy, I'll steal the glue." So we pushed our way past the mob which filled the hallway to her room.

"Isador," she smiled when she saw me at the door, "what are you doing at school so early?" She looked at Pico and Chueco, and a slight frown crossed her face.

"I came for the book," I reminded her. She was dressed in bright spring yellow, and the light shone through the windows glistened on her dress and her soft hair.

"Of course . . . I have it ready." I walked with her to the desk and she handed me the book. I glanced at the title, *The Arabian*

Nights. I shivered because out of the corner of my eye I saw Pico grab a bottle of glue and stick it under his shirt.

"Thank you," I mumbled. We turned and raced out of the room to the bathroom. A couple of eighth-graders stood by the windows, looking out and smoking cigarettes. They usually paid little attention to us seventh-graders, so we slipped unnoticed into one of the stalls. Pico closed the door. Even in the early morning the stall was already warm and the odor very bad.

"Okay, break the mirror," Pico whispered.

"Seven years bad luck," Chueco reminded me.

"Don't pay attention to him, break it!" Pico commanded.

I took the mirror from my pocket, recalled for a moment the warm, sweet fragrance which filled my parents' bedroom, the aroma of the vanity case, the sweet scent of the orchard, like Miss Brighton's cologne, and then I looked at Pico and Chueco's sweating faces and smelled the bad odor of the crowded stall and my hands broke out in a sweat.

"Break it!" Pico said sharply.

I looked at the mirror, briefly saw my face in it, saw my eyes which I knew would give everything away if we were caught, and I thought of the disgrace I would bring my father if he knew what I was about to do.

I can't, I said, but there was no sound. There was only the rancid odor which rose from the toilet stool, Chueco's heavy breathing, and Pico's eyes glued to the mirror as I turned my hand and let it fall. It fell slowly, as if in slow motion, reflecting us, changing our sense of time, which had moved so fast that morning, into a time which moved so slowly I thought the mirror would never hit the floor and break. But it did. The sound exploded, the mirror broke and splintered, and each piece seemed to bounce up to reflect our dark, sweating faces again.

"Shhhhhhhh," Pico whispered, finger to lips.

We held our breath and waited. Nobody moved outside the stall. No one had heard the breaking of the mirror which for me had been like the sound of thunder.

Then Pico reached down and picked up three well-shaped pieces, about the size of silver dollars. "Just right!" He grinned and handed each of us a piece. Then he put his right foot on the toilet seat, opened the bottle of glue, and smeared the white, sticky glue on the tip of his shoe. He placed the piece of mirror on the glue, looked down and saw his sharp, weasel face reflected in it, and smited. "Fits just right!"

We followed suit, first Chueco, then me.

"This is going to be fun!" Chueco giggled.

"Hot bloomers! Hot bloomers!" Pico slapped my back.

"Now what?"

"Wait for it to dry."

We stood with our feet on the toilet seat, pant legs up, waiting for the glue to dry.

"Whose panties are you going to see first?" Chueco asked Pico.

"Concha Panocha's," Pico leered. "She's got the biggest boobs!"

"If they have big boobs, does that mean they have it big downstairs?" Chueco asked.

"Damn right!"

"Zow-ee!" Chueco exclaimed, and spit all over me.

"Shhhh!" Pico whispered. Two boys had come in. They talked while they used the urinals, then they left.

"Ninth-graders," Pico said.

"Those guys know everything," Chueco said.

"Yeah, they know how to get it, but after today we'll know too."

"Yeah." Chueco smiled.

I turned away to escape another shower and his bad breath. The wall of the bathroom stall was covered with drawings of naked men and women. Old Plácido, the janitor, worked hard to keep the walls clean, but the minute he finished scrubbing off the drawings in one stall, others appeared next door. The drawings were crude, hastily done diagrams. The one in front of me showed two legs spread apart. A swollen tool hung down from two giant balloons. Everything was always dripping. I wondered why. And why had I joined Pico and Chueco in this crazy plan?

Last year the girls didn't seem to matter to us. We played freely with them. But the summer seemed to change everything. When we came back to school the girls had changed. They had grown bigger. Some of them began to wear lipstick and nail polish. They carried their bodies differently, and I couldn't help but notice for the first time their small, swollen breasts. Pico explained about brassieres to me. An air of mystery began to surround the girls we had once known so well.

I began to listen closely to the stories the ninth-grade boys told about girls. They gathered in the bathroom to smoke before class and during lunch break, and they talked about cars or sports or girls. Some of them already dated girls, and a few bragged about girls they had gotten naked. I guessed those were the ones who drew the pictures on the bathroom walls. They knew.

But their stories were incomplete, half whispered, and the crude drawings only aroused more curiosity. The more I thought about the change which was coming over us, the more troubled I became, and at night my sweaty dreams were filled with the images of women, phantasmal creatures who danced in a mist and removed their veils as they swirled around me. But always I awoke before the last veil was removed. I knew nothing. That's why I gave in to Pico's idea. I wanted to know.

He had said that if we glued a small piece of mirror to our shoes, we could push our feet between the girls' legs when they weren't watching, and then we could see everything.

"And they don't wear panties in the spring," he said. "Everybody knows that. So you can see everything!"

"Eehola!" Chueco whistled.

"And sometimes there's a little cherry there—"

"Really?" Chueco exclaimed. "Like a cherry from a cherry tree?"

"Sure," Pico said. "Watch for it, it's good luck." He reached down and tested the mirror on his shoes. "Hey, it's dry! Let's go!"

We piled out of the dirty stall and followed Pico toward the water fountain at the end of the hall. That's where the girls usually gathered, because it was right outside their bathroom.

"Watch me," he said daringly, then he worked his way carefully behind Concha Panocha, who stood talking to her friends. She wore a very loose skirt, perfect for Pico's plan. She was a big girl, and she wasn't very pretty, but Pico liked her. Now we watched as he slowly worked his foot between her feet until the mirror was in position. Then he looked down and we saw his eyes light up. He turned and looked at us and grinned. He had seen everything!

"Perfect! Perfect!" he shouted when he came back to us. "I could see everything! Panties! Nalgas! The spot!"

"Eee-heee-heeee," Chueco moaned. "Now it's my turn!"

They ran off to try Concha again, and I followed them. I felt the blood pounding in my head and a strange excitement ran through my body. If Pico could see everything, then I could too! I could solve the terrible mystery which had pulled me back and forth all year long. I slipped up behind a girl, not even knowing who she was, and with my heart pounding madly, I carefully pushed my foot between her feet. I worked cautiously, afraid to get caught, afraid of what I was about to see. Then I peered into the mirror, saw in a flash my guilty eyes, moved my foot to see more, but all I could see was darkness. I leaned closer to her, looked closely into the mirror, but there was nothing except the glimpse of her white panties and then the darkness.

I moved closer, accidentally bumped her, and she turned and looked puzzled and I said excuse me and pulled back and ran away. There was nothing to see; Pico had lied. I felt disappointed. So was Chueco when we met again at lunchtime.

"They all wear panties, you liar!" Chueco accused Pico.

"And most of them wear dirty panties," I added. That had been my only discovery.

"One girl caught me looking at her and she hit me with her purse," Chueco complained. His left eye was red. "What do we do now?" he asked.

"Let's forget the whole thing," I suggested. The excitement was gone, there was nothing to discover. The mystery which was changing the girls into women would remain unexplained. And not being responsible for the answer was even a relief. I reached down to pull the mirror from my foot. My leg was stiff from holding it between the girls' legs.

"No!" Pico exclaimed, and grabbed my arm. "Let's try one more thing!"

"What?"

He looked at me and grinned. "Let's look at one of the teachers."

"What? You're crazy!"

"No I'm not! The teachers are more grown up than the girls! They're really women!"

"Bah, they're old hags." Chueco frowned.

"Not Miss Brighton!" Pico smiled.

"Yeah." Chueco's eyes lit up and he wiped the white spittle that gathered at the edges of his mouth. "She reminds me of Wonder Woman!" He laughed and made a big curve with his hands.

"And she doesn't wear a bra. I know, I've seen her," Pico said.

"No." I shook my head. No, it was crazy. It would be as bad as looking at my mother. Again I reached down to tear the mirror from my shoe and again Pico stopped me.

"You can't back out now!" he hissed.

"Yeah," Chueco agreed, "we're in this together."

"If you back out now, you're out of the gang," Pico warned

me. He held my arm tightly, hard enough for it to hurt. Chueco nodded. I looked from one to the other, and I knew they meant it. I had grown up with them, known them even before we started school.

"This summer we'll be the kings of the apple orchard, and you won't be able to come in," Pico added to his threat.

"But I don't want to do it," I insisted.

"Who then?" Chueco asked, and looked at Pico. "We can't all do it, she'd know."

"So let's draw," Pico said, and drew three toothpicks out of his pocket. He always carried toothpicks and usually had one hanging from his lips. "Short man does it. Fair?"

Chueco nodded. "Fair." They looked at me. I nodded. Pico broke one toothpick in half, then he put one half with two whole ones in his hand, made a fist, and held it out for us to draw. I lost.

"Eho, Isador, you're lucky," Chueco said.

"I, I can't," I mumbled.

"You have to!" Pico said. "That was the deal!"

"Yeah, and we never break our deals," Chueco reminded me. "As long as we've been playing together we never broke a deal."

"If you back out now, that's the end . . . no more gang," Pico said seriously. Then he added, "Look, I'll help you. It's the last day of school, right, so there's going to be a lot of noise during last period. I'll call her to my desk, and when she bends over it'll be easy! She won't know!" He slapped my back.

"Yeah, she won't know!" Chueco repeated.

I finally nodded. Why argue with them, I thought. I'll just put my foot out and fake it, and later I'll make up a big story to tell them in the apple orchard. I'll tell them I saw everything. I'll say it was like the drawing in the bathroom.

But it wasn't that easy. The rest of the day my thoughts crashed into each other like wild goats. Fake it, one side said. Look and solve the mystery, others shouted. Now's your chance!"

By the time I got to last-period study hall I was very nervous. I slipped into my seat across the aisle from Pico and buried my head in the book Miss Brighton had lent me. I sat with my feet drawn in beneath my desk so the mirror wouldn't show. After a while my foot grew numb in its cramped position. I flipped through the pages and tried to read, but it was no use, my thoughts were on Miss Brighton. I wondered if she was the woman who danced in my dreams. And why did I always blush when I looked into her clear blue eyes, those eyes which even now seemed to be looking at me and waiting for me to dare to learn their secret.

"Ready," Pico whispered, and raised his hand. I felt my throat tighten and go dry. My hands broke out in a sweat. I slipped lower into my desk to try to hide as I heard her walk toward Pico's desk.

"I want to know this word," Pico pointed.

"Contradictory," she said. "Con-tra-dic-to-ry . . ."

"Cunt-try-dick-tory," Pico repeated.

I turned and looked at her. Beyond her, through the window, I could see the apple orchard. The buzz of the bees swarming over the blossoms filled my ears.

"It means 'to contradict.' Like if one thing is true, then the other is false," I heard her say.

I would have to confess, I thought . . . Forgive me, Father, but I have contradicted you. I stole from my mother. I looked in the mirror and saw the secret of the woman . . . And why shouldn't you, something screamed in my head. You have to know! It's the only way to become a man! Look now! See! Learn everything you can!

I took a deep breath and slipped my foot from beneath my desk. I looked down, saw her eyes reflected in the small mirror. I slid it quietly between her feet. I could almost touch her skirt, smell her perfume. Behind her the light of the window and the glow from the orchard was blinding. I will pull back now, won't go all the way, I thought.

"Con-tra . . . ," she repeated.

"Cunt-ra . . . ," Pico stuttered.

Then I looked, saw in a flash her long, tanned legs, leaned to get a better image, saw the white frill, then nothing. Nothing. The swirl of darkness and the secret. The mystery remainded hidden in darkness.

I gasped as she turned. She saw me pull my leg back, caught my eyes before I could bury myself in the book again, and in that brief instant I knew she had seen me. A frown crossed her face. She started to say something, then she stood up very straight.

"Get your books ready, the bell's about to ring" was all she said. Then she walked quickly to her desk and sat down.

"Did you see?" Pico whispered. I said nothing, but stared at pages of the book, which were a blur. The last few minutes of the class ticked by very slowly. I thought I could even hear the clock ticking, and each stroke was like a bell.

Then seconds before the bell rang I heard her say, "Isador, I want you to stay after school."

My heart sank. She knew my crime. I felt sick in the pit of my stomach. I cursed Pico and Chueco for talking me into the awful thing. Better to have let everything remain as it was. Let them keep their secret. Whatever it was, it wasn't worth the love I knew would end between me and Miss Brighton. She would tell my parents, everyone would know. I wished that I could reach down and rip the cursed mirror from my shoe, undo everything and set it right again.

But I couldn't. The bell rang. The room quickly emptied. I remained sitting at my desk. Long after the noise had cleared on the school grounds, she called me to her desk. I got up slowly, my legs weak and trembling, and I went to her desk. The room felt very big and empty, bigger than I could ever remember it. And it was very quiet.

She stood and came around her desk. Then she reached down, grabbed the small mirror on my shoe, and jerked it. It splintered when she pulled and cut her thumb, but she didn't cry out. She was trembling with anger. She let the pieces drop on the floor; I saw the blood as it smeared her skirt and formed red balls on the tip of her thumb.

"Why did you do it?" she asked. Her voice was angry. "I know that Pico and Chueco would do things like that, but not you, Isador, not you!"

I shook my head. "I wanted to know," I heard myself say, "I wanted to know . . ."

"To know what?" she asked.

"About women . . ."

"But what's there to know?" she said. "You saw the film the coach showed you . . . and later we talked in class when the nurse came. She showed you the diagrams, pictures!"

I could only shake my head. "It's not the same. I wanted to know how women are . . . why different? How?"

She stopped trembling. Her breathing became regular. She took my chin in her hand and made me look at her. Her eyes were clear, not angry, and the frown had left her face. I felt the blood wet my chin.

"There's stories . . . and drawings, everywhere . . . and at night I dream, but I still don't know, I don't know anything!" I cried.

She looked at me while my frustrations came pouring out, then she drew me close and put her arms around me and smoothed my hair. "I understand," she said, "I understand . . . but you don't need to hide and see through the mirror. That makes it dirty. There is no secret to hide . . . nothing to hide . . ."

She held me tight and I could hear her heart pounding, and I heard her sigh, as if she too was troubled by the questions which hounded me. Then she let me go and went to the window and pulled shut all the venetian blinds. Except for a ray of light streaming through the top, the room grew dark. Then she went to the door and locked it. She turned and looked at me, smiled with a look I had never seen before, then walked gracefully to the small elevated platform in the back of the room.

She stood in the center and very slowly and carefully she unbuttoned her blouse. She let it drop to her feet, then she undid her bra and let it fall. I held my breath and felt my heart pounding wildly. Never had I seen such beauty as I saw then in the pale light which bathed her naked shoulders and her small breasts. She unfastened her skirt and let it drop, then she lowered her panties and stepped out of them. When she was completely naked she called me.

"Come and see what a woman is like." She smiled.

I walked very slowly to the platform. Beneath me my legs trembled, and in my ears I began to hear a buzzing sound, the kind of sound the bees make when they are swarming around the new blossoms of the apple trees. I stood looking at her for a long time, and she stood very still, like a statue. Then I began to walk around the platform, still looking at her, noting every feature and every curse of her long, firm legs, her flat stomach with its dot of a navel, the small round behind that curved down between her legs then rose along her spine to her hair which fell over her shoulders . . . I walked around and I began to feel a swirling sensation, a very pleasant feeling, as if I was slowly getting drunk. And I continued to hear the humming sound; perhaps she was singing, or it was the sound of the bees in the orchard, I didn't know. But she was smiling, a distant, pleasant smile.

The glowing light of the afternoon slipped through the top of the blinds and rested on her hair. It was the color of honey, spun so fine I wanted to reach out and touch it. But I didn't. A part of her secret she would have to keep, I was content to look at the beauty of her soft curves. Once I had gone hunting with my uncles and I had seen a golden aspen forest which had entranced me with its beauty, but even it was not as beautiful as this. Not even the summer nights when I slept outside and watched the swirl of the

Milky Way in the dark sky could compare to the soft curves of her body. Not even the brilliant sunsets of the summer when the light seemed painted on the glowing clouds could be as full of wonder as the light which fell on her naked body. I looked until I thought I had memorized every curve, every nook and shadow, the color of her hair, the flesh tone of her skin . . . and I breathed in, deep, to inhale the aroma of her body. Then when I could no longer stand the beauty of the mystery unraveling itself before my eyes, I turned and ran.

I ran out the door into the bright setting sun, a cry of joy exploding at my lips. I ran as hard as I could, and I felt I was turning and leaping in the air like a ballet dancer.

"Now I know!" I shouted to myself. "Now I know the secret, and I'll keep it forever!"

I ran through the orchard, laughing with joy. All around me the bright white blossoms of the trees shimmered in the spring light. I heard music in the radiance which exploded around me; I thought I was dreaming.

I ran around the trees and then stopped to caress them, and the smooth trunks and branches reminded me of her body. Each curve developed a shope and shadow of its own, each twist was rich with the secret we now shared. The flowers smelled like her hair and reminded me of her smile. Then, gasping for breath and still trembling with excitement, I fell exhausted on the ground.

It's a dream, I thought, and I'll soon wake. But no, it had happened. For a few brief moments I had shared the secret of her body, her mystery. But even now as I tried to remember how she looked, her image was fading like a dream. I sat up straight and looked toward the school, tried to picture the room and the light which had fallen on her bare shoulders, but it was fuzzy, like a dream which fades as one awakens. Her smile, her golden hair, and the soft curves of her body were already fading into the sunset light, dissolving into the graceful curves of the trees. The image of her body, which just a short time ago had been so vivid, was working itself into the apple orchard, becoming the shape of trunks and branches . . . and her sweet fragrance blended into the damp earth smell of the orchard and its nettles and wild alfalfa.

For a moment I reached out to keep it from fading away, and that's when I realized that this was the real mystery. That she should fade and grow softer in my memory was the real beauty! That's why she told me to look! It was like the mystery of the apple orchard, changing before my eyes even as the sun set. All the curves and shadows, the sounds and smells, were changing form! In a few days the flowers would wilt and drop, then I would have to wait until next spring to see them again, but the memory would linger, parts of it would keep turning in my mind. Then next spring I could come back to the apple orchard to see the blossoms again. I would always keep coming back, to rediscover, to feel the smoothness of flesh and bark, to smell hair and flower, to linger as I bathed in beauty ... The mystery would always be there, and I would be exploring its form forever.

The China Venus Thinks About Making Love

Alicia Borinsky

she had adorned herself with sequins with cadavers pushed toward
    the fire.
she had made compresses talcum power on the buttocks rice
    powder

false eyelashes roughed nipples
perfectly outlined belly button

In the shower she swore an orgasm to come
She practiced the cry of pleasure
Plotted a meticulous wild love scene

red sheets pillows strewn around the floor half moon of perfume
Low-down music
What a taut crisscross of caresses
What burning bodies at the center of the world.

Translated by Cola Franzen

Rumor

Alicia Borinsky

oh guys she was red hot all night long without hope or rancor
touching her vagina   smoothing her legs
decorating her nipples
the whole night long red hot

they say what boleros
exclaim what tangos
I have a souvenir post card

naturally it was on a boat
naturally it was in technicolor

Translated by Cola Franzen

Invocation 13

Juan Cameron

What might your petticoat be like if the tide goes out
& your smile is left hanging in the closet?
What might your thighs be like when autumn comes
& summer & winter   or winter & spring?
I imainge colors slipping by lukewarm
the last funicular flickerings out on your face

What might your core be like correctly speaking
or in silence   with meadows   like a golf course?
How would it be if I say good evening and come in
with my damp discourse to turn on your light?

What might your letters asleep on your pillow be like
your knee   your nails   your hair when you wake up?
They all seem to me like a single note
of a song without a name
   How on earth can one know, one
or two
   or three
      or two.

Translated by Cola Franzen

The Mule Going Round the Well

Ethel Krauze

"Where are we going?"

He laughs and doesn't answer. Is he going to take me somewhere to do that? Who does he think he is? Is he trying to intimi-
date me? And what if I don't feel like it? What—does he think a
woman is always supposed to feel like it, with him? It's annoying.
Let's wait a while, I tell him, and I really mean it. Let's try doing
something else first, I don't know, maybe just be nice to each other
for a while, who knows. Because I really don't understand what's
going on with me. What if I don't get wet enough? Yesterday he
asked me to do it to him, well, he didn't ask me directly, he insinuated it, but it seemed like he was looking down on—was it himself
or me? Should I do it or not, I thought, do I want to or not, I don't
know if I want to or not. Well, I say O.K., he comes on me, he fills
me up good and then cool, real cool, he leans back on the steering
wheel. Is he happy? And what about me? It sort of disgusted me;
and what about me? He falls asleep, I think, for a minute, he turns
on the radio, lights a cigarette, I smooth my hair, dry off my—not
exactly my sweat, what sweat, after all; is it really true that you
sweat when you do it? He doesn't say a word. For a moment his
eyes sparkle. He starts the engine; should we go?; sure, why not,
you've already started the car; I don't care where we go, let's just go!

"Weren't we going to have a cup of coffee or a drink?"

"What?"

"Yeah, that's why we stopped in front of the bar, wasn't it?"

"Well, we're already here; I thought, well, what you told me."

"Yeah, I know—what I told you."

"So I guess you're not ready yet."

"No, it isn't that; I don't want to lay any trips on you; just give
me some time."

"O.K., O.K., O.K., that's fine."

Fine? What's fine, for me to cut them off? To somehow castrate
myself? Does that seem fine to you? I'll be damned! And to think
that I'm doing it for this beast, to see if we can have something and
not end up castrating each other so fast without getting anything out
of it. But I like his skin. He's an accountant or an engineer or what-

ever, but I don't give a shit what he is, at this point I don't give a shit what any of them are. I find him attractive; he's tall, real tall, with tanned arms, lots of body hair, and gray eyes. He's immense, enormous, almighty. I feel tiny beside him, as if people on the street were laughing at how we look together. And I love how he laughs and then he seems to look at me out of the corners of his eyes and then something glows inside him; that's the only time I think or feel or suppose I'm really interested. And he's affectionate, because he's also a gentleman, not like the snotty-nosed boys that have hung around me all my life, every single day of my life. Damn! I hope he's interested in me, I hope he's really interested in me.... But then he comes out with some shit; I'm not sure exactly what, but I don't give a damn; I'd like to fall in love with him and have him fall in love with me; I'd like to swoon and make him swoon. I hope I'm not going to blow it this time. Do you want it, baby? Sure, but let's do it right; sure, but it takes effort, you have to show some grace, some real desire.

"So there isn't any problem, is there? If you come home late and all that."

"Well ..."

There isn't any problem? You already did it, didn't you? All because of that time Irma introduced us at the bar and we were talking on and on with those girls you picked up, till four in the morning, then we got rid of the poor things and only Irma, me, you and your friend were left. How great, how fantastic! But I'm not going to blow it this time, I swear!

"Well, there won't really be a problem, but I don't want to do it until I like it. Why?"

"No, just in case we're late."

"Oh ... and I don't suppose you live at home anymore, do you?"

"I still go there to sleep, but I'm getting an apartment with some friends."

"Oh yeah? And I suppose you've got a job."

"Well, right now I'm still a student."

Right now, always right now; it's all bullshit; we don't know how to talk about anything but sex. If we leave out sex for the time being, everything is left out, it's all provisional, fleeting, useless, unimportant. He's already asked for the check; now he's going to take me to the car, make me do it so he won't have to go home in pain, so he won't have to pay money for what he's already bought with other things, and he'll be able to sleep like a baby after he comes a few minutes from now. And what about me? Who gives me orgasms and puts me to sleep all worn out?

It's definitely better to be a man. They come on to you, they have the power to call you when they feel like it and tell you to go to hell when they're tired of you. And they have that tiny but definite pleasure of their ejaculation, the freedom to always be what they are. But don't you dare take the initiative with them or they'll think you're desperate and easy, that you're spreading your legs wide for their sweet whip; but don't turn them down either, or they get tired of waiting. "You won't give it to me whenever and however I want it? Get lost, sweetheart; I've got another twenty girls waiting in line; it's up to you." And what do they give you in exchange: a little saliva, an incoherent grunt, a whitish secretion to toss in the toilet. And what about the magnificent orgasm? It stayed in there, stuck to your skin, or hidden deep inside you.

"We're going to do it today," I tell Irma.

"Really? You finally made up your mind?"

"Don't be silly; what do you think? I've seen him five or six times now, and I've already drawn it out to two weeks."

"Yeah, that's already a record, isn't it?"

"Uh-huh, but I think if I drag it out any longer I'll spoil it. The other day I told him we should wait a while, that day I told you about when he asked me why we didn't make love. What love? Since when do we love each other, I say, just out of curiosity, you know? So he said O.K., let's wait till you feel like it. He didn't get it at all, but I didn't want to lay any of my trips on him, but I've had it with getting really hung up on the first hunk I meet, because I swear—and you and I have already talked about his—I swear that I go home afterwards and feel like shit, ugly, stupid, empty, useless, because what do I get out of it, hell, just tell me what I get out of it. So I tell him to be patient, let's wait and see, O.K.? Let's wait and see if we do it or not, let's see if it's worth it. All right, fine, he says. I tell you he didn't get it at all; that's why he waited five days to call me again, supposedly because he had exams and was studying day and night and who knows what."

"O.K., O.K., but you said that now you've made up your mind."

"What choice do I have? Look, I really do want to now, I admit it, I want to, why not, I've been waiting for months and you know it; how much longer can I wait? And this guy I like comes along, he sort of gets stuck on me, I tell you he's been hitting on me for two weeks already, and I like him, I really like him, he's fascinating, I don't care but he's fascinating, so it's time, isn't it? If not now, when? It's all going to be ruined, you know?"

"Yes, come to think of it, if I had waited that long with that idiot I told you about, maybe things would have worked out for us, who knows."

"Look, I don't care if we break up, but let's get it over with; I'm fed up now, completely fed up!"

Today's the day. Shit. The marvelous day. And what if nothing happens? And what if he tells me to go to hell? And what if he doesn't turn me on anymore? And what if I don't feel anything? Well, it doesn't matter anymore; I already committed myself; we're on our way. Insurgentes Avenue after five P.M., the Manacar Theatre, San Angel, the university, the shitty high school, Tlalpan, where are we going? Down the old highway to Cuernavaca, what horrible places, how incredible the highway looks at this hour. And isn't this beast ever going to talk to me? He's content, on his way to paradise, and I feel like I'm on a nonstop flight to the slaughterhouse to find my mother. He looks at me, smiles, now I'm smiling too; you're going to get it in a minute, don't worry; all I ask is that you take a good look at it, that you see that mine is different, it's mine; it may not be very round or very good, but it's marvelous. And how can I get you to see this; now I don't know how to hand it to you on a silver platter, because if you don't see it, it isn't your fault. I don't know how to make you feel like mine is worth more than all the rest of them, because maybe it isn't worth it anymore, maybe it's never been worth it. Useless, imbeciles. Now we're arriving.

"What do you think? Nice, huh?"

"It isn't bad. I like that yellow skylight; it gives the place an atmosphere of . . . I don't know."

"Want a drink?"

"No."

". . . Because we could order room service."

"Yes, I know we could order room service."

"Well . . ."

"What are you laughing at?' '

"I don't know; all the high drama struck me as funny."

"What high drama?"

"Yeah, all the complications, when we know it's all going to lead up to this. Who was it that said that? I can't remember."

"But that's the whole point, isn't it?"

"There you go; exactly. And do you know why I'm laughing so hard?"

"You're really on my case."

"I'm nervous as hell—how stupid, how dumb can you be? But don't just stand there looking at me like that. Do something, big guy, do something; take my clothes off. . . ."

Come here, my love, I want to feel your burning skin and have you pour me out, light and wet, and make me feel so nice and thick, and everything the poets say when they turn into lovers. This is all so difficult. Come here, cover me with saliva, the enormous weight of your body, yes, please destroy me, my love, I don't know how to tell you any more, what to call you, since you really aren't mine. How awkward I am. And you aren't surprised, you don't suffer, don't scream; you only spill yourself out slowly, like you're doing it on demand. I don't know whether to touch you—where? And you, why don't you move across my body from head to toe, sweetly, you're going about your business, doing what you need to do, and I don't know how to stop you so we can look at each other first, so I can kiss you with all my heart. What am I saying! Come on in, then, let it hurt me, like a bull in heat, you seem to be coming closer and looking for me between my lips there, yes, yes, yes, more, your delicious fingers, you're doing it right, right, right, I'm sinking sinking, sweet cold sinking in the amazing heat of your crotch, sinking in seas, rivers of bellowing foam, no, no, no, wait, wait, wait you son of a bitch, don't go off yet, don't leave me like this, and now you're happily coming, hunched over your bitch's back with your little doggie's whimper, and me wiping off my belly button and my eyes and my legs ... Your pitiful drops, oh your goddamn love, why are you going this to me? ... Go ahead and smoke, you bastard, enjoy what you think you've achieved.

"Don't you want a cigarette?"

"No."

"Did you come?"

"I don't suppose I need to ask if you did, do I?"

You laugh; you're so cool. But it doesn't matter; I'll learn; I'm patient. I like to feel your skin; I'm satisfied with that for now, that you've enjoyed yourself; and I should tell you so! And I should say it without loving you, let you learn to love me, let me learn to love you and let us make some sort of sense of all this, and I've done it all for you, you believe that you've waited for me, that you've been patient with me, but you don't know anything about my patience. Waiting for you to discover that you can love me, then making me discover that I can love you. Patience to learn not to hate you, not to hate myself. And now you're coming again. And afterwards it's the same thing all over again, always the same, not knowing what we're doing or why.

"I'm going to take a shower."

"Yeah, let's take a shower!"

"Don't tell me you're going to take a shower; you can't go home with your hair wet. No, you wait here; I won't be long."

I can go home however I feel like it, wet or dry, and I almost always go home dry, and if I wanted to get my hair wet I'd know how to do it. You don't even let me enjoy what comes afterwards, because it all ends here, as if you had cleaned me off of you and here I haven't even gotten dirty yet, I'm still an immaculate virgin!

"And like I was saying, Irma, like I told you before, he wasn't even going to call me. We said good-bye as if nothing had happened; I was beside myself all the next day—should I call him or not, I don't understand how he can not call me the day after, to be polite if nothing else, he might at least thank me, don't you think? But no, on Thursday I finally called him because I couldn't stand it any longer; he wasn't home so I left him a message. And I waited . . . I think I was falling in love with him. I didn't go to school all week, I just couldn't, and that bastard acted as if nothing had happened; he didn't give a shit about me, Irma. He tossed me aside as if I weren't worth a damn! So then I said, This guy can go to hell. And it keeps happening to me again and again, like a mule going around a well, and it just isn't worth it. And tell me, please tell me where I went wrong, where I blew it. I waited. Be careful, I told myself, no kidding, and I didn't take the initiative, or talk dirty to him, believe me, I was even careful about that, I was patient. I wanted us to have something, and it was useless, don't you see, it was useless again. And me like a jerk, as if nothing had ever happened, there I was left high and dry, am I going to keep ending up there all my life? And what do you know, as if that wasn't bad enough, two weeks later the phone rings, and I'm all involved in other things by then. . . .

"Hello?"

"Hi! How about that, you're finally home."

"Oh, it's you."

"I called you a bunch of times but you were never home and I've been tied up with exams; they're really breaking my—"

"Yeah, I know, they're breaking your balls, uh-huh."

"They told me you called the other day. . . ."

"Did I? I don't remember. Oh yeah, it was that day I got shit-faced, it was really something."

"Well, they gave me your message, but like I say, I've been busy as hell, especially the last few days, 'cause I'm going out of town over Easter vacation."

"That's great. I'm thinking about making some plans of my own."

"Yeah, I'm going to Cancún with some buddies."

"All right! You're gonna have pussy coming outta your ears."

"Don't be silly; what's wrong with you?"

"And blond pussy, the kind that knows how to give great blow jobs. Far out!"

"Hey, what's with you?"

"Nothing, I really laid one on, it isn't worth talking about, it's really really awesome. Jesus!"

"Well, we should get together sometime."

"Right on; damn straight. Fuckin' A!"

Translated by Cynthia Steele

Home Movies

Ed Vega

The thing with Rosy was better than I expected. I was often at
odds with Dhread but his scheme paid off most of the time. I never
would've imagined Rosy Cruz to be so wild. I took her to Chum-
ley's, bought her a few drinks and something to eat. Afterward we
walked around the Village. I asked her if she wanted to go to The
Steps, a coffeehouse on Bleecker Street. She said she didn't feel like
it. It was about nine and the air had grown colder in the past hour.

"Whatever you want, Johnny," she said. "I feel funny in those
places. Like I don't belong. Anyway, I see so many people at work
that after a while I get tired of being in a crowd."

"It's a quiet place," I said.

"Don't be stupid, Johnny," Dhread said, breaking in.

"Would you like to go up to my place?" I said, taking Dhread's
cue. "I mean, I'm not trying to get you up there so I can seduce
you or anything."

"Oh, brother," Dhread said.

"I know, Johnny," Rosy said. "I trust you."

"See?" Dhread said.

I steered Rosy across Sheridan Square. She was quiet and
seemed a little tense. About a block from my apartment she put
her arm through mine and smiled when I looked down at her. Her
lips, still coral, were slightly open.

Dhread was going crazy.

"Oh, Jesus, Johnny," he said. "She's ready for it right now.
Don't start talking when you get upstairs. For Christ's sake, don't
do that to me. It's been four days."

"Things are slower down here, aren't they, Rosy," I said, ges-
turing at the tree-lined street and low buildings.

"Yeah, it's so quiet," she said. "Almost sad," she added, looking
up at the late-autumn trees, bare now of foliage. In the light of
the street lamp they looked like dancers, their arms and fingers
stretched skyward.

"Are you sad?" I said.

Rosy looked up at my face and shook her head. She didn't
say anything.

"You got a weeper, Johnny," Dhread said. "Don't start getting sentimental on me."

"What's the matter, Rosy?" I said.

"I don't know."

"Do you want me to take you home?" I said.

"Jesus, Johnny, cut out the bullshit," Dhread said in a mild panic. "Look at her. She wants you to take her upstairs and do a number on her. She's working herself up to make believe it was the mood."

"I'll be all right, Johnny," Rosy said, gripping my arm.

When we got inside the apartment, Rosy took off her coat, slipped out of her shoes and curled up on the sofa. She looked like a little girl, her large brown eyes opened wide in expectation of a treat.

"This is a nice place, Johnny," she said. "It's like one of those pads in the movies. Did you decorate it yourself?"

I said I had, even though it wasn't true. I had subleased it just like it was. The owner went off to Europe for two years. He was Carol's cousin—a film dealer or something. The apartment was a duplex in a remodeled brownstone. It was neat and modern. There were some movie star posters up on one wall. In the living room there were set lights. Here and there objects had been placed in such a way that they produced questions about the resident of the place. A water pipe, a huge Mayan stone with oblique, bulging eyes, an espresso machine on the bar, a slot machine with a bowlful of coins next to it. Along the far wall there was a floor-to-ceiling bookcase with at least six hundred books. Off to one side, within the bookcase, there was a stereo and several thousand dollars' worth of recording equipment. Rosy panned the room slowly, as if she didn't want to forget any of the details.

"Can I see the upstairs, Johnny?" she said.

"That's it, pal," Dhread said. "That's the word."

I gave Rosy my hand and led her to the wrought-iron spiral staircase. She went up and I followed, with Dhread commenting on Rosy's neat little buttocks as they swung back and forth up the coil of the steps. There were two bedrooms and a projection room on the second floor. Rosy was immediately drawn to the projection room. I had inadvertently left the lights on. She went into the room, looked around and then asked me if I showed my own movies.

"Sure," I said. "Sometimes." I didn't want to tell her they were all, except for some Road Runner cartoons, old stag films. "They're old silent films."

"But they're like what they call home movies, right?"

"Yeah, I guess so," I said, feeling deceitful.

"God," Dhread. "This one's a real yahoo."

"Can I see one?" Rosy asked. "Please." She took down a reel from one of the shelves where they were stacked and handed it to me. The movie was called *The Sheriff*. "Put it on," Rosy squealed in anticipation.

"Go ahead," Dhread said. "She'll cream right in her pants."

"Well, that's not a very good one," I said, moving to the other side of the shelves. "There's some good cartoons over here."

"No, no, this one," Rosy said. "I like westerns."

I had no choice. I began threading the film. Rosy sat down Indian style on the water bed in front of the projector. When I finished, I turned on the projector, turned off the lights and joined Rosy. She giggled as the water shifted and the titles came on. I was ready to apologize but Dhread let loose with a string of indictments about my lack of courage and my hypocrisy.

On the screen, a very tall man in a 1930s cowboy outfit was walking down the middle of a western town. He had a star on his shirt. He went into a saloon called Mame's, asked the bartender a question and went upstairs. The people in the bar, as well as the bartender, all had wide-eyed looks of fear on their faces. Once upstairs the sheriff knocked on a door and a seductive madam type answered. She motioned the sheriff in with a Mae West sort of gesture and, without the least ceremony, unbuttoned his pants and began blowing him. The guy had an enormous penis.

At this point Rosy gasped and buried her face in her hands.

"I'm sorry," I said. "I should've told you."

"Oh, Johnny," she said through a sob. "How horrible." She was shaking all over and I couldn't help putting my arms around her. Dhread was mocking her and urging me to touch her breasts. "I can't look," Rosy said. "It's so ugly."

"Listen to this bitch," Dhread said. "There's no question that the dude's ugly, but where does she get off with all this prudery?"

"Shall I turn it off?" I said.

"No, no," Rosy cried. "Just hold me, Johnny."

I was leaning up against the wall and Rosy was curled up against me, her head resting underneath my chin. I stroked her hair and kissed her forehead.

"I'm sorry I didn't tell you," I said again.

"It's okay, Johnny," she said. "It's so big."

The sheriff had now taken off all his clothes except for his boots, hat and gun belt and was plowing away at Mame's supple buttocks. The camera focused on his enormous organ as it worked in and out of Mame's vagina.

"Jesus, Johnny," Dhread said. "I can't hold on much longer. Do something."

I moved closer to Rosy and detected just the slightest movement of her body towards mine. It could've been the motion of the water bed. Slowly, I began kissing her face. In the light from the projector I could see one of her eyes focused on my face, the other one on the screen.

"That's so awful," she said. "I can't even look."

I ran my hands over her hips and thighs and she moaned softly. A minute later she was breathing heavily and her pelvis was moving against my left leg.

"Take off her blouse," Dhread whispered.

I reached for the buttons.

"No, Johnny, please," Rosy said, but offered no resistance. Her hands clawed at my back and her pelvis moved with more determination against me. When I had removed her blouse and bra, I bent down and kissed her miniature breasts. She smelled sweetly of spices and perfume as I kissed her. Pit was humming, as he usually does when I'm kissing a woman. The film ended. I reached up and turned off the projector. I again tried to apologize but Rosy put two fingers to my lips and slushed me.

"It wasn't your fault," she said. "I forced you."

She was kneeling on the water bed, her tiny breasts pointed at my face.

"What a fucking come-on," Dhread said. "Take off her pants, stupid."

"Why don't you take off all your clothes," I said, suddenly.

"Here on the water bed?" Rosy asked.

"No, on the fucking kitchen table, dummy," Dhread said.

"Sure," I said, and began undressing. "Why not?"

"You're not like the guy in the film, are you, Johnny?" Rosy said when I had stripped down to my jockey shorts.

"Here we go again," Dhread said. "Let me get in her mouth so she can see."

"Don't worry, Rosy," I said. "I won't hurt you."

"I'm scared," she said.

"We'll go slowly," I whispered.

"Like hell we will," Dhread said.

I gently urged Rosy to lie back on the bed, then pulled down her pants and her panties, her hips raising to my touch. She was lying on the water bed, her body swaying from the undulating motion of the water. Pit was humming and he went immediately for Rosy's clitoris. She smelled sweet and tasted salty, he told me later. He was humming "Oh, Happy Day."

Dhread was now screaming and cursing, his body flailing up and down crazily.

"Me, you bastard," he was saying. "Me, me."

"Wait a while," I said out loud.

"What?" Rosy said.

"Nothing," I mumbled. "It's all right."

"Oh, happy day," Pit hummed.

"Shut up, faggot," Dhread screamed.

"Oh, happy daaay," Pit went on.

"Oh, Johnny," Rosy said, passionately. "Oh, baby, baby. Oh, Johnny."

"Oh, happy daaay."

"Oh, God, I'm dying," Dhread moaned. "Now, now. I can't wait. I'll do it on the water bed."

"Oh, happy day," Pit slobbered on.

"I think I'm going to come, Johnny," Rosy said hoarsely.

She was alternately panting and moaning and moving up against my face, my mustache becoming entwined with her soft pubic hairs. Pit was still humming and Dhread was hysterical.

"You bastard. You rotten, hypocritical bastard. I can't wait. I can't."

"Now, Johnny," said Rosy. "Johnny, oh God. *Ay, Dios mio. Ay, papi*. Ay, ay. Oh, Johnny. Ay, ay. It feels so good. Yes, yes, yes. That's it, Johnny. Oh, my God."

Against all reason Dhread had managed to get his way and was now cursing wildly and driving ferociously against Rosy's body.

"You cunt. You lousy, fucking, spic bitch," he was saying. "There, there, there. Take it. Take it all, you mealy-mouthed hamburger clerk. Two all-beef-patties, special-sauce, lettuce, cheese, pickles, onions-on-a-Sesame-Street-bun bitch."

"Bun-burr-on-bun," Pit hummed deeply as he imitated the *Dragnet* theme.

"Shut up," Dhread screamed.

"Oh, Johnny, I'm coming again," Rosy said.

Dhread screamed when he heard her. He was like a maniac. Like a monster. *AGHR!* Only louder and wilder. He drove uncontrollably against Rosy's pelvis until he was exhausted. I lay panting atop Rosy. She was moaning softly and saying yes over and over again, her pelvis still moving in small rotating thrusts. After a few moments she was still. I kissed her mouth and eyes. She felt hot and sweet. Pit reached out and licked her face. Rosy let out a little laugh and squeezed Dhread.

"Oh, my head," Dhread said in considerable pain. "My head."

Pit laughed and sang, "You Go to My Head."

"Tell him to shut up, Johnny," Dhread said.

I ignored him and asked Rosy if she was all right.

"Uhmn," she said, and kissed me. Her lips were swollen and hot, her tongue fresh and cool as it brushed mine. "My goodness," she said. "What a trip. On a water bed."

"I'm sorry about the film," I said, beginning to hate myself for being a phony.

"It scared me. You're pretty tall so I thought you'd be like that."

"Tell her to cut the shit," Dhread said. "I don't feel good. I want to get out. This muff's driving me crazy. She can't keep her mouth shut. Switching back and forth from English to Spanish and she wants to start up again. 'Les do it one mole tine, honee.' "

I ignored Dhread and in time he fell asleep. I eventually turned over and lay back on the water bed. Rosy was caressing my chest with her hands, her fingers sending tiny shivers up and down my body. I felt sleepy in that funny kind of way you get after sex. I could hear everything going on and feel everything but my body was asleep. I don't think I was asleep like that for more than twenty minutes before Dhread was screaming at me to wake up.

"We got a live one, Johnny," he said. Dhread could recuperate quite well when he wanted to.

"I want to do you now, Johnny," Rosy said as I opened my eyes. She was licking my stomach and Dhread was laughing and making wisecracks. I held her head in my hands, touching her hair as it streamed around my thighs. I could hear him laughing cavernously from within Rosy's mouth.

This went on for a while. Pit was humming and Dhread was in his glory. It was his contention that the phenomenon afflicting the young woman in *Deep Throat* was not an isolated incident of female anatomy. A couple of times Rosy gasped, choked and pulled away as Dhread threatened to destroy her larynx.

Pit was humming "*Allá en el Rancho Grande.*"

Along with a rather violent act in which Dhread attempted to bugger Rosy, this went on for about an hour. About one in the morning I took Rosy home to Avenue C. At her doorway she kissed me, as passionate as if we were still locked in sexual embrace. Her face was still flushed from the excitement of our lovemaking.

"I'll see you," she said. "Call me, okay?"

"Okay, Rosy," I said.

"Selfish bitch," Dhread said. "She can't wait for the next time."

I went quickly down the stairs and out into the street, walked through the Lower East Side back to my apartment.

"Why the hell do you pretend?" Dhread said as I walked.

"Don't start, okay, Dhread?"

"Don't give me that crap. Why did you stop me?"

"From what?"

"Oh, brother. I was going to give it to her in the rear exit and you pulled back."

"Well, I don't think that's the kind of thing you expose a girl to on the first date, Dhread. Especially a Puerto Rican girl."

"Bullshit. Where are you going now?"

"Home to sleep. I'm wasted."

As we walked west on Houston Street, a group of hippies approached us. Dhread eyed the woman, their hair in disarray, their breasts hanging loose inside their flowing robes and blouses.

"I bet that frizzy-haired broad would go for a toilet job, Johnny. Go ahead and ask her."

"Shut up, okay?" I said.

I continued walking quickly until I felt safe again in the West Village. I kept thinking Rosy had a boyfriend. Some olive-skinned little guy with a mustache, a ducktail haircut, pointy shoes and a knife and he was coming after me. I walked up Avenue of the Americas, turned the corner and was back in my apartment.

"You're feeling guilty, right?" Dhread said as soon as I sat down.

"I don't feel guilty," I said. "She was a lot of fun, Dhread. She's a nice girl."

"You're a real psycho, Johnny Angleson."

"You're the one that goes crazy and can't control himself."

"That's because of the broads you pick. This Rosy talks real nice and she seems like the most innocent thing that ever left San Juan, but she's got the most indecent muff I've ever met. Carmen's a fucking animal. She likes rough sex and she practically tried to choke me. The second time in she even tried to get me to say dirty words in Spanish. 'Say *criquita linda,* babee.' I told her to shut up."

"Dhread!"

"What?"

"You're really a puritan at heart. I'm touched."

"You got it all wrong, pal. It's just that I hate it when chicks are hypocritical. This Rosy muchacha is a total phony. Violent, too."

"It was great, Dhread. Admit it."

"Yeah, sure. I do all the work and you get all the pleasure."

"What's the matter?" I said, recalling a joke. "Did she have teeth down there?"

"Very funny," Dhread said. "I could hardly move, she was squeezing so hard. That's why I was banging into her. It hurt like hell."

"No pain, no gain," I said, dozing off.

"Hey, you're not going to sleep, are you?" Dhread said.

"You got it, buddy."

"We're friends, right?"

"Yeah, I guess so."

"Well, let's shake hands."

"Yeah, sure, Dhread," I said.

"C'mon," he said, seductively.

"Give me a break, Dhread," I said. "After all the action you've seen tonight. Go to sleep."

Dhread was insulted. I took a shower and went to bed. It was Friday night and I didn't have to be at work until noon the next day.

In the middle of the night Dhread began tossing and turning, screaming that some Puerto Rican muff had hidden a razor blade in her and was trying to get him involved. He was so excited that I had no choice but to calm him down. Afterward, I felt stupid and as usual extremely guilty.

Our Language

Brenda Cárdenas

When I sigh
I am breathing you
back out of me.
Like smoke you pause,
then fleet, melt into air.
You are often this intangible,
the silent *e* of love
or *hache* or *hábito.*
Hablame, you say,
yet my next breath
draws you in with the hiss of air
sliding past teeth
because I do not know
where I want you in this syntax
or what you are veiling
in the semantics of loss.

Can you diagram our migration
toward this hour?
Do the syllables fall
into furrows like kernels
beneath a perfect husk of pain?
The hush of your hands
reaches me from every shadow
in this room. You kiss
the slats of skin open
to the striped dawn
of the window blind.
You kiss these warm *l's* of light
and are gone.

In the caesura of hours and days, weeks
of *palabras,* sentences and paragraphs,

I stroke watercolor onto porous paper.
The blue sinks deep
as the resonant pitch
of your vocal cords.
It spread far as the anaphora
of sound waves
lapping phrases to the shore.
It curls the edges of the painting
like a question mark
until the paper is satiated.
I am not.

We work in English,
make love in Spanish
and code switch past our indecisions.
But in your absence,
all sounds are guttural,
days filled with glottal stops.
So I think in *sinalefas*
and trace you in the ring left
by my morning coffee cup.
If only I could touch
the amber circles of your eyes,
kiss your liquid pupils
when they dilate, enticed.
Then I'd be inside of you
as you so easily
fall into me.

I feel the constriction
of an *x* we cannot name,
the multilingual moan of *o's,*
tense Spanish vowels
awaiting release.
Then the loose
twirling of an *erre*
down our spines,
down the soft sides of our arms,
las líquidas vibrantes
of our blood.

This is how I want you—
at once within
and without
like a breath,
a sigh,
a language.

A Lover's Resolution on the New Year to Thaw Our Winter Blood

Brenda Cárdenas

You are the eclipse
the pause
the silence that falls
between drops sliding
down icicles
clutching my roof.

You sneak wet, naked
beneath flannel sheets,
rub your sleek fur
against the backs of my thighs
while kissing a stripe
along the part in my hair.

Down my spine, you tongue
this mark of the badger
who took shelter in the boathouse—
neighbors afraid of its teeth
of its lone tracks
in the acres of snow.

You coax the frozen lake
groaning as it pushes against shore,
ice mounds heaped
like tiny, scattered glaciers.
You slip into the silhouette
edging those slick cliffs.

While we hold this hour,
first dusk settles white everywhere.
A moon swollen with milk
is licked by stars and snowflakes
that flit like fireflies alighting
the ice-covered earth.

One black pine brushes the sky.
You are this black form
tickling, fingerpainting
the moon until it bursts,
spills blue all over
its own white light.

Egyptian Tango

Saúl Yurkievich

rancid air of Luxor
between columns of papyrus
the sun's glare
            gilds the turgid torso
your tremulous velvet gleams
          fuzzy orchid
and a black perfume
             overwhelms me
             in your honied indolence
             rosy silk
             in your softness
enthralling me
          with the wanton garden
          where the palm
          sifts
your radiance
          superb your satiny skin
          over the brocade
lascivious siesta   oasis   I go
like a cobra
in search of your aroma to the open being
between your thighs   fiery
            spikenard
crossing your shielded door
            befuddles
I go to your navel
            to the purple mound
to become aroused
            to engorge the lower parts
            the flank to gorge you
desire
     to find myself in thee to find
your innermost substance
grape that bursts and oozes
            its milky balm

regales   enlivens
                        opal stone and sandalwood
perfumed bole of your rump
I will anoint you with my nectars
                        turquoise and lapis lazuli

in your heron eyes
                    sybylline magnets
                                amulets

Nubian languor   feline ador
ibis   iris   raptors
                    falconry that I figure
                                flight

to lure you into the air of desire
into the shadow of my bliss
                        lodge you
I go to thee   I say   to touch you
to awaken you
                gawker's chimera
                gasps of smoke
tint   your flesh
    in vivid tints   I invoke you
                pipe dreamlet of my dream
                my painted ellipse

your pulp
                I want to bring to light
                        the mark of your kiss
                I want to show
                        you breathless
your breath   less

Translated by Cola Franzen

Two Flowers and My Tongue

John Juan Domingo

Oceanic waves in patterns rippling are moving toward the center. I draw inward. All awareness is imploding. From my fingers, belly, and thighs, awareness moves like dense fire, to the region between my earth-colored legs. My balls have eyes and my heart has vocal cords. From here I shall write with my passion a memory, a snippet of sensual continuum.

As she undressed a fire was started, near venetian blinds partially open. Light and shadow marked the contours of her body in black and white strips. Over the sharp turn in the small of her back, to ripe full buttocks, I lingered. The stripes came closer together, then moved farther apart, then disappeared into the crevice far from her sight. With clothes piled at her feet, she stretched like a cat satisfied expelling a sigh, as pink as her nipples, lips, and toes.

I had to kiss her, standing, wet in my mouth, like kissing a dandelion—tongue lightly touching the delicate entry, the rim of scalloped edge, pollen dusting lips pressing and sinking into one-another for a moment, ending as if never beginning.

Blood was giving her skin pleasure. Blood was holding its sanguine truth as utterly true. Blood asked for terror and pleasure, for warriors to engage in ritual war. If warriors met at their edges, they could humbly pass through. Yes, death asked for terror and warring, then ease through the touch. Sensuality as death asked us to fall . . . into the arms of Our Lady.

Mictecacihuatl was pulling us down, into her realm of bones, asking for the offering of our bodies. In the earthen pit, sperm gave life to bones, and egg echoed a condensed version of earth. In that spherical and life-giving form, souls could enter to find sustenance and a home.

But my lover wanted peace. The thought of death brought the fear of losing a loved one. Too many loved ones had already died. We had had that conversation and I could sense the hesitation putting an edge to her movements. Sinuous lines of longing were replaced with the lines of erratic jerks, not quite sure whether "here" was ok, or if "somewhere else" was in fact preferred.

Our Lady of the Dead seemed hideous with her arms reaching

up like straight arrows beckoning, her boney tits, her balloon eyes, her teeth bared showing a grimace. Her jewelry worn proudly seemed ghastly, as did the severed arm tied to her waist hanging below her ass.

And I had already begun to die. I was becoming a heap of senses reaching for odors, tastes, visions, sounds, and the titillation of hair standing on end. I became the *calavera* seen so many times in ancient pictographs, eyes bulging, a skull with tongue erect, jutting and cutting through the air in front of it, descending along the contours of my lover's body.

My teeth, I am sure, shone fluorescent in the dim light of the street lamp outside the window. A bus drove by, flashing a bright light like a flashbulb, sparked from a break in the connection, between bus on the street and electrical wire in the sky. The black and white stripes on her body disappeared. All was white light obliterating the distinction between woman, room, and skull, my skull, my tongue continuing its jutting search into the pubic forest, as the black and white stripes once again appeared on her body.

I touched her other flower with the tip of my tongue, as lightly as I had touched the dandelion on her lips, so as to retain the pollen, on a moistened and erect tip. My jutting motion had ceased. Nectar was flowing. I could see it forming a drip on the ends of her pubic hair. I tasted it.

Saltwater seepage from the ocean of nascent life, reminder that water gives in reverence to the great earth mother. Salt, life, and death ... for the sultry existence of those who sweat profusely, I tasted as brine ... from my lover's saltwater depths. I tasted the body of crustaceans, the grasses moist on a windswept hill, the musty smell of redwoods, lichen, and red wine.

She moaned, then bit down holding her lips between her teeth. Her motions became sinuous once again. I pressed my tongue and held it softly against her moisture, warmth to warmth, water to water, my tongue rolling, then retracting to release her taste and scent through the chambers of my mouth and throat.

She moaned, resounded on the walls of her bedroom and in the towers of buildings growing upward. Sutro tower, like a trident reaching for the sky, was blinking red lights on Twin Peaks ... through the haze of low clouds and ocean fog. My hands followed the back of her legs with caresses.

She moaned, I stood up and my erection found its way to where my lips had left the iridescent tracks of snails, glistening in the subdued light of street lamps, inching their way back to the first water source.

Her mouth, her mouth. Our tongues prodded, teased, and danced with oneanother, moved to find ears and necks, places where clavicles love to go, sinking always into her lips and mouth presently descending on my body composed of brightly firing neurons.

I moaned, my brain melted into receptivity. I was in the precortical realm of lizards. There was no yesterday, no tomorrow. I saw a lizard licking the folds of a pecan, the pecan positioned between legs of vermilion. The vulva of pecan, the vertical color of lizard, the bursting colors of what I wanted desperately . . .

She moaned; the flask of our combined skin held silence streaming from the sacred. The patches of sunlight peeked through the leaves of an oak, to grasses of green below. Between rain and moist earth, I could smell her, my entire body between two pubic hairs. I had become so small, so unimportant. I felt every pore of my skin sucking in unison with my mouth, sucking life-giving liquids, earth saltiness, juices from the depths of an ocean in concentric circles.

We moaned, and died into our bodies. We exploded into the night. *Mictecacihuatl* sang her song, and played drums with the bones of our ancestors watching. She pulled us down into the earth. She embraced us . . . we entered her womb . . . as a woman spun yarn . . . on her life-giving lap.

I Tell You This

Omar Castañeda

I have been awake for hours. Annie has just curled up behind me. The hairs of her pussy are nestled between my cheeks. Perhaps in her sleep she has forgotten that we went to bed angry, hating, swearing this would be the end, our thing together. Perhaps the sleep seeping through her has made her forget who she's in bed with.

The walls are slashed with light from the venetian blinds and the street lamp on the corner. Her Indian batiks are dark, indistinguishable in night except for the longer light bands streaking one. Once more, it is the cut of the street in our lives. The cut of street. Light now that is razoring through our windows, our blinds that should be stopping any bit of New York from creeping in.

I have said the place is seedy. Everything in New York is seedy. Even the best here is somehow outgrowth from the compost around it. I try not to think of our fight.

Instead, I listen to the plastic cup turning outside. The window is open because the radiator is too hot. It is cold as infidelity outside. Cold as a single goldfish, cold as the Saharan night.

We are on the fifth floor, yet from the street in front, we seem to be on the first. The second floor, if you count street level as one. It is because we live on Haven in the upper west side. The lower floors descend into the cliff below and behind us to overlook the Hudson River, the George Washington Bridge and the twin nightmares of Riverside Drive and Henry Hudson Parkway. The plastic cup in the street is loud because it is late.

We live at the joint of a "T." 173rd is straight in front. Haven curves south to bcome 168th and north to a ramp for the Henry Hudson P. Whether because of the T of Haven or because of the park like a plateau on one side and the straight-faced tenements on the other, the plastic cup is merely circling in the street. I know it will circle for days. The trash outside never really moves, it only circles in little whirlwinds or larger whirlwinds that may seem to the unaware or to those agog at surfaces as if there is real movement, but none of it really moves.

I have watched trash for days from my window because I cannot write these days. I watched a manila envelope, an SASE—is it "an" SASE or is it "a" SASE?: Now you see why I cannot write; it is the difference between the rules of the written and the rules of the spoken, how something sounds and how something is supposed to be. Christ! It is self-indulgence.

So I watched it swirl on the street for ten days until it was accidentally swallowed by the streetsweeper. On Monday and Thursday the cars on this side double-park on the other side for the sweeper. On Tuesday and Friday the other side double-parks on this side. The sweepers push the garbage from one side to the other. I have learned to get up from my desk whenever I hear the machines come because I want to see which pieces of trash will happen to be pulled into the brushes of the machines. I have learned to guess correctly. It all depends on where they are in the whirlwind when the cars are moved or not really moved, depending on your breadth of vision. The shift in currents alters the tiny maelstrom and then the sweeper machine comes whirring on. This is how the SASE is eaten. Yet the plastic cup swirls still. It is surviving the same way a fly survives between panes of glass.

I try to imagine its path. Annie mewls against me like a cat. Her translucent blond hairs tickle me. Her breasts are warm. Her breath smells bad. The leaves have fallen for days and they too enter the circuit outside. I can imagine the leaves from the park, mostly yellow and orange-red elm leaves now, the newspaper that a passerby dropped two days ago, the plastic cup that appeared one day while I was deep in thought and oblivious to the noise sweeping up from the street, and the bags and paper that are shit-stained because dog owners pick up their pets' droppings only to drop them surreptitiously a few feet away. It is 4:30 in the goddamned morning.

I do not want to recall our argument. I do not want to think about the plastic cup. I do not want to see how the streetlight is appropriately cutting through our window. I remember instead the story I read in my new journal before Annie came home and we had our marathon fight. It is really cold in here. It is a mistake to leave the window open even that little bit. I told her. Closed it is hot, but hot is better than cold. I am from Florida. Annie is from Chicago. You see. It is fall and I do not know if I will be able to take winter in New York. Altanta is too cold for me. New York is what?—freezing and filthy! It is freezing, filthy and a fucking mess. It makes people like itself. All of this is part of the argument that I do not want to think about. I do not want to think about it.

Whatever happened to the garbage barge we heard so much about? Is there some man piloting it still? Is his face and body disintegrating because of the fumes from that tonnage of NYC refuse? Is the barge circling forever the seven seas? Is this by someone's order, circling, until all of it just decomposes; atom upon atom lifting away into the air, each to become a single neural tick in someone's respiratory system?

I've looked over the walls along the walkway between our apartment building and the ramp to the drives below. I have seen barges moving up and down the Hudson. From the top of our building I can see a sewage treatment plant on the river. Once, I walked down the walking bridge by our building and down to Riverside Park. I discovered an entire community of street people living under the overpasses and the bridges and cloverleaves that make up the Washington Bridge, Henry Hudson P. and Riverside Drive. One woman even had a bed and dresser against an embankment. Several fires were going. People were just eating their meals from cans, smoking dope and drinking. For the most part they didn't give a shit about me. Some asked me for a cigarette. At the bottom, in the median between the walkway of Haven Cliffs and the park, dozens of wrecked and stripped cars served as shelters. In the park more cars had been left. The wrecks were ravaged so that only the most useless of wires and hardware was left. By the Hudson River, car seats littered the rock banks as if people used them to leisurely take in the splendor of this grimy river lapping Manhattan.

There is human shit everywhere. There are clear markings where a person has made a temporary home. I have come to recognize them. The distinguishing marks are easy: a plastic bag of clothes, nearby a campfire made of broken cinderblock, a rusty hibachi, scrapmetal from a car or major appliance, and empty cans of Vienna sausage, pork and beans, chili-dog mix, dog food. There is a bottle somewhere close by. Sometimes a bag of empty aluminums, some glass and plastic bottles, large ones. When I see bags of cans left I know that something awful has happened because they would not have left these by choice. These things are money.

I do not like this train of thought either. I do not like much of anything anymore. I did not want to come to New York. I do not want to stay. Annie is making her way into things here, but I am not. My writing is not going well. I lean against the windowsill and watch the happenings far too much. I see the trash swirl; she moves and out of it.

OMAR CASTAÑEDA • 339

I think maybe I should get up and close the window because it is really cold outside. My whole body feels like its shriveling. The cup swirls. The sound of leaves whirling. I get up and close the window.

I look at the cover of the journal by my feeble notes. The first story is terrible. It is first person present tense and I hate it. Like purple or spiked hair, first person present tense is the face of things. I write in past tense. I hate the story because I know that today everything is on the surface. Everything that matters is just on the face of things. This is what postmodernism is. Fiction in journals swirls like the trash outside, only seeming to move and change, when it does not. And I know that this is what I must do or I will just have to set up my own hibachi, hunt for aluminum fiction to sell to journals, find a stoop to sleep near.

But this is just another diversion because really it is the fight that has brought me to this point and not the writing. The fight may draw these things too. Yet it is not the state of literature, but the fact that New York City is the filthiest place I have ever lived in, including places all over the goddamned world. And it is looking to be colder than betrayal, colder than stupidity in power, colder than having to give in, than the plethora of M.F.A. editors of literary journals. What do they know of anything?

Right here I crumple this story. Because present tense is something beyond sense, I can say that I take this story and crumple it. Yes this one. I crumple this very story. I despise what I am doing. I think I will rip the pages apart but I do not. I think about it for some time more and I think without using contractions in my language because that too is part of it all. And instead I throw the paper into the trash can. I bend down and swirl the pages I have dropped. A comma is the furthest thing from my mind. This is vestige. This is indulgence.

Back in bed it is warmer. I feel Annie's pussy hair against my buttocks and know that we are nearing the end. Maybe this is what is happening to us. This swirling. I feel the cold again and put my hand between my legs. My hand curls around my penis because I ams still so cold. The head of my penis is cold. My penis is shriveled because of the cold. It feels like a chicken heart taken from a thawing bird. It feel so small. I wonder how it could ever make anyone happy, it is so small. I remember something that says that men's penises are getting larger. Perhaps evolution is doing this. Women are choosing large penises more and more and so the smaller penises are becoming maladaptive. Culled out, evolutionarily speaking. The large penis is adaptive. The large penis is breeding more and perpetuating itself. Who can blame a woman for dumping a small penis? The fittest survive in nature's order. Are vaginas enlarging—or would that be maladaptive? No, it is the inverse relationship that is being perpetuated. The little penis in my hand gets colder and smaller. I am convinced that what I have between my legs is nothing more than a chicken neck with a chicken heart attached to it. Under them there is a cold and tiny octopus sac. How could anyone like what I have here?

I would be better if I were a woman and Annie my husband. Would I be able to take misfortune better? Would my sorrow be something easily petted away by my husband? Would I be absolved of guilt and anything I did be acceptable because of the tyranny of men, the liberation of women, the confines of everything? Would infidelity never be my fault? Would betrayal be a sharp bone to merely pluck from my mouth and place on the rim of the plate?

I think I am a woman and Annie is my husband:

I am like we are now, but instead of hair I feel her thick and flaccid penis lolling against my buttocks. In the morning, when we are stirring from sleep I stretch and yawn. My cheeks press against her and her penis slowly unfurls, fills and looms against my buttocks and lower back. She has a very large penis. I did not marry her because of it, but I am glad that she does. Her arms drops around me, gathers up my breasts and she hugs me. I feel her lips kissing against my cheek, searching in the morning laziness for my mouth. She is being lazy, half asleep. I shift and the length of her penis plops between my legs so that I can feel it lightly rub both my pussy and my anus. I feels wonderful. I know that she loves me. She doesn't say it much, but she is always rubbing my ass, petting me and kissing my neck when we are alone. We have been fighting but yesterday she said that my needs really did matter. She said she loved me.

So today I allow her to do something that she likes. I raise up so she can move closer. The head of her penis slowly pushes against my anus, bending the muscle in. I feel her pressing forward and the heaviness slides gently into my pussy from behind. It hurts a little because she is so big. Huge. But I get used to it fast because I can feel her pleasure just in the sounds coming from her mouth. Her pleasure is important to me. Her arms feel light around me, full of a genuine satisfaction because I have allowed her to do this. She begins rocking. Her penis reaches far up inside me, so that my breath is gone. Annie turns my face with the flat of her hand so that our lips join. She does not move fast or hard, but I know she is enjoying how tight it feels around her and how I am completely soft for her. Receptive. She does not want to hurt me. It is only something she likes, wants to try like anal sex.

Because of this scene, I get up from bed and go to the trash can. I take out this story from among the newspaper and junk and unfold the pages for you. You.

At the end of the story there is another whirlwind. The flurry is not unlike Dorothy's Kansas storm. I can see inside it. I tell you there are people whirling about inside it. There are hibachis and plastic coffee cups and chickens and penises, large and small, and *The Iowa Review* and bombed-out cars with AIDS-bitten-drug-addicted-mentally-unstable streetpeople and the *AWP Newsletter,* the word "grammar," and Annie rolling like a hoopsnake so that her enormously long penis wraps around her back and enters her mouth. All of these things are at the end, in the end of this story that I uncrumple from the trash. All these things are in this final paragraph, this vertiginous whorl that finally stops at a very curious "you."

Sisters

Alma Luz Villanueva

(wo)man
    Yes Woman!
I celebrate our bodies,
our wombs,
intact and perfect even as
we're born
out of our mother's
    womb
I celebrate
because most   . . . If man is out
men have forgotten   of touch with
how to   the earth,
he is afraid   how can he
of us, he   touch woman)
denies us,
   —but in the process
     denies his own existence;
     when will he re/learn
     this ancient fact—

I rejoice in the slick/red walls of our
     wombs,
     the milk of our breasts
     the ecstasy of our clitoris
and our need of man when we
open our legs and womb
to him
     the bloody circle thru our daughters
     and sons

I want to fly and sing
of our beauty and power.
to re/awaken this joy
in us all;
        our power lies in being Woman

ALMA LUZ VILLANUEVA • 343

I celebrate the absence of mystery of
the "eternal mystery of woman":
we are.

we are the trees of the earth
our roots stetching deep and strong,
the stone of the firmament,
sister to the stars
that gave birth to the soil.

Let us never forget the dance
or lose the song
or cease to dream
or efface the mystery

zero in on life
myth
magic
mystery
revel in the extra ordinary
fill your
be
ing with it,

a bird is skimming the water
lands on a smooth surface,
the snow falls softly on a mountain
chilling the earth's crust,
a sapling smiles at the wind,
a cloud gathers and spills its rain
on a hungry field—

cock your head
and listen
it calls
      everyman
        not everyone
            hears

Sassy

Alma Luz Villanueva

I love myself when I want
everything—when I know
everything, in my self, in
my own heart. The world does

not condone this, this kind
of knowing—the smallest child
gets whacked for such behavior.
Just this morning my three-year-
old and I fought it out at the
door—he wanted to open it,

so did I. I opened it—we both
walked through. Sometimes, I
just want to be alone in my heart,
in my soul, in my body—sometimes,

I just want to open the damn door
myself without thinking of someone
else. Sometimes, I think the best
thing we can do for our children is

to teach them how to fight
for what they want—because
if they, too, want everything,
and dare to love themselves, they'd
better grab that handle, and when
the way is clear, pass through.

And when the way is clear, you
are alone, even if a billion
people are on your heels,
or one small child, we enter
different rooms. We could
each describe it differently—

why we came, why we stay.
Why we leave. I've been in many
rooms, and have come to realize
the fullest room was empty. To
get there you must sass back
God and fight him for the door.
And when you enter, you must
laugh at the empty fullness,
greet your perfect self in the
corner—and when she, the Goddess,
asks you what you see, as clouds,
thin air, float by: you must
answer: I see the

freedom. She isn't pleased
or displeased—she's been expecting
you forever. She knows what
you had

to do
to love
your
self.

Violation

Alma Luz Villanueva

Do you want me to tell you
what I know? I know

the grass bends in the wind.
I know the rain is wet and

loves the living. I know
children must play, even in war.

I know cruelty is not human
(it is learned, it is learned).

I know there is a terrible
secret in love (the terrible

desire to destroy the loved
one, the one who destroys

our sweet solitude, our freedom—
and yet we seek him/her out, we long

and weep, we plead to be loved,
but then our singularity,

our hard-earned androgyny,
ecstatic one-in-one-self is

touched, is loved, is violated).
This desire to be

violated.
This desire to

violate
and know every

taste, touch, smell, memory
of the one we

love.

The Lover

Alma Luz Villanueva

What is the difference
between sexuality and sensuality,

we discuss oh so
calmly . . . I spin

on the words
sexuality   sensuality

as though they were
worlds, civilizations

I've been studying:
"Sexuality is localized in

the genitals," I say ...
"an energy that keeps

us hungry, hunting,
stalking. Sexuality seizes,

tames, conquers, gloats
and howls with victory,

and we are all proof of this
momentary victory, the trophy."

I pause
and continue:

"Sensuality. Rose petals, thick
grass, deep water, fragrant neck,

newborn-in-the-arms, suckling
milk and light, lover's lips, tender

tongues, frying onions, luscious
sauce simmering, to be poured over

meat slid from bone,
done, perfect, surrendered,

cooked, for, your, pleasure,
the perpetual sound of the sea,

aching, longing, roaring, singing,
singing, roaring, longing, aching,

the never ever ever ending
delight, no trophies,

delight, no proof;
I give my children back

to their lives, their senses,
their most private and secret

dreams, where we conquer worlds
and then wisely relinquish them

in order to praise the Lover
(delight),

worlds without ever
ending," I murmur

as I watch summer disrobing
and   oh   so   slowly

enter the irresistible coolness
on the 26th of June.

St. John of the Divine Cathedral

H. Emilia Paredes

Celestial hands, *la ilusión*
de los cumbres celestes
stained glass, granite
wafts of purple, gold, blood red
sangre dorado heart shudder
through solar plexus
vulva, hooded clitoris
arch of spine, cool cathedral marble
smooth to first *caricia*
fingertips explore each subtle imperfection
each anti-christ quaking
fine-veined and also holy
snarl of beast
come to wrestle the divine
from quick of throat
currents of *espiritu santo* illumine
breasts, pelvis, limbs, palms and feet
fingers take wing
toes point in glorious conception of the invisible
your image, not graven, but sensate
ripples of adulation
una lagrima se cae, single tear
single bead of sweat
oceans cry out
wind and thunder ignite
lover to belovéd
fingers grasping rays of light, *la luz*
breath of god on mortal flesh
she sings. . . .

Ode to the Firmament
Her Right Shoulder

H. Emilia Paredes

For B. Brown

Beneath the light
of the brightest star
your hands and fingers
doves flying
over vistas
of body, *corpus sanctus*
I give to you
an unnamed constellation
on your right shoulder
to map the firmament
of your right shoulder
where the moons of my fingernails
press faint rose
petals down milky
contours of your skin.
I whisper in a language
you cannot understand
cannot break down into reason
but perhaps your heart suspects
perhaps the nerve endings of the flesh
a just perceptible flutter
to tongue sweet ripening
warm jewel tucked soft
against your pelvis suspects.

I witness *el misterio*
mystery of your sleep
tremor of your right shoulder
moan of your lips
what dreams
take you

to the brink of self
break from your body
in worlds you breathe beneath me
and I discover
the font of paradise
believe
one star sent light to guide
the fit of our bodies
I slip nameless into your firmament
my hand faint on your shoulder.

Woman in Prayer

H. Emilia Paredes

For V. Gonzales

Her face radiant
knowing she will meet her lover
in a place where touch becomes spirit
and flesh speaks.

She closes her eyes
to go there
moistens her lips
and smiles a secret
light of what it is
to feast the eyes on one so dear
in a glance, *el mundo entero*
the world.

God listens to this woman
leans close to hear
each breathless pause.

Woman in a Velvet Dress

H. Emilia Paredes

the color of a deep rosé. It takes a discriminating palate
to appreciate the body and fragrance of a fine
red wine, and her dark eyes laughing with the turn
of the season.

> In the vineyard
> before harvest
> it is almost enough
> to imbibe the scent
> of the fruit
> quickening on the vine
> her lips
> ripe and sweet
> her wine
> tints the heavens
> inebriates the gods
> reminds us of ourselves
>
> drink of sun-warm
> liquid in a moment
> of incarnation.

Acknowledgments

"Spring Shining" and "Pétalos Negros" by Pat Mora. Originally published in *Agua Santa: Holy Water* by Pat Mora, Beacon Press, 1995. Copyright © by Pat Mora, 1995. Reprinted by permission of the author and publisher.

"You Are Naked" and "El Inicio" by Verónica Volkow. "You Are Naked" Copyright © 1983 by Verónica Volkow. Originally published in *El Inicio,* Joaquin Mortiz Publishers, 1983. Reprinted by permission of City Lights Books, publishers of *Light From a Nearby Window: Contemporary Mexican Poetry,* edited by Juvenal Acosta, 1993. "El Inicio" Copyright © 1983 by Verónica Volkow. Originally published in *El Inicio,* Joaquin Mortiz Publishers, 1983. Reprinted by permission of Milkweed Editions, publishers of *Mouth to Mouth: Poems by Twelve Contemporary Mexican Women,* edited by Forrest Gander, 1993.

"Free Women," "The Receiving Blanket," "Sisters," "Sassy," "Violation," and "The Lover" by Alma Luz Villanueva. "Free Women" originally appeared in *Weeping Woman: La Llorona and Other Stories* by Alma Luz Villanueva, Bilingual Press, 1994. Copyright © by Alma Luz Villanueva, 1994. Reprinted by permission of the author and publisher. "The Receiving Blanket" by Alma Luz Villanueva. Copyright © by Alma Luz Villanueva, 1995. Used by permission of the author. "Sisters" and "Sassy" originally appeared in *She Rises Like the Sun: Contemporary Women's Poetry,* Crossing Press, 1984. Copyright © by Alma Luz Villanueva, 1984. Used by permission of the author. "Violation" and "The Lover" by Alma Luz Villanueva. Copyright © by Alma Luz Villanueva, 1995. Used by permission of the author.

"Happiness" by Elena Poniatowska. Copyright © by Elena Poniatowska, 1993. Originally appeared in *Pleasure in the Word: Erotic Writings by Latin American Women,* edited by Margarite Fernandez Olmos

Fernandez Olmos and Lizabeth Paravisini-Gebert, White Pine Press, 1993. Reprinted by permission of White Pine Press.

"Firefly Under the Tongue," "Your Borders: Crevices That Uncover Me," "Untitled," and "On the Facets: The Flashing" by Coral Bracho. "Firefly Under the Tongue" and "Untitled" originally appeared in *The Fertile Rhythms: Contemporary Women Poets of Mexico,* edited by Thomas Hoeksema, Latin American Literary Review Press, 1989. Copyright © by Coral Bracho, 1989. Reprinted by permission of Latin American Literary Review Press. "Your Borders: Crevices That Uncover Me" and "On the Facets: The Flashing" originally appeared in *Mouth to Mouth: Poems by Twelve Contemporary Mexican Women,* edited by Forrest Gander, Milkweed Editions, 1993. Copyright © by Coral Bracho, 1993. Reprinted by permission of Milkweed Editions.

"Collections of Navels" and "Trying Trying" by Daniel de Burgos. Copyright © by Daniel de Burgos, 1995. Used by permission of the author.

"Portrait / Nude #30 / 4 x 6," "Portrait / Nude #9 / 7 x 11," "Saguaro," "Arc," "The Boy of Seventeen," and "Reversible Lovers" by Juan Felipe Herrera. "Portrait / Nude #30 / 4 x 6," "Portrait / Nude #9 / 7 x 11," "Saguaro," "Arc," and "The Boy of Seventeen" originally appeared in *Akrilica* by Juan Felipe Herrera, Alcatraz Editions, 1989. Copyright © by Juan Felipe Herrera, 1989. Used by permission of the author. "Reversible Lovers" by Juan Felipe Herrera. Copyright © by Juan Felipe Herrera, 1995. Used by permission of the author.

"Bellas Artes" and "My Flaws Among the Peach Blossoms" by Kyra Galvan. "Bellas Artes" originally appeared in *Mouth to Mouth: Poems by Twelve Contemporary Mexican Women,* edited by Forrest Gander, Milkweed Editions, 1993. Copyright © by Kyra Galvan, 1993. Reprinted by permission of Milkweed Editions. "My Flaws Among the Peach Blossoms" originally appeared in *The Fertile Rhythms: Contemporary Women Poets of Mexico,* edited by Thomas Hoeksema, Latin American Literary Review Press, 1989. Copyright © by Kyra Galvan, 1989. Reprinted by permission of Latin American Literary Review Press.

"The Thing in My Mouth" and "Avocado Blues Avocado Greens" by Carlotta Sanchez. Copyright © by Carlotta Sanchez, 1995. Used by permission of the author.

"Blessed the Hungry" by Demetria Martínez. Originally appeared in *Three Times a Woman* by Demetria Martínez, Bilingual Press, 1990. Copyright © by Demetria Martínez, 1990. Reprinted by permission of the author and publisher.

"Circle of Friends" by Ricardo Lopez Masarillo. Copyright © by Richardo Lopez Masarillo. Used by permission of the author.

"Crossfire" by J. E. Pardo. Copyright © by J. E. Pardo, 1995. Used by permission of the author.

"Researching Frida Kahlo" by Markanthony Alvidrez. Copyright © by Markanthony Alvidrez, 1995. Used by permission of the author.

"The Apple Orchard" by Rudolfo Anaya. Copyright © by Rudolfo Anaya, 1995. Used by permission of Susan Bergholz Literary Services.

"The China Venus Thinks About Making Love" and "Rumor" by Alicia Borinsky. Originally appeared in *Timorous Women* by Alicia Borinsky, translated by Cola Franzen, Spectacular Diseases Press, 1992. Copyright © by Alicia Borinsky and Cola Franzen, 1992. Reprinted by permission of Cola Franzen.

"Invocation 13" by Juan Cameron, translated by Cola Franzen. Copyright © by Juan Cameron and Cola Franzen. Used by permission of Cola Franzen.

"The Mule Going Round the Well" by Ethel Krauze. Originally appeared in *New Writing From Mexico,* edited by Reginald Gibbons, special issue of *TriQuarterly,* 1992. Copyright © by Ethel Krauze, 1992. Reprinted by permission of Reginald Gibbons.

"Home Movies" by Ed Vega. Copyright © by Ed Vega, 1995. Used by permission of Susan Bergholz Literary Services.

"Our Language" and "A Lover's Resolution on the New Year to Thaw Our Winter Blood" by Brenda Cárdenas. Copyright © by Brenda Cárdenas, 1995. Used by permission of the author.

"Egyptian Tango" by Saúl Yurkievich, translated by Cola Franzen. Copyright © by Saúl Yurkievich and Cola Franzen. Used by permission of Cola Franzen.